Learn Docker – Fundamentals of Docker 18.x

Everything you need to know about containerizing your applications and running them in production

Gabriel N. Schenker

BIRMINGHAM - MUMBAI

Learn Docker – Fundamentals of Docker 18.x

Commissioning Editor: Gebin George
Acquisition Editor: Shrilekha Inani
Content Development Editor: Ronn Kurien
Technical Editor: Swathy Mohan
Copy Editor: Safis Editing
Project Coordinator: Judie Jose
Proofreader: Safis Editing
Indexer: Priyanka Dhadke
Graphics: Tom Scaria
Production Coordinator: Nilesh Mohite

First published: April 2018

Production reference: 1240418

Published by Packt Publishing Ltd.
Livery Place
35 Livery Street
Birmingham
B3 2PB, UK.

ISBN 978-1-78899-702-7

www.packtpub.com

`mapt.io`

Mapt is an online digital library that gives you full access to over 5,000 books and videos, as well as industry leading tools to help you plan your personal development and advance your career. For more information, please visit our website.

Why subscribe?

- Spend less time learning and more time coding with practical eBooks and Videos from over 4,000 industry professionals

- Improve your learning with Skill Plans built especially for you

- Get a free eBook or video every month

- Mapt is fully searchable

- Copy and paste, print, and bookmark content

PacktPub.com

Did you know that Packt offers eBook versions of every book published, with PDF and ePub files available? You can upgrade to the eBook version at `www.PacktPub.com` and as a print book customer, you are entitled to a discount on the eBook copy. Get in touch with us at `service@packtpub.com` for more details.

At `www.PacktPub.com`, you can also read a collection of free technical articles, sign up for a range of free newsletters, and receive exclusive discounts and offers on Packt books and eBooks.

Contributors

About the author

Gabriel N. Schenker has more than 25 years of experience as an independent consultant, architect, leader, trainer, mentor, and developer. Currently, Gabriel works as Senior Curriculum Developer at Confluent after coming from a similar position at Docker. Gabriel has a Ph.D. in Physics, and he is a Docker Captain, a Certified Docker Associate, and an ASP Insider. When not working, Gabriel enjoys time with his wonderful wife Veronicah and his children.

About the reviewer

Peter McKee is a Software Architect and Senior Software Engineer at Docker, Inc. He leads the technical team that delivers the Docker Success Center. He's been leading and mentoring teams for more than 20 years. When not building things with software, he spends his time with his wife and seven kids in beautiful Austin, TX.

Packt is searching for authors like you

If you're interested in becoming an author for Packt, please visit authors.packtpub.com and apply today. We have worked with thousands of developers and tech professionals, just like you, to help them share their insight with the global tech community. You can make a general application, apply for a specific hot topic that we are recruiting an author for, or submit your own idea.

Table of Contents

Preface

Docker containers have revolutionized the software supply chain in small and big enterprises. Never before has a new technology so rapidly penetrated the top 500 enterprises worldwide. Companies that embrace containers and containerize their traditional mission-critical applications have reported savings of at least 50% in total maintenance costs and a reduction of 90% (or more) in deploying new versions of those applications. Furthermore, they are benefiting from increased security by using containers rather than running applications outside containers.

This book starts from scratch, introducing you to Docker fundamentals and setting up an environment to work with it. Then, we delve into concepts such as Docker containers, Docker images, and Docker Compose. We will also cover the concepts of deployment, orchestration, networking, and security. Furthermore, we explain Docker functionalities on public clouds, such as AWS.

By the end of this book, you will have hands-on experience working with Docker containers and orchestrators, such as SwarmKit and Kubernetes.

Who this book is for

This book is targeted at system administrators, operations engineers, DevOps engineers, and developers or stakeholders who are interested in getting started with Docker from scratch. No prior experience with Docker containers is required.

What this book covers

Chapter 1, *What Are Containers and Why Should I Use Them?*, focuses on the software supply chain and the friction within it. It then presents containers as a means to reduce this friction and add enterprise-grade security on top of it. In this chapter, we also look into how containers and the ecosystem around them are assembled. We specifically point out the distinction between the upstream OSS components (Moby) that form the building blocks of the downstream products of Docker and other vendors.

Chapter 2, *Setting up a Working Environment*, discusses in detail how to set up an ideal environment for developers, DevOps engineers, and operators that can be used when working with Docker containers.

Chapter 3, *Working with Containers*, teaches how start, stop, and remove containers. The chapter also teaches how to inspect containers to retrieve additional metadata. Furthermore, it introduces how to run additional processes and how to attach to the main process in an already running container. It also shows how to retrieve logging information from a container that is produced by the processes running inside it.

Chapter 4, *Creating and Managing Container Images*, introduces the different ways to create container images, which serve as templates for containers. It introduces the inner structure of an image and how it is built.

Chapter 5, *Data Volumes and System Management*, introduces data volumes that can be used by stateful components running in containers. The chapter also introduces system-level commands that are used to gather information about Docker and the underlying OS, as well as commands to clean the system from orphaned resources. Finally, it introduces the system events generated by the Docker engine.

Chapter 6, *Distributed Application Architecture*, introduces the concept of a distributed application architecture and discusses the various patterns and best practices that are required to run a distributed application successfully. Finally, it discusses the additional requirements that need to be fulfilled to run such an application in production.

Chapter 7, *Single-Host Networking*, introduces the Docker container networking model and its single-host implementation in the form of the bridge network. The chapter introduces the concept of software-defined networks (SDNs) and how they are used to secure containerized applications. Finally, it introduces how container ports can be opened to the public and thus how to make containerized components accessible from the outside world.

Chapter 8, *Docker Compose*, introduces the concept of an application consisting of multiple services, each running in a container, and how Docker Compose allows us to easily build, run, and scale such an application using a declarative approach.

Chapter 9, *Orchestrators*, introduces the concept of orchestrators. It teaches why orchestrators are needed and how they work. The chapter also provides an overview of the most popular orchestrators and explores a few of their pros and cons.

Chapter 10, *Introduction to Docker Swarm*, introduces Docker's native orchestrator called SwarmKit. It elaborates on all the concepts and objects SwarmKit uses to deploy and run a distributed, resilient, robust, and highly available application in a cluster on-premise, or in the cloud. The chapter also introduces how SwarmKit ensures secure applications using SDNs to isolate containers and secrets to protect sensitive information.

Chapter 11, *Zero Downtime Deployments and Secrets*, teaches how to deploy services or applications onto a Docker swarm with zero downtime and automatic rollback capabilities. It also introduces secrets as a means to protect sensitive information.

Chapter 12, *Introduction to Kubernetes*, introduces the currently most popular container orchestrator. It introduces the core Kubernetes objects that are used to define and run a distributed, resilient, robust, and highly available application in a cluster. Finally, it introduces Minikube as a way to locally deploy a Kubernetes application and also the integration of Kubernetes with Docker for Mac and Docker for Windows.

Chapter 13, *Deploying, Updating, and Securing an Application with Kubernetes*, teaches how to deploy, update, and scale applications into a Kubernetes cluster. It also explains how zero-downtime deployments are achieved to enable disruption free updates and rollbacks of mission-critical applications. This chapter also introduces Kubernetes secrets as a means to configure services and protect sensitive data.

Chapter 14, *Running a Containerized App in the Cloud*, gives an overview over some of the most popular ways of running containerized applications in the cloud. We have a closer look to what the most popular cloud vendor, AWS, offers in this regard. We include self-hosting and hosted solutions and discuss their pros and cons. Offerings of other vendors, such as Microsoft Azure and Google Cloud Engine, are also briefly discussed.

To get the most out of this book

Ideally you have access to a laptop or personal computer with Windows 10 Professional or a recent version of Mac OS X installed. A computer with any popular Linux OS installed works too. If you're on a Mac you should install Docker for Mac and if you're on Windows then install Docker for Windows. You can download them from here: `https://www.docker.com/community-edition`

If you are on an older version of Windows or are using Windows 10 Home edition, then you should install Docker Toolbox. You can find the Docker Toolbox here: `https://docs.docker.com/toolbox/toolbox_install_windows/`

On the Mac, use the Terminal application, and on Windows, use a PowerShell console to try out the commands you will be learning. You also need a recent version of a browser such as Google Chrome, Safari or Internet Explorer. Of course you will need internet access to download tools and container images that we are going to use and explore in this book.

Download the example code files

You can download the example code files for this book from your account at `www.packtpub.com`. If you purchased this book elsewhere, you can visit `www.packtpub.com/support` and register to have the files emailed directly to you.

You can download the code files by following these steps:

1. Log in or register at `www.packtpub.com`.
2. Select the **SUPPORT** tab.
3. Click on **Code Downloads & Errata**.
4. Enter the name of the book in the **Search** box and follow the onscreen instructions.

Once the file is downloaded, please make sure that you unzip or extract the folder using the latest version of:

- WinRAR/7-Zip for Windows
- Zipeg/iZip/UnRarX for Mac
- 7-Zip/PeaZip for Linux

The code bundle for the book is also hosted on GitHub at `https://github.com/fundamentalsofdocker/labs`. If there's an update to the code, it will be updated on the existing GitHub repository.

We also have other code bundles from our rich catalog of books and videos available at `https://github.com/PacktPublishing/`. Check them out!

Download the color images

We also provide a PDF file that has color images of the screenshots/diagrams used in this book. You can download it from `https://www.packtpub.com/sites/default/files/downloads/LearnDockerFundamentalsofDocker18x_ColorImages.pdf`.

Conventions used

There are a number of text conventions used throughout this book.

`CodeInText`: Indicates code words in text, database table names, folder names, filenames, file extensions, pathnames, dummy URLs, user input, and Twitter handles. Here is an example: "The content of each layer is mapped to a special folder on the host system, which is usually a subfolder of `/var/lib/docker/`."

A block of code is set as follows:

```
COPY . /app
COPY ./web /app/web
COPY sample.txt /data/my-sample.txt
ADD sample.tar /app/bin/
ADD http://example.com/sample.txt /data/
```

When we wish to draw your attention to a particular part of a code block, the relevant lines or items are set in bold:

```
FROM python:2.7
RUN mkdir -p /app
WORKDIR /app
COPY ./requirements.txt /app/
RUN pip install -r requirements.txt
CMD ["python", "main.py"]
```

Any command-line input or output is written as follows:

```
$ mkdir ~/FundamentalsOfDocker
$ cd ~/FundamentalsOfDocker
```

Bold: Indicates a new term, an important word, or words that you see onscreen. For example, words in menus or dialog boxes appear in the text like this. Here is an example: "Select **System info** from the **Administration** panel."

 Warnings or important notes appear like this.

 Tips and tricks appear like this.

Get in touch

Feedback from our readers is always welcome.

General feedback: Email `feedback@packtpub.com` and mention the book title in the subject of your message. If you have questions about any aspect of this book, please email us at `questions@packtpub.com`.

Errata: Although we have taken every care to ensure the accuracy of our content, mistakes do happen. If you have found a mistake in this book, we would be grateful if you would report this to us. Please visit `www.packtpub.com/submit-errata`, selecting your book, clicking on the Errata Submission Form link, and entering the details.

Piracy: If you come across any illegal copies of our works in any form on the Internet, we would be grateful if you would provide us with the location address or website name. Please contact us at `copyright@packtpub.com` with a link to the material.

If you are interested in becoming an author: If there is a topic that you have expertise in and you are interested in either writing or contributing to a book, please visit `authors.packtpub.com`.

Reviews

Please leave a review. Once you have read and used this book, why not leave a review on the site that you purchased it from? Potential readers can then see and use your unbiased opinion to make purchase decisions, we at Packt can understand what you think about our products, and our authors can see your feedback on their book. Thank you!

For more information about Packt, please visit `packtpub.com`.

1
What Are Containers and Why Should I Use Them?

This first chapter of this book will introduce you to the world of containers and their orchestration. The book starts from the beginning, assuming no prior knowledge in the area of containers, and will give you a very practical introduction into the topic.

In this chapter, we are focusing on the software supply chain and the friction within it. We then present containers as a means to reduce this friction and add enterprise-grade security on top of it. In this chapter, we also look into how containers and the ecosystem around them are assembled. We specifically point out the distinction between the upstream **Operations Support System (OSS)** components, united under the code name Moby, that form the building blocks of the downstream products of Docker and other vendors.

The chapter covers the following topics:

- What are containers?
- Why are containers important?
- What's the benefit for me or for my company?
- The Moby project
- Docker products
- The container ecosystem
- Container architecture

After completing this module, you will be able to:

- Explain in a few simple sentences to an interested layman what containers are, using an analogy such as physical containers
- Justify to an interested layman why containers are so important, using an analogy such as physical containers versus traditional shipping, or apartment homes versus single family homes, and so on
- Name at least four upstream open source components that are used by the Docker products, such as Docker for Mac/Windows
- Identify at least three Docker products

Technical requirements

This chapter is a theoretical introduction into the topic. Therefore, there are no special technical requirements for this chapter.

What are containers?

A software container is a pretty abstract thing and thus it might help if we start with an analogy that should be pretty familiar to most of the readers. The analogy is a shipping container in the transportation industry. Throughout history, people have been transporting goods from one location to another by various means. Before the invention of the wheel, goods would most probably have been transported in bags, baskets, or chests on the shoulders of the humans themselves, or they might have used animals such as donkeys, camels, or elephants to transport them.

With the invention of the wheel, transportation became a bit more efficient as humans would built roads on which they could move their carts along. Many more goods could be transported at a time. When we then introduced the first steam-driven machines, and later gasoline driven engines, transportation became even more powerful. We now transport huge amounts of goods in trains, ships, and trucks. At the same time, the type of goods became more and more diverse, and sometimes complex to handle.

In all these thousands of years, one thing did not change though, and that was the necessity to unload the goods at the target location and maybe load them onto another means of transportation. Take, for example, a farmer bringing a cart full of apples to a central train station where the apples are then loaded onto a train, together with all the apples from many other farmers. Or think of a winemaker bringing his barrels of wine with a truck to the port where they are unloaded, and then transferred to a ship that will transport the barrels overseas.

This unloading from one means of transportation and loading onto another means of transportation was a really complex and tedious process. Every type of good was packaged in its own way and thus had to be handled in its own way. Also, loose goods risked being stolen by unethical workers, or goods could be damaged in the process.

Then, there came the container, and it totally revolutionized the transportation industry. The container is just a metallic box with standardized dimensions. The length, width, and height of each container is the same. This is a very important point. Without the world agreeing on a standard size, the whole container thing would not have been as successful as it is now.

Now, with standardized containers, companies who want to have their goods transported from A to B package those goods into these containers. Then, they call a shipper which comes with a standardized means for transportation. This can be a truck that can load a container or a train whose wagons can each transport one or several containers. Finally, we have ships that are specialized in transporting huge amounts of containers. The shippers never need to unpack and repackage goods. For a shipper, a container is a black box and they are not interested in what is in it nor should they care in most cases. It is just a big iron box with standard dimensions. The packaging of goods into containers is now fully delegated to the parties that want to have their goods shipped, and they should know best on how to handle and package those goods.

Since all containers have the same standardized shape and dimensions, the shippers can use standardized tools to handle containers, that is, cranes that unload containers, say from a train or a truck, and load them onto a ship or vice versa. One type of crane is enough to handle all the containers that come along over time. Also, the means of transportation can be standardized, such as container ships, trucks, and trains.

Because of all this standardization, all the processes in and around shipping goods could also be standardized and thus made much more efficient than they were before the age of containers.

I think by now you should have a good understanding of why shipping containers are so important and why they revolutionized the whole transportation industry. I chose this analogy purposefully, since the software containers that we are going to introduce here fulfill the exact same role in the so-called software supply chain as shipping containers do in the supply chain of physical goods.

In the old days, developers would develop a new application. Once that application was completed in the eyes of the developers, they would hand this application over to the operations engineers that were then supposed to install it on the production servers and get it running. If the operations engineers were lucky, they even got a somewhat accurate document with installation instructions from the developers. So far so good, and life was easy.

But things got a bit out of hand when in an enterprise, there were many teams of developers that created quite different types of applications, yet all needed to be installed on the same production servers and kept running there. Usually, each application has some external dependencies such as which framework it was built on or what libraries it uses and so on. Sometimes, two applications would use the same framework but in different versions that might or might not be compatible between each other. Our operations engineer's life became much harder over time. They had to be really creative on how they could load their ship, which is of course their servers with different applications without breaking something.

Installing a new version of a certain application was now a complex project on its own and often needed months of planning and testing. In other words, there was a lot of friction in the software supply chain. But these days, companies rely more and more on software and the release cycles become shorter and shorter. We cannot afford anymore to just have a new release maybe twice a year. Applications need to be updated in a matter of weeks or days, or sometimes even multiple times per day. Companies that do not comply risk going out of business due to the lack of agility. So, *what's the solution?*

A first approach was to use **virtual machines (VMs)**. Instead of running multiple applications all on the same server, companies would package and run a single application per VM. With it, the compatibility problems were gone and life seemed good again. Unfortunately, the happiness didn't last for long. VMs are pretty heavy beasts on their own since they all contain a full-blown OS such as Linux or Windows Server and all that for just a single application. This is as if in the transportation industry you would use a gigantic ship just to transport a truck load of bananas. What a waste. That can never be profitable.

The ultimate solution to the problem was to provide something much more lightweight than VMs but also able to perfectly encapsulate the goods it needed to transport. Here, the goods are the actual application written by our developers plus (and this is important) all the external dependencies of the application, such as framework, libraries, configurations, and more. This holy grail of a software packaging mechanism was the Docker container.

Developers use Docker containers to package their applications, frameworks, and libraries into them, and then they ship those containers to the testers or to the operations engineers. For the testers and operations engineers, the container is just a black box. It is a standardized black box, though. All containers, no matter what application runs inside them, can be treated equally. The engineers know that if any container runs on their servers, then any other containers should run too. And this is actually true, apart from some edge cases which always exist.

Thus, Docker containers are a means to package applications and their dependencies in a standardized way. Docker then coined the phrase—*Build, ship and run anywhere.*

Why are containers important?

These days, the time between new releases of an application become shorter and shorter, yet the software itself doesn't become any simpler. On the contrary, software projects increase in complexity. Thus, we need a way to tame the beast and simplify the software supply chain.

We also hear every day how much more cyber crimes are on the rise. Many well-known companies are affected by security breaches. Highly sensitive customer data gets stolen, such as social security numbers, credit card information, and more. But not only customer data is compromised, sensitive company secrets are also stolen.

Containers can help in many ways. First of all, Gartner has found in a recent report that applications running in a container are more secure than their counterparts not running in a container. Containers use Linux security primitives such as Linux kernel namespaces to sandbox different applications running on the same computers and **control groups (cgroups)**, to avoid the noisy neighbor problem where one bad application is using all available resources of a server and starving all other applications.

Due to the fact that container images are immutable, it is easy to have them scanned for known vulnerabilities and exposures, and in doing so, increase the overall security of our applications.

Another way we can make our software supply chain more secure when using containers is to use **content trust**. Content trust basically ensures that the author of a container image is who they pretend to be and that the consumer of the container image has a guarantee that the image has not been tampered with in transit. The latter is known as a **man-in-the-middle (MITM)** attack.

All that I have just said is of course technically also possible without using containers, but since containers introduce a globally accepted standard, it makes it so much easier to implement those best practices and enforce them.

OK, but security is not the only reason why containers are important. There are other reasons:

One of them is the fact that containers make it easy to simulate a production-like environment, even on a developer's laptop. If we can containerize any application, then we can also containerize, say, a database such as Oracle or MS SQL Server. Now, everyone who has ever had to install an Oracle database on a computer knows that this is not the easiest thing to do and it takes a lot of space away on your computer. You wouldn't want to do that to your development laptop just to test whether the application you developed really works end to end. With containers at hand, I can run a full-blown relational database in a container as easily as saying 1, 2, 3. And when I'm done with testing, I can just stop and delete the container and the database is gone without leaving a trace on my computer.

Since containers are very lean compared to VMs, it is not uncommon to have many containers running at the same time on a developer's laptop without overwhelming the laptop.

A third reason why containers are important is that operators can finally concentrate on what they are really good at, provisioning infrastructure, and running and monitoring applications in production. When the applications they have to run on a production system are all containerized, then operators can start to standardize their infrastructure. Every server becomes just another Docker host. No special libraries of frameworks need to be installed on those servers, just an OS and a container runtime such as Docker.

Also, the operators do not have to have any intimate knowledge about the internals of the applications anymore since those applications run self-contained in containers that ought to look like black boxes to the operations engineers, similar to how the shipping containers look to the personnel in the transportation industry.

What's the benefit for me or for my company?

Somebody once said that today, every company of a certain size has to acknowledge that they need to be a software company. Software runs all businesses, period. As every company becomes a software company, there is a need to establish a software supply chain. For the company to remain competitive, their software supply chain has to be secure and efficient. Efficiency can be achieved through thorough automation and standardization. But in all three areas, security, automation, and standardization, containers have shown to shine. Large and well-known enterprises have reported that when containerizing existing legacy applications (many call them traditional applications) and establishing a fully automated software supply chain based on containers, they can reduce the cost used for maintenance of those mission-critical applications by a factor of 50 to 60% and they can reduce the time between new releases of these traditional applications by up to 90%.

That said, the adoption of container technology saves these companies a lot of money, and at the same time it speeds up the development process and reduces the time to market.

The Moby project

Originally, when the company Docker introduced Docker containers, everything was open source. Docker didn't have any commercial products at this time. The Docker engine which the company developed was a monolithic piece of software. It contained many logical parts, such as the container runtime, a network library, a RESTful API, a command-line interface, and much more.

Other vendors or projects such as Red Hat or Kubernetes were using the Docker engine in their own products, but most of the time they were only using part of its functionality. For example, Kubernetes did not use the Docker network library of the Docker engine but provided its own way of networking. Red Hat in turn did not update the Docker engine frequently and preferred to apply unofficial patches to older versions of the Docker engine, yet they still called it the **Docker engine**.

Out of all these reasons and many more, the idea emerged that Docker had to do something to clearly separate the Docker open source part from the Docker commercial part. Furthermore, the company wanted to prevent competitors from using and abusing the name Docker for their own gains. This was the main reason why the Moby project was born. It serves as the umbrella for most of the open source components Docker developed and continues to develop. These open source projects do not carry the name Docker in them anymore.

Part of the Moby project are components for image management, secret management, configuration management, and networking and provisioning, to name just a few. Also, part of the Moby project are special Moby tools that are, for example, used to assemble components into runnable artifacts.

Some of the components that technically would belong to the Moby project have been donated by Docker to the **Cloud Native Computing Foundation** (**CNCF**) and thus do not appear in the list of components anymore. The most prominent ones are `containerd` and `runc` which together form the container runtime.

Docker products

Docker currently separates its product lines into two segments. There is the **Community Edition** (**CE**) which is closed source yet completely free, and then there is the **Enterprise Edition** (**EE**) which is also a closed source and needs to be licensed on a yearly basis. The enterprise products are backed by 24 x 7 support and are supported with bug fixes much longer than their CE counterparts.

Docker CE

Part of the Docker community edition are products such as the Docker Toolbox, Docker for Mac, and Docker for Windows. All these three products are mainly targeting developers.

Docker for Mac and Docker for Windows are easy-to-install desktop applications that can be used to build, debug, and test Dockerized applications or services on a Mac or on Windows. Docker for Mac and Docker for Windows are complete development environments which deeply integrated with their respective hypervisor framework, networking, and filesystem. These tools are the fastest and most reliable way to run Docker on a Mac or on Windows.

Under the umbrella of the CE, there are also two products that are more geared towards operations engineers. Those products are Docker for Azure and Docker for AWS.

For example, with Docker for Azure, which is a native Azure application, you can set up Docker in a few clicks, optimized for and integrated to the underlying Azure **Infrastructure as a Service (IaaS)** services. It helps operations engineers to accelerate time to productivity in building and running Docker applications in Azure.

Docker for AWS works very similar but for Amazon's cloud.

Docker EE

The Docker EE consists of the two products **Universal Control Plane (UCP)** and **Docker Trusted Registry (DTR)** that both run on top of Docker Swarm. Both are Swarm applications. Docker EE builds on top of the upstream components of the Moby project and adds enterprise-grade features such as **role-based access control (RBAC)**, multi tenancy, mixed clusters of Docker Swarm and Kubernetes, web-based UI, and content trust, as well as image scanning on top of it.

The container ecosystem

There has never been a new technology introduced in IT that penetrated the landscape so quickly and so thoroughly than containers. Any company that doesn't want to be left behind cannot ignore containers. This huge interest in containers from all sectors of the industry has triggered a lot of innovation in this sector. Numerous companies have specialized in containers and either provide products that build on top of this technology or build tools that support it.

Initially, Docker didn't have a solution for container orchestration thus other companies or projects, open source or not, tried to close this gap. The most prominent one is Kubernetes which was initiated by Google and then later donated to the CNCF. Other container orchestration products are Apache Mesos, Rancher, Red Hat's Open Shift, Docker's own Swarm, and more.

More recently, the trend goes towards a service mesh. This is the new buzz word. As we containerize more and more applications, and as we refactor those applications into more microservice-oriented applications, we run into problems that simple orchestration software cannot solve anymore in a reliable and scalable way. Topics in this area are service discovery, monitoring, tracing, and log aggregation. Many new projects have emerged in this area, the most popular one at this time being Istio, which is also part of the CNCF.

Many say that the next step in the evolution of software are functions, or more precisely, **Functions as a Service (FaaS)**. Some projects exist that provide exactly this kind of service and are built on top of containers. One prominent example is OpenFaaS.

We have only scratched the surface of the container ecosystem. All big IT companies such as Google, Microsoft, Intel, Red Hat, IBM, and more are working feverishly on containers and related technologies. The CNCF that is mainly about containers and related technologies, has so many registered projects, that they do not all fit on a poster anymore. It's an exciting time to work in this area. And in my humble opinion, this is only the beginning.

Container architecture

Now, let's discuss on a high level how a system that can run Docker containers is designed. The following diagram illustrates what a computer on which Docker has been installed looks like. By the way, a computer which has Docker installed is often called a Docker host, because it can run or host Docker containers:

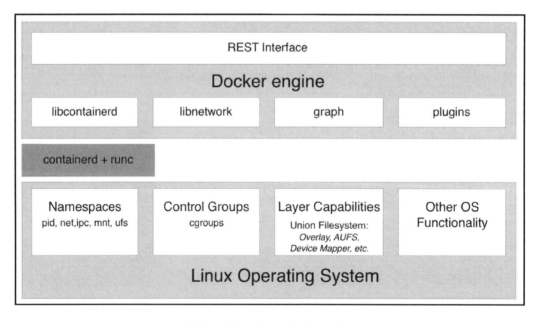

High-level architecture diagram of the Docker engine

In the preceding diagram, we see three essential parts:

- On the bottom, we have the Linux operating system
- In the middle dark gray, we have the container runtime
- On the top, we have the Docker engine

Containers are only possible due to the fact that the Linux OS provides some primitives, such as namespaces, control groups, layer capabilities, and more which are leveraged in a very specific way by the container runtime and the Docker engine. Linux kernel namespaces such as **process ID (pid)** namespaces or **network (net)** namespaces allow Docker to encapsulate or sandbox processes that run inside the container. Control groups make sure that containers cannot suffer from the noisy neighbor syndrome, where a single application running in a container can consume most or all of the available resources of the whole Docker host. Control groups allow Docker to limit the resources, such as CPU time or the amount of RAM that each container gets maximally allocated.

The container runtime on a Docker host consists of `containerd` and `runc`. `runc` is the low-level functionality of the container runtime and `containerd`, which is based on `runc`, provides the higher-level functionality. Both are open source and have been donated by Docker to the CNCF.

The container runtime is responsible for the whole life cycle of a container. It pulls a container image (which is the template for a container) from a registry if necessary, creates a container from that image, initializes and runs the container, and eventually stops and removes the container from the system when asked.

The Docker engine provides additional functionality on top of the container runtime, such as network libraries or support for plugins. It also provides a REST interface over which all container operations can be automated. The Docker command-line interface that we will use frequently in this book is one of the consumers of this REST interface.

Summary

In this chapter, we looked at how containers can massively reduce the friction in the software supply chain and on top of that, make the supply chain much more secure.

In the upcoming chapter, we will familiarize ourselves with containers. We will learn how to run, stop, and remove containers and otherwise manipulate them. We will also have a pretty good overview over the anatomy of containers. For the first time, we're really going to get our hands dirty and play with these containers, so stay tuned.

Questions

Please solve the following questions to assess your learning progress:

1. Which statements are correct (multiple answers are possible)?
    1. A container is kind of a lightweight VM
    2. A container only runs on a Linux host
    3. A container can only run one process
    4. The main process in a container always has PID 1
    5. A container is one or more processes encapsulated by Linux namespaces and restricted by cgroups
2. Explain to an interested layman in your own words, maybe using analogies, what a container is.
3. Why are containers considered to be a game changer in IT? Name three to four reasons.
4. What does it mean when we claim: *If a container runs on a given platform then it runs anywhere...*? Name two to three reasons why this is true.
5. True or False: *Docker containers are only really useful for modern greenfield applications based on microservices*. Please justify your answer.
6. How much does a typical enterprise save when containerizing their legacy applications?
    1. 20%
    2. 33%
    3. 50%
    4. 75%
7. Which two core concepts of Linux are containers based on?

Further reading

Here is a list of links that lead to more detailed information regarding topics we have discussed in this chapter:

- *Docker overview* at `https://docs.docker.com/engine/docker-overview/`
- *The Moby project* at `https://mobyproject.org/`
- *Docker products* at `https://www.docker.com/get-docker`
- *Cloud Native Computing Foundation* at `https://www.cncf.io/`
- *containerd – industry standard container runtime* at `https://containerd.io/`

Setting up a Working Environment

2

In the last chapter, we learned what Docker containers are and why they're important. We learned what kinds of problem containers solve in a modern software supply chain.

In this chapter, we are going to prepare our personal or working environment to work efficiently and effectively with Docker. We will discuss in detail how to set up an ideal environment for developers, DevOps, and operators that can be used when working with Docker containers.

This chapter covers the following topics:

- The Linux command shell
- PowerShell for Windows
- Using a package manager
- Choosing a code editor
- Docker Toolbox
- Docker for Mac and Docker for Windows
- Minikube

After completing this chapter, you will be able to do the following:

- Use an editor on your laptop that is able to edit simple files such as a Dockerfile or a `docker-compose.yml` file
- Use a shell such as Bash on Mac and PowerShell on Windows to execute Docker commands and other simple operations, such as navigating the folder structure or creating a new folder
- Install Docker for Mac or Docker for Windows on your computer
- Execute simple Docker commands such as `docker version` or `docker container run` on your Docker for Mac or Docker for Windows

- Successfully install Docker Toolbox on your computer
- Use `docker-machine` to create a Docker host on VirtualBox
- Configure your local Docker CLI to remote access a Docker host running in VirtualBox

Technical requirements

For this chapter, you will need a laptop or a workstation with either macOS or Windows, preferably Windows 10 Professional, installed. You should also have free internet access to download applications and the permission to install those applications on your laptop.

The Linux command shell

Docker containers were first developed on Linux for Linux. It is thus natural that the primary command-line tool used to work with Docker, also called a shell, is a Unix shell; remember, Linux derives from Unix. Most developers use the Bash shell. On some lightweight Linux distributions, such as Alpine, Bash is not installed and consequently one has to use the simpler Bourne shell, just called **sh**. Whenever we are working in a Linux environment, such as inside a container or on a Linux VM, we will use either `/bin/bash` or `/bin/sh`, depending on their availability.

Although macOS X is not a Linux OS, Linux and OS X are both flavors of Unix and thus support the same types of tools. Among those tools are the shells. So, when working on a Mac, you will probably be using the Bash shell.

In this book, we expect from the readers a familiarity with the most basic scripting commands in Bash, and PowerShell if you are working on Windows. If you are an absolute beginner, then we strongly recommend that you familiarize yourself with the following cheat sheets:

- *Linux Command Line Cheat Sheet* by Dave Child at `http://bit.ly/2mTQr8l`
- *PowerShell Basic Cheat Sheet* at `http://bit.ly/2EPHxze`

PowerShell for Windows

On a Windows computer, laptop, or server, we have multiple command-line tools available. The most familiar is the command shell. It has been available on any Windows computer for decades. It is a very simple shell. For more advanced scripting, Microsoft has developed PowerShell. PowerShell is very powerful and very popular among engineers working on Windows. On Windows 10, finally, we have the so-called **Windows Subsystem for Linux**, which allows us to use any Linux tool, such as the Bash or Bourne shells. Apart from this, there also exist other tools that install a Bash shell on Windows, for example, the Git Bash shell. In this book, all commands will use Bash syntax. Most of the commands also run in PowerShell.

Our recommendation for you is thus to either use PowerShell or any other Bash tool to work with Docker on Windows.

Using a package manager

The easiest way to install software on a Mac or Windows laptop is to use a good package manager. On a Mac, most people use **Homebrew** and on Windows, **Chocolatey** is a good choice.

Installing Homebrew on a Mac

Installing Homebrew on a Mac is easy; just follow the instructions at https://brew.sh/.

The following is the command to install Homebrew:

```
/usr/bin/ruby -e "$(curl -fsSL
https://raw.githubusercontent.com/Homebrew/install/master/install)"
```

Once the installation is finished, test whether Homebrew is working by entering brew --version in the Terminal. You should see something like this:

```
$ brew --version
Homebrew 1.4.3
Homebrew/homebrew-core (git revision f4e35; last commit 2018-01-11)
```

Now, we are ready to use Homebrew to install tools and utilities. If we, for example, want to install the Vi text editor, we can do so like this:

```
$ brew install vim
```

This will then download and install the editor for you.

Installing Chocolatey on Windows

To install the Chocolatey package manager on Windows, please follow the instructions at `https://chocolatey.org/` or just execute the following command in a PowerShell Terminal that you have run as administrator:

```
PS> Set-ExecutionPolicy Bypass -Scope Process -Force; iex ((New-Object
System.Net.WebClient).DownloadString('https://chocolatey.org/install.ps1'))
```

Once Chocolatey is installed, test it with the command `choco` without additional parameters. You should see output similar to the following:

```
PS> choco
Chocolatey v0.10.3
```

To install an application such as the Vi editor, use the following command:

```
PS> choco install -y vim
```

The `-y` parameter makes sure that the installation happens without asking for reconfirmation. Please note that once Chocolatey has installed an application, you need to open a new PowerShell window to use it.

Choosing a code editor

Using a good code editor is essential to working productively with Docker. Of course, which editor is the best is highly controversial and depends on your personal preference. A lot of people use Vim, or others such as Emacs, Atom, Sublime, or **Visual Studio (VS)** Code, to just name a few. If you have not yet decided which editor is best suited for you, then I highly recommend that you try VS Code. This is a free and lightweight editor, yet it is very powerful and is available for Mac, Windows, and Linux. Give it a try. You can download VS Code from `https://code.visualstudio.com/download`.

But if you already have a favorite code editor, then please continue using it. As long as you can edit text files, you're good to go. If your editor supports syntax highlighting for Dockerfiles and JSON and YAML files, then even better.

Docker Toolbox

Docker Toolbox has been available for developers for a few years. It precedes the newer tools such as Docker for Mac and Docker for Windows. The toolbox allows a user to work very elegantly with containers on any Mac or Windows computer. Containers must run on a Linux host. Neither Windows or Mac can run containers natively. Thus, we need to run a Linux VM on our laptop, where we can then run our containers. Docker Toolbox installs VirtualBox on our laptop, which is used to run the Linux VMs we need.

 As a Windows user, you might already be aware that there exists so-called Windows containers that run natively on Windows. And you are right. Recently, Microsoft has ported the Docker engine to Windows and it is now possible to run Windows containers directly on a Windows Server 2016 without the need for a VM. So, now we have two flavors of containers, Linux containers and Windows containers. The former only run on Linux host and the latter only run on a Windows Server. In this book, we are exclusively discussing Linux containers, but most of the things we learn also apply to Windows containers.

Let's use `docker-machine` to set up our environment. Firstly, we list all Docker-ready VMs we have currently defined on our system. If you have just installed Docker Toolbox, you should see the following output:

NAME	ACTIVE	DRIVER	STATE	URL	SWARM	DOCKER	ERRORS
default	-	virtualbox	Running	tcp://192.168.99.100:2376		v18.04.0-ce	

List of all Docker-ready VMs

The IP address used might be different in your case, but it will be definitely in the `192.168.0.0/24` range. We can also see that the VM has Docker version `18.04.0-ce` installed.

If, for some reason, you don't have a default VM or you have accidentally deleted it, you can create it using the following command:

```
$ docker-machine create --driver virtualbox default
```

The output you should see looks as follows:

```
$ docker-machine create --driver virtualbox default
Running pre-create checks...
Creating machine...
(default) Copying /Users/gabriel/.docker/machine/cache/boot2docker.iso to /Users/gabriel/.docker/machine/
machines/default/boot2docker.iso...
(default) Creating VirtualBox VM...
(default) Creating SSH key...
(default) Starting the VM...
(default) Check network to re-create if needed...
(default) Waiting for an IP...
Waiting for machine to be running, this may take a few minutes...
Detecting operating system of created instance...
Waiting for SSH to be available...
Detecting the provisioner...
Provisioning with boot2docker...
Copying certs to the local machine directory...
Copying certs to the remote machine...
Setting Docker configuration on the remote daemon...
Checking connection to Docker...
Docker is up and running!
To see how to connect your Docker Client to the Docker Engine running on this virtual machine, run: docke
r-machine env default
$ 
```

Creating the VM called default in VirtualBox

To see how to connect your Docker client to the Docker Engine running on this virtual machine, run the following command:

```
$ docker-machine env default
```

Once we have our VM called default ready, we can try to SSH into it:

```
$ docker-machine ssh default
```

When executing the preceding command, we are greeted by a boot2docker welcome message.

Type docker --version in the Command Prompt as follows:

```
docker@default:~$ docker --version
Docker version 17.12.1-ce, build 7390fc6
```

Now, let's try to run a container:

```
docker@default:~$ docker run hello-world
```

This will produce the following output:

```
docker@default:~$ docker run hello-world
Unable to find image 'hello-world:latest' locally
latest: Pulling from library/hello-world
ca4f61b1923c: Pull complete
Digest: sha256:97ce6fa4b6cdc0790cda65fe7290b74cfebd9fa0c9b8c38e979330d547d22ce1
Status: Downloaded newer image for hello-world:latest

Hello from Docker!
This message shows that your installation appears to be working correctly.

To generate this message, Docker took the following steps:
 1. The Docker client contacted the Docker daemon.
 2. The Docker daemon pulled the "hello-world" image from the Docker Hub.
    (amd64)
 3. The Docker daemon created a new container from that image which runs the
    executable that produces the output you are currently reading.
 4. The Docker daemon streamed that output to the Docker client, which sent it
    to your terminal.

To try something more ambitious, you can run an Ubuntu container with:
 $ docker run -it ubuntu bash

Share images, automate workflows, and more with a free Docker ID:
 https://cloud.docker.com/

For more examples and ideas, visit:
 https://docs.docker.com/engine/userguide/

docker@default:~$ █
```

Running the Docker Hello World container

Docker for Mac and Docker for Windows

If you are using a Mac or have Windows 10 Professional installed on your laptop, then we strongly recommend that you install Docker for Mac or Docker for Windows. These tools give you the best experience when working with containers. Note, older versions of Windows or Windows 10 Home edition cannot run Docker for Windows. Docker for Windows uses Hyper-V to run containers transparently in a VM but Hyper-V is not available on older versions of Windows nor is it available in the Home edition.

Installing Docker for Mac

Navigate to the following link to download Docker for Mac at `https://docs.docker.com/docker-for-mac/install/`.

 There is a stable version and a so-called edge version of the tool available. In this book, we are going to use some newer features and Kubernetes, which at the time of writing are only available in the edge version. Thus, please select this version.

To start the installation, click on the **Get Docker for Mac (Edge)** button and follow the instructions.

Once you have successfully installed Docker for Mac, please open a Terminal. Press *command* + *spacebar* to open Spotlight and type `terminal`, then hit *Enter*. The Apple Terminal will open as follows:

```
⌂ gabriel — gabriel@Anubis — ~ — -zsh — 80×24
Last login: Sat Feb  3 12:49:33 on ttys005
➜  ~ ▊
```

Apple Terminal window

Type `docker --version` in the Command Prompt and hit *Enter*. If Docker for Mac is correctly installed, you should get an output similar to the following:

```
$ docker --version
Docker version 18.02.0-ce-rc2, build f968a2c
```

To see whether you can run containers, enter the following command into the Terminal and hit *Enter*:

```
$ docker run hello-world
```

If all goes well, your output should look something like the following:

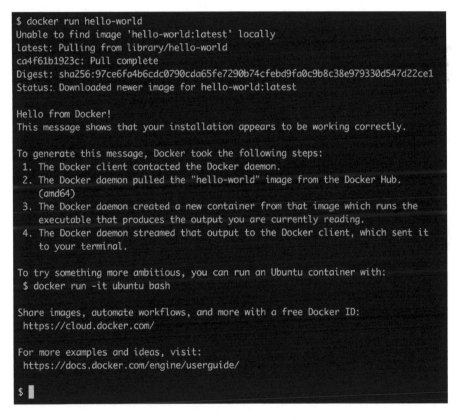

Running the Hello World container on Docker for Mac

Congratulations, you are now ready to work with Docker containers.

Installing Docker for Windows

Note, you can only install Docker for Windows on Windows 10 Professional or Windows Server 2016 since it requires Hyper-V, which is not available on older Windows versions or on the Home edition of Windows 10. If you are using Windows 10 Home or an older version of Windows, you will need to stick with Docker Toolbox.

Navigate to the following link to download Docker for Windows at `https://docs.docker.com/docker-for-windows/install/`.

 There is a stable version and a so-called edge version of the tool available. In this book, we are going to use some newer features and Kubernetes, which at the time of writing are only available in the edge version. Thus, please select this version.

To start the installation, click on the **Get Docker for Windows (Edge)** button and follow the instructions.

With Docker for Windows, you can develop, run, and test Linux containers and Windows containers. In this book, though, we are only discussing Linux containers.

Once you have successfully installed Docker for Windows, open a PowerShell window and type `docker --version` in the Command Prompt. You should see something like the following:

```
PS> docker --version
Docker version 18.04.0-ce, build 3d479c0
```

Using docker-machine on Windows with Hyper-V

If you have Docker for Windows installed on your Windows laptop, then you also have Hyper-V enabled. In this case, you can't use Docker Toolbox since it uses VirtualBox, and Hyper-V and VirtualBox cannot coexist and run at the same time. In this case, you can use `docker-machine` with the Hyper-V driver.

Open a PowerShell console as an administrator. Install `docker-machine` using Chocolatey as follows:

```
PS> choco install -y docker-machine
```

Create a VM called `boot2docker` in Hyper-V with the following command:

```
PS> docker-machine create --driver hyperv --hyperv-virtual-switch "My
Internal Switch" boot2docker
```

Note, you must run the preceding command in administrator mode or it will fail.

You should see the following output generated by the preceding command:

```
Running pre-create checks...
(boot2docker) Image cache directory does not exist, creating it at
C:\Users\Docker\.docker\machine\cache...
(boot2docker) No default Boot2Docker ISO found locally, downloading the
latest release...
(boot2docker) Latest release for github.com/boot2docker/boot2docker is
v18.01.0-ce
....
....
Checking connection to Docker...
Docker is up and running!
To see how to connect your Docker Client to the Docker Engine running on
this virtual machine, run: C:\Program Files\Doc
ker\Docker\Resources\bin\docker-machine.exe env boot2docker
```

To see how to connect your Docker client to the Docker Engine running on this virtual machine, run the following:

```
C:\Program Files\Docker\Docker\Resources\bin\docker-machine.exe env
boot2docker
```

Listing all VMs generated by `docker-machine` gives us the following output:

```
PS C:\WINDOWS\system32> docker-machine ls
NAME            ACTIVE   DRIVER   STATE     URL                 SWARM   DOCKER
ERRORS
boot2docker     -        hyperv   Running   tcp://[...]:2376
v18.01.0-ce
```

Now, let's SSH into our `boot2docker` VM:

```
PS> docker-machine ssh boot2docker
```

You should be greeted by the welcome screen.

We can test the VM by executing our `docker version` command, which is shown as follows:

```
$ docker version
Client:
 Version:      18.03.0-ce-rc4
 API version:  1.37
 Go version:   go1.9.4
 Git commit:   fbedb97
 Built: Thu Mar 15 07:33:28 2018
 OS/Arch:      darwin/amd64
 Experimental: false
 Orchestrator: swarm

Server:
 Engine:
  Version:      18.03.0-ce-rc4
  API version:  1.37 (minimum version 1.12)
  Go version:   go1.9.4
  Git commit:   fbedb97
  Built:        Thu Mar 15 07:42:29 2018
  OS/Arch:      linux/amd64
  Experimental: true
$
```

Version of the Docker client (CLI) and server

This is definitely a Linux VM, as we can see on the `OS/Arch` entry, and has Docker `18.03.0-ce-rc4` installed.

Minikube

If you cannot use Docker for Mac or Windows or, for some reason, you only have access to an older version of the tool that does not yet support Kubernetes, then it is a good idea to install Minikube. Minikube provisions a single-node Kubernetes cluster on your workstation and is accessible through **kubectl**, which is the command-line tool used to work with Kubernetes.

Installing Minikube on Mac and Windows

To install Minikube for Mac or Windows, navigate to the following link at `https://kubernetes.io/docs/tasks/tools/install-minikube/`.

Follow the instructions carefully. If you have the Docker Toolbox installed, then you already have a hypervisor on your system since the Docker Toolbox installer also installed VirtualBox. Otherwise, I recommend that you install VirtualBox first.

If you have Docker for Mac or Windows installed, then you already have `kubectl` installed with it, thus you can skip that step too. Otherwise, follow the instructions on the site.

Finally, select the latest binary for Minikube for Mac or Windows and install it. For Mac, the latest binary is called `minikube-darwin-amd64` and for Windows it is `minikube-windows-amd64`.

Testing Minikube and kubectl

Once Minikube is successfully installed on your workstation, open a Terminal and test the installation. First, we need to start Minikube. Enter `minikube start` at the command line. The output should look like the following:

```
Starting local Kubernetes v1.9.0 cluster...
Starting VM...
Downloading Minikube ISO
 142.22 MB / 142.22 MB [============================================] 100.00% 0s
Getting VM IP address...
Moving files into cluster...
Downloading localkube binary
 162.41 MB / 162.41 MB [============================================] 100.00% 0s
 0 B / 65 B [------------------------------------------------------]   0.00%
 65 B / 65 B [============================================] 100.00% 0sSetting up certs...
Connecting to cluster...
Setting up kubeconfig...
Starting cluster components...
Kubectl is now configured to use the cluster.
Loading cached images from config file.
$
```

Starting Minikube

Now, enter `kubectl version` and hit *Enter* to see something like the following screenshot:

```
$ kubectl version
Client Version: version.Info{Major:"1", Minor:"9", GitVersion:"v1.9.0", GitCommit:"925c127ec6b946659ad0fd596fa959be43f0cc05"
, GitTreeState:"clean", BuildDate:"2017-12-15T21:07:38Z", GoVersion:"go1.9.2", Compiler:"gc", Platform:"darwin/amd64"}
Server Version: version.Info{Major:"", Minor:"", GitVersion:"v1.9.0", GitCommit:"925c127ec6b946659ad0fd596fa959be43f0cc05",
GitTreeState:"clean", BuildDate:"2018-01-26T19:04:38Z", GoVersion:"go1.9.1", Compiler:"gc", Platform:"linux/amd64"}
$
```

Determining the version of the Kubernetes client and server

If the preceding command fails, for example, by timing out, then it could be that your `kubectl` is not configured for the right context. `kubectl` can be used to work with many different Kubernetes clusters. Each cluster is called a context. To find out which context `kubectl` is currently configured for, use the following command:

```
$ kubectl config current-context
minikube
```

The answer should be `minikube`, as shown in the preceding output. If this is not the case, use `kubectl config get-contexts` to list all contexts that are defined on your system and then set the current context to `minikube` as follows:

```
$ kubectl config use-context minikube
```

The configuration for `kubectl`, where it stores the contexts, is normally found in `~/.kube/config`, but this can be overridden by defining an environment variable called `KUBECONFIG`. You might need to unset this variable if it is set on your computer.

For more in-depth information about how to configure and use Kubernetes contexts, consult the link at `https://kubernetes.io/docs/concepts/configuration/organize-cluster-access-kubeconfig/`.

Assuming Minikube and `kubectl` work as expected, we can now use `kubectl` to get information about the Kubernetes cluster. Enter the following command:

```
$ kubectl get nodes
NAME        STATUS    ROLES     AGE       VERSION
minikube    Ready     <none>    47d       v1.9.0
```

Evidently, we have a cluster of one node, which in my case has Kubernetes `v1.9.0` installed on it.

Summary

In this chapter, we set up and configured our personal or working environment so that we can productively work with Docker containers. This equally applies for developers, DevOps, and operations engineers. In that context, we made sure that we use a good editor, have Docker for Mac or Windows installed, and can also use `docker-machine` to create VMs in VirtualBox or Hyper-V which we can use to run and test containers.

In the next chapter, we're going to learn all the important facts about containers. For example, we will explore how we can run, stop, list, and delete containers, but more than that, we will also dive deep into the anatomy of containers.

Questions

On the basis of your reading of this chapter, please answer the following questions:

1. What is `docker-machine` used for? Name three to four scenarios.
2. True or false? With Docker for Windows, one can develop and run Linux containers.
3. Why are good scripting skills (such as Bash or PowerShell) essential for a productive use of containers?
4. Name three to four Linux distributions on which Docker is certified to run.
5. Name all the Windows versions on which you can run Windows containers.

Further reading

Consider the following link for further reading:

- *Run Docker on Hyper-V with Docker Machine* at `http://bit.ly/2HGMPiI`

3

Working with Containers

In the previous chapter, you learned how to optimally prepare your working environment for the productive and frictionless use of Docker. In this chapter, we are going to get our hands dirty and learn everything that is important to work with containers. Here are the topics we're going to cover in this chapter:

- Running the first container
- Starting, stopping, and removing containers
- Inspecting containers
- Exec into a running container
- Attaching to a running container
- Retrieving container logs
- Anatomy of containers

After finishing this chapter you will be able to do the following things:

- Run, stop, and delete a container based on an existing image, such as NGINX, busybox, or alpine
- List all containers on the system
- Inspect the metadata of a running or stopped container
- Retrieve the logs produced by an application running inside a container
- Run a process such as `/bin/sh` in an already-running container.
- Attach a Terminal to an already-running container
- Explain in your own words to an interested layman the underpinnings of a container

Technical requirements

For this chapter, you should have installed Docker for Mac or Docker for Windows. If you are on an older version of Windows or are using Windows 10 Home Edition, then you should have Docker Toolbox installed and ready to use. On macOS, use the Terminal application, and on Windows, a PowerShell console to try out the commands you will be learning.

Running the first container

Before we start, we want to make sure that Docker is installed correctly on your system and ready to accept your commands. Open a new Terminal window and type in the following command:

```
$ docker -v
```

If everything works correctly, you should see the version of Docker installed on your laptop output in the Terminal. At the time of writing, it looks like this:

```
Docker version 17.12.0-ce-rc2, build f9cde63
```

If this doesn't work, then something with your installation is not right. Please make sure that you have followed the instructions in the previous chapter on how to install Docker for Mac or Docker for Windows on your system.

So, you're ready to see some action. Please type the following command into your Terminal window and hit return:

```
$ docker container run alpine echo "Hello World"
```

When you run the preceding command the first time, you should see an output in your Terminal window similar to this:

```
Unable to find image 'alpine:latest' locally
latest: Pulling from library/alpine
2fdfe1cd78c2: Pull complete
Digest: sha256:ccba511b...
Status: Downloaded newer image for alpine:latest
Hello World
```

Now that was easy! Let's try to run the very same command again:

```
$ docker container run alpine echo "Hello World"
```

The second, third, or nth time you run the preceding command, you should see only this output in your Terminal:

```
Hello World
```

Try to reason about why the first time you run a command you see a different output than all the subsequent times. But don't worry if you can't figure it out, we will explain the reasons in detail in the following sections of the chapter.

Starting, stopping, and removing containers

You have successfully run a container in the previous section. Now we want to investigate in detail what exactly happened and why. Let's look again at the command we used:

```
$ docker container run alpine echo "Hello World"
```

This command contains multiple parts. First and foremost, we have the word `docker`. This is the name of the Docker **command-line interface (CLI)**, which we are using to interact with the Docker engine that is responsible to run containers. Next, we have the word `container`, which indicates the context we are working with. As we want to run a container, our context is the word `container`. Next is the actual command we want to execute in the given context, which is `run`.

Let me recap—so far, we have `docker container run`, which means, *Hey Docker, we want to run a container....*

Now we also need to tell Docker which container to run. In this case, this is the so-called `alpine` container. Finally, we need to define what kind of process or task shall be executed inside the container when it is running. In our case, this is the last part of the command, `echo "Hello World"`.

Maybe the following figure can help you to get a better approach to the whole thing:

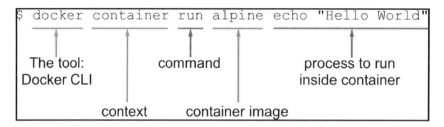

Anatomy of the docker container run expression

Now that we have understood the various parts of a command to run a container, let's try to run another container with a different process running inside it. Type the following command into your Terminal:

```
$ docker container run centos ping -c 5 127.0.0.1
```

You should see output in your Terminal window similar to the following:

```
Unable to find image 'centos:latest' locally
latest: Pulling from library/centos
85432449fd0f: Pull complete
Digest: sha256:3b1a65e9a05...
Status: Downloaded newer image for centos:latest
PING 127.0.0.1 (127.0.0.1) 56(84) bytes of data.
64 bytes from 127.0.0.1: icmp_seq=1 ttl=64 time=0.022 ms
64 bytes from 127.0.0.1: icmp_seq=2 ttl=64 time=0.019 ms
64 bytes from 127.0.0.1: icmp_seq=3 ttl=64 time=0.029 ms
64 bytes from 127.0.0.1: icmp_seq=4 ttl=64 time=0.030 ms
64 bytes from 127.0.0.1: icmp_seq=5 ttl=64 time=0.029 ms

--- 127.0.0.1 ping statistics ---
5 packets transmitted, 5 received, 0% packet loss, time 4103ms
rtt min/avg/max/mdev = 0.021/0.027/0.029/0.003 ms
```

What changed is that, this time, the container image we're using is centos and the process we're executing inside the centos container is ping -c 5 127.0.0.1, which pings the loopback address for five times until it stops.

- The first line is as follows:

  `Unable to find image 'centos:latest' locally`

  This tells us that Docker didn't find an image named `centos:latest` in the local cache of the system. So, Docker knows that it has to pull the image from some registry where container images are stored. By default, your Docker environment is configured such as that images are pulled from the Docker Hub at `docker.io`. This is expressed by the second line, as follows:

  `latest: Pulling from library/centos`

- The next three lines of output are as follows:

  ```
  85432449fd0f: Pull complete
  Digest: sha256:3b1a65e9a05...
  Status: Downloaded newer image for centos:latest
  ```

  This tells us that Docker has successfully pulled the image `centos:latest` from the Docker Hub.

All the subsequent lines of the output are generated by the process we ran inside the container, which is the ping tool in this case. If you have been attentive so far, then you might have noticed the keyword `latest` occurring a few times. Each image has a version (also called a tag), and if we don't specify a version explicitly, then Docker automatically assumes it as latest.

If we run the preceding container again on our system, the first five lines of the output will be missing since, this time, Docker will find the container image cached locally and thus won't have to download it first. Try it out and verify what I just told.

Running a random quotes container

For the subsequent sections of this chapter, we need a container that runs continuously in the background and produces some interesting output. That's why, we have chosen an algorithm that produces random quotes. The API that produces those free random quotes can be found at `https://talaikis.com/random_quotes_api/`.

Now the goal is to have a process running inside a container that produces a new random quote every five seconds and outputs the quote to STDOUT. The following script will do exactly that:

```
while :
do
    wget -qO- https://talaikis.com/api/quotes/random
    printf 'n'
    sleep 5
done
```

Try it in a Terminal window. Stop the script by pressing *Ctrl+ C*. The output should look similar to this:

```
{"quote":"Martha Stewart is extremely talented. Her designs are picture
perfect. Our philosophy is life is messy, and rather than being afraid of
those messes we design products that work the way we live.","author":"Kathy
Ireland","cat":"design"}

{"quote":"We can reach our potential, but to do so, we must reach within
ourselves. We must summon the strength, the will, and the faith to move
forward - to be bold - to invest in our future.","author":"John
Hoeven","cat":"faith"}
```

Each response is a JSON-formatted string with the quote, its author, and its category.

Now, let's run this in an `alpine` container as a daemon in the background. For this, we need to compact the preceding script into a one-liner and execute it using the `/bin/sh -c "..."` syntax. Our Docker expression will look as follows :

```
$ docker container run -d --name quotes alpine \
    /bin/sh -c "while :; do wget -qO-
https://talaikis.com/api/quotes/random; printf '\n'; sleep 5; done"
```

In the preceding expression, we have used two new command-line parameters, `-d` and `--name`. The `-d` tells Docker to run the process running in the container as a Linux daemon. The `--name` parameter in turn can be used to give the container an explicit name. In the preceding sample, the name we chose is `quotes`.

If we don't specify an explicit container name when we run a container, then Docker will automatically assign the container a random but unique name. This name will be composed of the name of a famous scientist and and adjective. Such names could be `boring_borg` or `angry_goldberg`. Quite humorous our Docker engineers, *isn't it?*

One important takeaway is that the container name has to be unique on the system. Let's make sure that the quotes container is up and running:

```
$ docker container ls -l
```

This should give us something like this:

Listing the last run container

The important part of the preceding output is the STATUS column, which in this case is Up 16 seconds. That is, the container has been up and running for 16 seconds now.

Don't worry if the last Docker command is not yet familiar to you, we will come back to it in the next section.

Listing containers

As we continue to run containers over time, we get a lot of them in our system. To find out what is currently-running on our host, we can use the container `list` command as follows:

```
$ docker container ls
```

This will list all currently-running containers. Such a list might look similar to this:

List of all containers running on the system

By default, Docker outputs seven columns with the following meanings:

Column	Description
Container ID	The unique ID of the container. It is a SHA-256.
Image	The name of the container image from which this container is instantiated.
Command	The command that is used to run the main process in the container.
Created	The date and time when the container was created.
Status	The status of the container (created, restarting, running, removing, paused, exited, or dead).
Ports	The list of container ports that have been mapped to the host.
Names	The name assigned to this container (multiple names are possible).

If we want to list not only the currently running containers but all containers that are defined on our system, then we can use the command-line parameter -a or --all as follows:

```
$ docker container ls -a
```

This will list containers in any state, such as created, running, or exited.

Sometimes, we want to just list the IDs of all containers. For this, we have the parameter -q:

```
$ docker container ls -q
```

You might wonder where this is useful. I show you a command where it is very helpful right here:

```
$ docker container rm -f $(docker container ls -a -q)
```

Lean back and take a deep breath. Then, try to find out what the preceding command does. Don't read any further until you find the answer or give up.

Right: the preceding command deletes all containers that are currently defined on the system, including the stopped ones. The rm command stands for remove, and it will be explained further down.

In the previous section, we used the parameter -1 in the list command. Try to use Docker help to find out what the -1 parameter stands for. You can invoke help for the list command as follows:

```
$ docker container ls -h
```

Stopping and starting containers

Sometimes, we want to (temporarily) stop a running container. Let's try this out with the quotes container we used previously. Run the container again with this command:

```
$ docker container run -d --name quotes alpine \
    /bin/sh -c "while :; do wget -qO-
https://talaikis.com/api/quotes/random; printf '\n'; sleep 5; done"
```

Now, if we want to stop this container then we can do so by issuing this command:

```
$ docker container stop quotes
```

When you try to stop the quotes container, you will probably note that it takes a while until this command is executed. To be precise, it takes about 10 seconds. *Why is this the case?*

Docker sends a Linux SIGTERM signal to the main process running inside the container. If the process doesn't react to this signal and terminate itself, Docker waits for 10 seconds and then sends SIGKILL, which will kill the process forcefully and terminate the container.

In the preceding command, we have used the name of the container to specify which container we want to stop. But we could also have used the container ID instead.

How do we get the ID of a container? There are several ways of doing so. The manual approach is to list all running containers and find the one that we're looking for in the list. From there, we copy its ID. A more automated way is to use some shell scripting and environment variables. If, for example, we want to get the ID of the quotes container, we can use this expression:

```
$ export CONTAINER_ID = $(docker container ls | grep quotes | awk '{print
$1}')
```

Now, instead of using the container name, we can use the variable $CONTAINER_ID in our expression:

```
$ docker container stop $CONTAINER_ID
```

Once we have stopped the container, its status change to `Exited`.

If a container is stopped, it can be started again using the `docker container start` command. Let's do this with our quotes container. It is good to have it running again, as we'll need it in the subsequent sections of this chapter:

```
$ docker container start quotes
```

Removing containers

When we run the `docker container ls -a` command, we can see quite a few containers that are in status `Exited`. If we don't need these containers anymore, then it is a good thing to remove them from memory, otherwise they unnecessarily occupy precious resources. The command to remove a container is:

```
$ docker container rm <container ID>
```

Another command to remove a container is:

```
$ docker container rm <container name>
```

Try to remove one of your exited containers using its ID.

Sometimes, removing a container will not work as it is still running. If we want to force a removal, no matter what the condition of the container currently is, we can use the command-line parameter `-f` or `--force`.

Inspecting containers

Containers are runtime instances of an image and have a lot of associated data that characterizes their behavior. To get more information about a specific container, we can use the `inspect` command. As usual, we have to provide either the container ID or name to identify the container of which we want to obtain the data. So, let's inspect our sample container:

```
$ docker container inspect quotes
```

The response is a big JSON object full of details. It looks similar to this:

```
[
    {
        "Id": "c5c1c68c87...",
```

```
        "Created": "2017-12-30T11:55:51.223271182Z",
        "Path": "/bin/sh",
        "Args": [
            "-c",
            "while :; do wget -qO-
https://talaikis.com/api/quotes/random; printf '\n'; sleep 5; done"
        ],
        "State": {
            "Status": "running",
            "Running": true,
            ...
        },
        "Image": "sha256:e21c333399e0...",
        ...
        "Mounts": [],
        "Config": {
            "Hostname": "c5c1c68c87dd",
            "Domainname": "",
            ...
        },
        "NetworkSettings": {
            "Bridge": "",
            "SandboxID": "2fd6c43b6fe5...",
            ...
        }
    }
]
```

The output has been shortened for readability.

Please take a moment to analyze what you got. You should see information such as:

- The ID of the container
- The creation date and time of the container
- From which image the container is built and so on

Many sections of the output, such as `Mounts` or `NetworkSettings` don't make much sense right now, but we will certainly discuss those in the upcoming chapters of the book. The data you're seeing here is also named the **metadata** of a container. We will be using the `inspect` command quite often in the remainder of the book as a source of information.

Sometimes, we need just a tiny bit of the overall information, and to achieve this, we can either use the **grep tool** or a **filter**. The former method does not always result in the expected answer, so let's look into the latter approach:

```
$ docker container inspect -f "{{json .State}}" quotes | jq
```

The `-f` or `--filter` parameter is used to define the filter. The filter expression itself uses the **Go template** syntax. In this example, we only want to see the state part of the whole output in the JSON format.

To nicely format the output, we pipe the result into the jq tool:

```
{
  "Status": "running",
  "Running": true,
  "Paused": false,
  "Restarting": false,
  "OOMKilled": false,
  "Dead": false,
  "Pid": 6759,
  "ExitCode": 0,
  "Error": "",
  "StartedAt": "2017-12-31T10:31:51.893299997Z",
  "FinishedAt": "0001-01-01T00:00:00Z"
}
```

Exec into a running container

Sometimes, we want to run another process inside an already-running container. A typical reason could be to try to debug a misbehaving container. *How can we do this?* First, we need to know either the ID or the name of the container, and then we can define which process we want to run and how we want it to run. Once again, we use our currently-running quotes container and we run a shell interactively inside it with the following command:

```
$ docker container exec -i -t quotes /bin/sh
```

The flag `-i` signifies that we want to run the additional process interactively, and `-t` tells Docker that we want it to provide us with a TTY (a terminal emulator) for the command. Finally, the process we run is `/bin/sh`.

If we execute the preceding command in our Terminal, then we will be presented with a new prompt. We're now in a shell inside the quotes container. We can easily prove that by, for example, executing the `ps` command, which will list all running processes in the context:

```
# / ps
```

The result should look somewhat similar to this:

```
/ # ps
PID   USER     TIME   COMMAND
   1 root      0:00 /bin/sh -c while :; do wget -q0- https://talaikis.com/api
  85 root      0:00 /bin/sh
 110 root      0:00 sleep 5
 111 root      0:00 ps
```

List of Processes running inside the quotes Container

We can clearly see that the process with `PID 1` is the command that we have defined to run inside the quotes container. The process with `PID 1` is also named the main process.

Leave the container by entering `exit` at the prompt. We cannot only execute additional processes interactive in a container. Please consider the following command:

```
$ docker container exec quotes ps
```

The output evidently looks very similar to the preceding output:

```
$ docker container exec quotes ps
PID   USER     TIME   COMMAND
   1 root      0:00 /bin/sh -c while :; do wget -q0- https://talaikis.com/api
 520 root      0:00 sleep 5
 521 root      0:00 ps
$
```

List of Processes running inside the quotes Container

We can even run processes as daemon using the flag `-d` and define environment variables using the `-e` flag variables as follows:

```
$ docker container exec -it \
    -e MY_VAR="Hello World" \
    quotes /bin/sh
# / echo $MY_VAR
Hello World
# / exit
```

Attaching to a running container

We can use the `attach` command to attach our Terminal's standard input, output, and error (or any combination of the three) to a running container using the ID or name of the container. Let's do this for our quotes container:

```
$ docker container attach quotes
```

In this case, we will see every five seconds or so a new quote appearing in the output.

To quit the container without stopping or killing it, we can press the key combination *Ctrl+P Ctrl+Q*. This detaches us from the container while leaving it running in the background. On the other hand, if we want to detach and stop the container at the same time, we can just press *Ctrl+C*.

Let's run another container, this time an Nginx web server:

```
$ docker run -d --name nginx -p 8080:80 nginx:alpine
```

Here, we run the Alpine version of Nginx as a daemon in a container named `nginx`. The `-p 8080:80` command-line parameter opens port `8080` on the host for access to the Nginx web server running inside the container. Don't worry about the syntax here as we will explain this feature in more detail in the `Chapter 7`, *Single-Host Networking*.

Let's see whether we can access Nginx, using the `curl` tool and running this command:

```
$ curl -4 localhost:8080
```

If all works correctly, you should be greeted by the welcome page of Nginx:

```
<html>
<head>
<title>Welcome to nginx!</title>
<style>
    body {
        width: 35em;
        margin: 0 auto;
        font-family: Tahoma, Verdana, Arial, sans-serif;
    }
</style>
</head>
<body>
<h1>Welcome to nginx!</h1>
<p>If you see this page, the nginx web server is successfully installed and
working. Further configuration is required.</p>
```

```
<p>For online documentation and support please refer to
<a href="http://nginx.org/">nginx.org</a>.<br/>
Commercial support is available at
<a href="http://nginx.com/">nginx.com</a>.</p>

<p><em>Thank you for using nginx.</em></p>
</body>
</html>
```

Now, let's attach our Terminal to the `nginx` container to observe what's happening:

```
$ docker container attach nginx
```

Once you are attached to the container, you first will not see anything. But now open another Terminal, and in this new Terminal window, repeat the `curl` command a few times, for example, using the following script:

```
$ for n in {1..10}; do curl -4 localhost:8080; done
```

You should see the logging output of Nginx, which looks similar to this:

```
172.17.0.1 - - [06/Jan/2018:12:20:00 +0000] "GET / HTTP/1.1" 200 612 "-"
"curl/7.54.0" "-"
172.17.0.1 - - [06/Jan/2018:12:20:03 +0000] "GET / HTTP/1.1" 200 612 "-"
"curl/7.54.0" "-"
172.17.0.1 - - [06/Jan/2018:12:20:05 +0000] "GET / HTTP/1.1" 200 612 "-"
"curl/7.54.0" "-"
...
```

Quit the container by pressing *Ctrl+C*. This will detach your Terminal and, at the same time, stop the `nginx` container.

To clean up, remove the `nginx` container with the following command:

```
$ docker container rm nginx
```

Retrieving container logs

It is a best practice for any good application to generate some logging information that developers and operators alike can use to find out what the application is doing at a given time, and whether there are any problems to help pinpoint the root cause of the issue.

When running inside a container, the application should preferably output the log items to STDOUT and STDERR and not into a file. If the logging output is directed to STDOUT and STDERR, then Docker can collect this information and keep it ready for consumption by a user or any other external system.

To access the logs of a given container, we can use the `docker container logs` command. If, for example, we want to retrieve the logs of our `quotes` container, we can use the following expression:

```
$ docker container logs quotes
```

This will retrieve the whole log produced by the application from the very beginning of its existence.

Stop, wait a second—this is not quite true, what I just said. By default, Docker uses the so-called `json-file` logging driver. This driver stores the logging information in a file. And if there is a file rolling policy defined, then `docker container logs` only retrieves what is in the current active log file and not what is in previous, rolled files that might still be available on the host.

If we want to only get a few of the latest entries, we can use the `-t` or `--tail` parameter, as follows:

```
$ docker container logs --tail 5 quotes
```

This will retrieve only the last five items the process running inside the container produced.

Sometimes, we want to follow the log that is produced by a container. This is possible when using the parameter `-f` or `--follow`. The following expression will output the last five log items and then follow the log as it is produced by the containerized process:

```
$ docker container logs --tail 5 --follow quotes
```

Logging drivers

Docker includes multiple logging mechanisms to help us get information from running containers. These mechanisms are named **logging drivers**. Which logging driver is used can be configured at the Docker daemon level. The default logging driver is `json-file`. Some of the drivers that are currently supported natively are:

Driver	Description
none	No log output for the specific container is produced.
json-file	This is the default driver. The logging information is stored in files, formatted as JSON.
journald	If the journals daemon is running on the host machine, we can use this driver. It forwards logging to the `journald` daemon.
syslog	If the `syslog` daemon is running on the host machine, we can configure this driver, which will forward the log messages to the `syslog` daemon.
gelf	When using this driver, log messages are written to a **Graylog Extended Log Format (GELF)** endpoint. Popular examples of such endpoints are Graylog and Logstash.
fluentd	Assuming that the `fluentd` daemon is installed on the host system, this driver writes log messages to it.

If you change the logging driver, please be aware that the `docker container logs` command is only available for the `json-file` and `journald` drivers.

Using a container-specific logging driver

We have seen that the logging driver can be set globally in the Docker daemon configuration file. But we can also define the logging driver on a container by container basis. In the following example, we are running a `busybox` container and use the `--log-driver` parameter to configure the `none` logging driver:

```
$ docker container run --name test -it \
    --log-driver none \
    busybox sh -c 'for N in 1 2 3; do echo "Hello $N"; done'
```

We should see the following:

```
Hello 1
Hello 2
Hello 3
```

Now, let's try to get the logs of the preceding container:

```
$ docker container logs test
```

The output is as follows:

```
Error response from daemon: configured logging driver does not support
reading
```

This is to be expected, since the none driver does not produce any logging output. Let's clean up and remove the test container:

```
$ docker container rm test
```

Advanced topic – changing the default logging driver

Let's change the default logging driver of a Linux host. The easiest way to do this is on a real Linux host. For this purpose, we're going to use Vagrant with an Ubuntu image:

```
$ vagrant init bento/ubuntu-17.04
$ vagrant up
$ vagrant ssh
```

Once inside the Ubuntu VM, we want to edit the Docker daemon configuration file. Navigate to the folder /etc/docker and run vi as follows:

```
$ vi daemon.json
```

Enter the following content:

```
{
  "Log-driver": "json-log",
  "log-opts": {
    "max-size": "10m",
    "max-file": 3
  }
}
```

Save and exit Vi by first pressing *Esc* and then typing `:w:q` and finally hitting the *ENTER* key.

The preceding definition tells the Docker daemon to use the `json-log` driver with a maximum log file size of 10 MB before it is rolled, and the maximum number of log files that can be present on the system is 3 before the oldest file gets purged.

Now we have to send a `SIGHUP` signal to the Docker daemon so that it picks up the changes in the configuration file:

```
$ sudo kill -SIGHUP $(pidof dockerd)
```

Note that the preceding command only reloads the config file and does not restart the daemon.

Anatomy of containers

Many individuals wrongly compare containers to VMs. However, this is a questionable comparison. Containers are not just lightweight VMs. OK then, *what is the correct description of a container?*

Containers are specially encapsulated and secured processes running on the host system.

Containers leverage a lot of features and primitives available in the Linux OS. The most important ones are **namespaces** and **cgroups**. All processes running in containers share the same Linux kernel of the underlying host operating system. This is fundamentally different compared with VMs, as each VM contains its own full-blown operating system.

The startup times of a typical container can be measured in milliseconds, while a VM normally needs several seconds to minutes to startup. VMs are meant to be long-living. It is a primary goal of each operations engineer to maximize the uptime of their VMs. Contrary to that, containers are meant to be ephemeral. They come and go in a quick cadence.

Let's first get a high-level overview of the architecture that enables us to run containers.

Architecture

Here, we have an architectural diagram on how this all fits together:

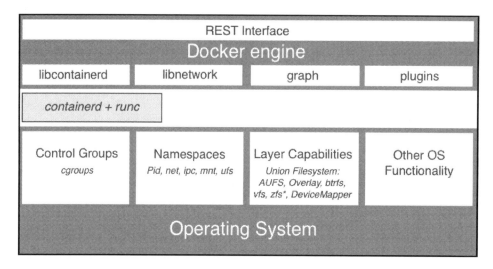

High level architecture of Docker

On the lower part of the the preceding figure, we have the Linux operating system with its cgroups, namespaces, and layer capabilities as well as other functionality that we do not need to explicitly mention here. Then, there is an intermediary layer composed of **containerd** and **runc**. On top of all that now sits the Docker engine. The Docker engine offers a RESTful interface to the outside world that can be accessed by any tool, such as the Docker CLI, Docker for Mac, and Docker for Windows or Kubernetes to just name a few.

Let's now describe the main building blocks in a bit more detail.

Namespaces

Linux namespaces had been around for years before they were leveraged by Docker for their containers. A namespace is an abstraction of global resources such as filesystems, network access, process tree (also named PID namespace) or the system group IDs, and user IDs. A Linux system is initialized with a single instance of each namespace type. After initialization, additional namespaces can be created or joined.

The Linux namespaces originated in 2002 in the 2.4.19 kernel. In kernel version 3.8, user namespaces were introduced and with it, namespaces were ready to be used by containers.

If we wrap a running process, say, in a filesystem namespace, then this process has the illusion that it owns its own complete filesystem. This of course is not true; it is only a virtual FS. From the perspective of the host, the contained process gets a shielded subsection of the overall FS. It is like a filesystem in a filesystem:

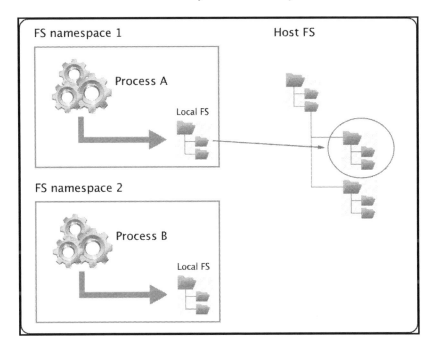

The same applies for all the other global resources for which namespaces exist. The user ID namespace is another example. Having a user namespace, we can now define a user `jdoe` many times on the system as long at it is living in its own namespace.

The PID namespace is what keeps processes in one container from seeing or interacting with processes in another container. A process might have the apparent PID **1** inside a container, but if we examine it from the host system, it would have an ordinary PID, say **334**:

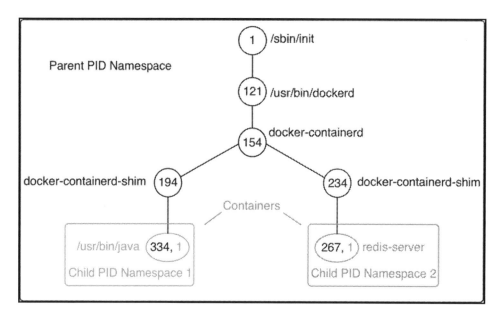

Process tree on a Docker host

In a given namespace, we can run one to many processes. That is important when we talk about containers, and we have experienced that already when we executed another process in an already-running container.

Control groups (cgroups)

Linux cgroups are used to limit, manage, and isolate resource usage of collections of processes running on a system. Resources are CPU time, system memory, network bandwidth, or combinations of these resources, and so on.

Engineers at Google have originally implemented this feature starting in 2006. The cgroups functionality was merged into the Linux kernel mainline in kernel version 2.6.24, which was released in January 2008.

Using cgroups, administrators can limit the resources that containers can consume. With this, one can avoid, for example, the classical *noisy neighbor* problem, where a rogue process running in a container consumes all CPU time or reserves massive amounts of RAM and, as such, starves all the other processes running on the host, whether they're containerized or not.

Union filesystem (UnionFS)

The UnionFS forms the backbone of what is known as container images. We will discuss container images in detail in the next chapter. At this time, we want to just understand a bit better what a UnionFS is and how it works. UnionFS is mainly used on Linux and allows files and directories of distinct filesystems to be overlaid and with it form a single coherent file system. In this context, the individual filesystems are called branches. Contents of directories that have the same path within the merged branches will be seen together in a single merged directory, within the new, virtual filesystem. When merging branches, the priority between the branches is specified. In that way, when two branches contain the same file, the one with the higher priority is seen in the final FS.

Container plumbing

The basement on top of which the Docker engine is built; we can also call it the **container plumbing** and is formed by the two component—**runc** and **containerd**.

Originally, Docker was built in a monolithic way and contained all the functionality necessary to run containers. Over time, this became too rigid and Docker started to break out parts of the functionality into their own components. Two important components are runc and containerd.

Runc

Runc is a lightweight, portable container runtime. It provides full support for Linux namespaces as well as native support for all security features available on Linux, such as SELinux, AppArmor, seccomp, and cgroups.

Runc is a tool for spawning and running containers according to the **Open Container Initiative (OCI)** specification. It is a formally specified configuration format, governed by the **Open Container Project (OCP)** under the auspices of the Linux Foundation.

Containerd

Runc is a low-level implementation of a container runtime; containerd builds on top of it, and adds higher-level features, such as image transfer and storage, container execution, and supervision, as well as network and storage attachments. With this, it manages the complete life cycle of containers. Containerd is the reference implementation of the OCI specifications and is by far the most popular and widely-used container runtime.

Containerd has been donated to and accepted by the CNCF in 2017. There exist alternative implementations of the OCI specification. Some of them are rkt by CoreOS, CRI-O by RedHat, and LXD by Linux Containers. However, containerd at this time is by far the most popular container runtime and is the default runtime of Kubernetes 1.8 or later and the Docker platform.

Summary

In this chapter, you learned how to work with containers that are based on existing images. We showed how to run, stop, start, and remove a container. Then, we inspected the metadata of a container, extracted the logs of it, and learned how to run an arbitrary process in an already-running container. Last but not least, we dug a bit deeper and investigated how containers work and what features of the underlying Linux operating system they leverage.

In the next chapter, you're going to learn what container images are and how we can build and share our own custom images. We're also discussing the best practices commonly used when building custom images, such as minimizing their size and leveraging the image cache. Stay tuned!

Questions

To assess your learning progress please answer the following questions:

1. What are the states of a container?
2. Which command helps us to find out what is currently running on our host?
3. Which command is used to list the IDs of all containers?

Further reading

The following articles give you some more information related to the topics we discussed in this chapter:

- *Docker container* at `http://dockr.ly/2iLBV2I`
- *Getting started with containers* at `http://dockr.ly/2gmxKWB`
- *Isolate containers with a user namespace* at `http://dockr.ly/2gmyKdf`
- *Limit container's resources* at `http://dockr.ly/2wqN5Nn`

4
Creating and Managing Container Images

In the previous chapter, we learned what containers are and how to run, stop, remove, list, and inspect them. We extracted the logging information of some containers, ran other processes inside an already running container, and finally we dived deep into the anatomy of containers. Whenever we ran a container, we created it using a container image. In this chapter, we will be familiarizing ourselves with these container images. We will learn in detail what they are, how to create them, and how to distribute them.

This chapter will cover the following topics:

- What images are?
- Creating images
- Sharing or shipping images

After completing this chapter, you will be able to do the following:

- Name three of the most important characteristics of a container image
- Create a custom image by interactively changing the container layer and committing it
- Author a simple Dockerfile using keywords such as `FROM`, `COPY`, `RUN`, `CMD`, and `ENTRYPOINT` to generate a custom image
- Export an existing image using `docker image save` and import it into another Docker host using `docker image load`
- Write a two-step Dockerfile that minimizes the size of the resulting image by only including the resulting artifacts (binaries) in the final image

What are images?

In Linux, everything is a file. The whole operating system is basically a filesystem with files and folders stored on the local disk. This is an important fact to remember when looking at what container images are. As we will see, an image is basically a big tarball containing a filesystem. More specifically, it contains a layered filesystem.

The layered filesystem

Container images are templates from which containers are created. These images are not just one monolithic block, but are composed of many layers. The first layer in the image is also called the base layer:

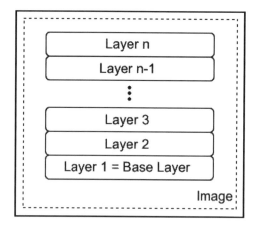

The image as a stack of layers

Each individual layer contains files and folders. Each layer only contains the changes to the filesystem with respect to the underlying layers. Docker uses a union filesystem—as discussed in `Chapter 3`, *Working with Containers*—to create a virtual filesystem out of the set of layers. A storage driver handles the details regarding the way these layers interact with each other. Different storage drivers are available that have advantages and disadvantages in different situations.

The layers of a container image are all immutable. Immutable means that once generated, the layer cannot ever be changed. The only possible operation affecting the layer is the physical deletion of it. This immutability of layers is important because it opens up a tremendous amount of opportunities, as we will see.

In the following image, we can see what a custom image for a web application using Nginx as a web server could look like:

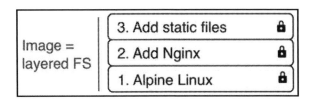

A sample custom image based on Alpine and Nginx

Our base layer here consists of the Alpine Linux distribution. Then, on top of that, we have a layer where Nginx is added on top of Alpine. Finally, the third layer contains all the files that make up the web application, such as HTML, CSS, and JavaScript files.

As has been said previously, each image starts with a base image. Typically, this base image is one of the official images found on Docker Hub, such as a Linux distro, Alpine, Ubuntu, or CentOS. However, it is also possible to create an image from scratch.

 Docker Hub is a public registry for container images. It is a central hub ideally suited for sharing public container images.

Each layer only contains the delta of changes in regard to the previous set of layers. The content of each layer is mapped to a special folder on the host system, which is usually a subfolder of `/var/lib/docker/`.

Since layers are immutable, they can be cached without ever becoming stale. This is a big advantage, as we will see.

The writable container layer

As we have discussed, a container image is made of a stack of immutable or read-only layers. When the Docker engine creates a container from such an image, it adds a writable container layer on top of this stack of immutable layers. Our stack now looks as follows:

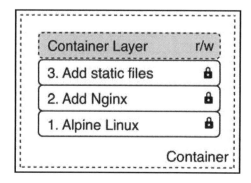

The writable container layer

The container layer is marked as read/write. Another advantage of the immutability of image layers is that they can be shared among many containers created from this image. All that is needed is a thin, writable container layer for each container:

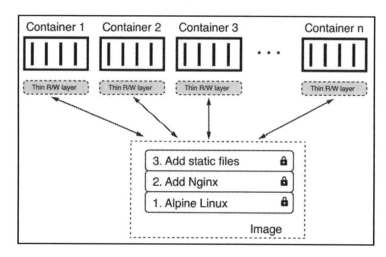

Multiple containers sharing the same image layers

This technique, of course, results in a tremendous reduction of resources that are consumed. Furthermore, this helps to decrease the loading time of a container since only a thin container layer has to be created once the image layers have been loaded into memory, which only happens for the first container.

Copy-on-write

Docker uses the copy-on-write technique when dealing with images. Copy-on-write is a strategy of sharing and copying files for maximum efficiency. If a layer uses a file or folder that is available in one of the low-lying layers, then it just uses it. If, on the other hand, a layer wants to modify, say, a file from a low-lying layer, then it first copies this file up to the target layer and then modifies it. In the following figure, we can see a glimpse of what this means:

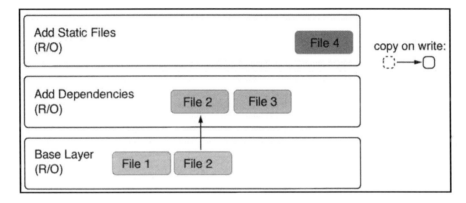

Copy-on-write

The second layer wants to modify **File 2**, which is present in the base layer. Thus, it copied it up and then modified it. Now, let's say that we're sitting in the top layer of the preceding figure. This layer will use **File 1** from the base layer and **File 2** and **File 3** from the second layer.

Graph drivers

Graph drivers are what enable the union filesystem. Graph drivers are also called storage drivers and are used when dealing with the layered container images. A graph driver consolidates the multiple image layers into a root filesystem for the mount namespace of the container. Or, put differently, the driver controls how images and containers are stored and managed on the Docker host.

Docker supports several different graph drivers using a pluggable architecture. The preferred driver is overlay2 followed by overlay.

Creating images

There are three ways to create a new container image on your system. The first one is by interactively building a container that contains all the additions and changes one desires and then committing those changes into a new image. The second and most important way is to use a Dockerfile to describe what's in the new image and then build this image using that Dockerfile as a manifest. Finally, the third way of creating an image is by importing it into the system from a tarball.

Now, let's look at these three ways in detail.

Interactive image creation

The first way we can create a custom image is by interactively building a container. That is, we start with a base image that we want to use as a template and run a container of it interactively. Let's say that this is the `alpine` image. The command to run the container would then be as follows:

```
$ docker container run -it --name sample alpine /bin/sh
```

By default, the alpine container does not have the `ping` tool installed. Let's assume we want to create a new custom image that has `ping` installed. Inside the container, we can then run the following command:

```
/ # apk update && apk add iputils
```

This uses the Alpine package manager `apk` to install the `iputils` library, of which `ping` is a part. The output of the preceding command should look as follows:

```
fetch http://dl-cdn.alpinelinux.org/alpine/v3.7/main/x86_64/APKINDEX.tar.gz
fetch
http://dl-cdn.alpinelinux.org/alpine/v3.7/community/x86_64/APKINDEX.tar.gz
v3.7.0-50-gc8da5122a4 [http://dl-cdn.alpinelinux.org/alpine/v3.7/main]
v3.7.0-49-g06d6ae04c3 [http://dl-cdn.alpinelinux.org/alpine/v3.7/community]
OK: 9046 distinct packages available
(1/2) Installing libcap (2.25-r1)
(2/2) Installing iputils (20121221-r8)
Executing busybox-1.27.2-r6.trigger
OK: 4 MiB in 13 packages
```

Now, we can indeed use `ping`, as the following snippet shows:

```
/ # ping 127.0.0.1
PING 127.0.0.1 (127.0.0.1) 56(84) bytes of data.
64 bytes from 127.0.0.1: icmp_seq=1 ttl=64 time=0.028 ms
64 bytes from 127.0.0.1: icmp_seq=2 ttl=64 time=0.044 ms
64 bytes from 127.0.0.1: icmp_seq=3 ttl=64 time=0.049 ms
^C
--- 127.0.0.1 ping statistics ---
3 packets transmitted, 3 received, 0% packet loss, time 2108ms
rtt min/avg/max/mdev = 0.028/0.040/0.049/0.010 ms
```

Once we have finished our customization, we can quit the container by typing `exit` at the prompt. If we now list all containers with `docker container ls -a`, we can see that our sample container has a status of `Exited`, but still exists on the system:

```
$ docker container ls -a | grep sample
eff7c92a1b98    alpine    "/bin/sh"    2 minutes ago    Exited (0) ...
```

If we want to see what has changed in our container in relation to the base image, we can use the `docker container diff` command as follows:

```
$ docker container diff sample
```

The output should present a list of all modifications done on the filesystem of the container:

```
C /bin
C /bin/ping
C /bin/ping6
A /bin/traceroute6
C /etc/apk
C /etc/apk/world
C /lib/apk/db
```

```
C /lib/apk/db/installed
C /lib/apk/db/lock
C /lib/apk/db/scripts.tar
C /lib/apk/db/triggers
C /root
A /root/.ash_history
C /usr/lib
A /usr/lib/libcap.so.2
A /usr/lib/libcap.so.2.25
C /usr/sbin
C /usr/sbin/arping
A /usr/sbin/capsh
A /usr/sbin/clockdiff
A /usr/sbin/getcap
A /usr/sbin/getpcaps
A /usr/sbin/ipg
A /usr/sbin/rarpd
A /usr/sbin/rdisc
A /usr/sbin/setcap
A /usr/sbin/tftpd
A /usr/sbin/tracepath
A /usr/sbin/tracepath6
C /var/cache/apk
A /var/cache/apk/APKINDEX.5022a8a2.tar.gz
A /var/cache/apk/APKINDEX.70c88391.tar.gz
C /var/cache/misc
```

In the preceding list, A stands for *added*, and C for *changed*. If we had any deleted files, then those would be prefixed with D.

We can now use the `docker container commit` command to persist our modifications and create a new image from them:

```
$ docker container commit sample my-alpine
sha256:44bca4141130ee8702e8e8efd1beb3cf4fe5aadb62a0c69a6995afd49c2e7419
```

With the preceding command, we have specified that the new image shall be called `my-alpine`. The output generated by the preceding command corresponds to the ID of the newly generated image. We can verify this by listing all images on our system, as follows:

```
$ docker image ls
```

We can see this image ID (shortened) as follows:

```
REPOSITORY  TAG      IMAGE ID        CREATED            SIZE
my-alpine   latest   44bca4141130    About a minute ago  5.64MB
...
```

We can see that the image named `my-alpine`, has the expected ID of `44bca4141130` and automatically got a tag `latest` assigned. This happens since we did not explicitly define a tag ourselves. In this case, Docker always defaults to the tag `latest`.

If we want to see how our custom image has been built, we can use the `history` command as follows:

```
$ docker image history my-alpine
```

This will print the list of layers our image consists of:

```
IMAGE              CREATED          CREATED BY          SIZE       COMMENT
44bca4141130       3 minutes ago    /bin/sh             1.5MB
e21c333399e0       6 weeks ago      /bin/sh -c #...     0B
<missing>          6 weeks ago      /bin/sh -c #...     4.14MB
```

The first layer in the preceding list is the one that we just created by adding the `iputils` package.

Using Dockerfiles

Manually creating custom images as shown in the previous section of this chapter is very helpful when doing exploration, creating prototypes, or making feasibility studies. But it has a serious drawback: it is a manual process and thus is not repeatable or scalable. It is also as error-prone as any task executed manually by humans. There must be a better way.

This is where the so-called Dockerfile comes into play. The Dockerfile is a text file that is usually literally called Dockerfile. It contains instructions on how to build a custom container image. It is a declarative way of building images.

Declarative versus imperative:
In computer science, in general and with Docker specifically, one often uses a declarative way of defining a task. One describes the expected outcome and lets the system figure out how to achieve this goal, rather than giving step-by-step instructions to the system on how to achieve this desired outcome. The latter is the imperative approach.

Let's look at a sample Dockerfile:

```
FROM python:2.7
RUN mkdir -p /app
WORKDIR /app
COPY ./requirements.txt /app/
RUN pip install -r requirements.txt
CMD ["python", "main.py"]
```

This is a Dockerfile as it is used to containerize a Python 2.7 application. As we can see, the file has six lines, each starting with a keyword such as FROM, RUN, or COPY. It is a convention to write the keywords in all caps, but that is not a must.

Each line of the Dockerfile results in a layer in the resulting image. In the following image, the image is drawn upside down compared to the previous illustrations in this chapter, showing an image as a stack of layers. Here, the base layer is shown on top. Don't let yourself be confused by this. In reality, the base layer is always the lowest layer in the stack:

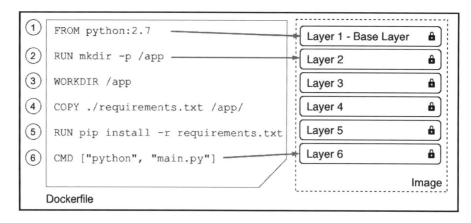

The relation of Dockerfile and layers in an image

Now let's look at the individual keywords in more detail.

The FROM keyword

Every Dockerfile starts with the FROM keyword. With it, we define which base image we want to start building our custom image from. If we want to build starting with CentOS 7, for example, we would have the following line in the Dockerfile:

```
FROM centos:7
```

On Docker Hub, there are curated or official images for all major Linux distros, as well as for all important development frameworks or languages, such as Python, Node JS, Ruby, Go, and many more. Depending on our need, we should select the most appropriate base image.

For example, if I want to containerize a Python 2.7 application, I might want to select the relevant official `python:2.7` image.

If we really want to start from scratch, we can also use the following statement:

```
FROM scratch
```

This is useful in the context of building super minimal images that only, for example, contain a single binary, the actual statically linked executable, such as `Hello-World`. The scratch image is literally an empty base image.

`FROM scratch` is a no-op in the Dockerfile, and as such does not generate a layer in the resulting container image.

The RUN keyword

The next important keyword is RUN. The argument for RUN is any valid Linux command, such as the following:

```
RUN yum install -y wget
```

The preceding command is using the CentOS package manager `yum` to install the `wget` package into the running container. This assumes that our base image is CentOS or RHEL. If we had Ubuntu as our base image, then the command would look similar to the following:

```
RUN apt-get update && apt-get install -y wget
```

It would look like this because Ubuntu uses `apt-get` as a package manager. Similarly, we could define a line with RUN like this:

```
RUN mkdir -p /app && cd /app
```

We could also do this:

```
RUN tar -xJC /usr/src/python --strip-components=1 -f python.tar.xz
```

Here, the former creates a `/app` folder in the container and navigates to it, and the latter untars a file to a given location. It is completely fine, and even recommended, for you to format a Linux command using more than one physical line, such as this:

```
RUN apt-get update \
    && apt-get install -y --no-install-recommends \
    ca-certificates \
    libexpat1 \
    libffi6 \
    libgdbm3 \
    libreadline7 \
    libsqlite3-0 \
    libssl1.1 \
    && rm -rf /var/lib/apt/lists/*
```

If we use more than one line, we need to put a backslash (\) at the end of the lines to indicate to the shell that the command continues on the next line.

Try to find out what the preceding command does.

The COPY and ADD keywords

The COPY and ADD keywords are very important since, in the end, we want to add some content to an existing base image to make it a custom image. Most of the time, these are a few source files of, say, a web application or a few binaries of a compiled application.

These two keywords are used to copy files and folders from the host into the image that we're building. The two keywords are very similar, with the exception that the ADD keyword also lets us copy and unpack TAR files, as well as provide a URL as a source for the files and folders to copy.

Let's look at a few examples of how these two keywords can be used:

```
COPY . /app
COPY ./web /app/web
COPY sample.txt /data/my-sample.txt
ADD sample.tar /app/bin/
ADD http://example.com/sample.txt /data/
```

In the preceding lines of code:

- The first line copies all files and folders from the current directory recursively to the `/app` folder inside the container image

- The second line copies everything in the `web` subfolder to the target folder, `/app/web`
- The third line copies a single file, `sample.txt`, into the target folder, `/data`, and at the same time, renames it to `my-sample.txt`
- The fourth statement unpacks the `sample.tar` file into the target folder, `/app/bin`
- Finally, the last statement copies the remote file, `sample.txt`, into the target file, `/data`

Wildcards are allowed in the source path. For example, the following statement copies all files starting with `sample` to the `mydir` folder inside the image:

```
COPY ./sample* /mydir/
```

From a security perspective, it is important to know that by default, all files and folders inside the image will have a **user ID (UID)** and a **group ID (GID)** of `0`. The good thing is that for both `ADD` and `COPY`, we can change the ownership that the files will have inside the image using the optional `--chown` flag, as follows:

```
ADD --chown=11:22 ./data/files* /app/data/
```

The preceding statement will copy all files starting with the name `web` and put them into the `/app/data` folder in the image, and at the same time assign user `11` and group `22` to these files.

Instead of numbers, one could also use names for the user and group, but then these entities would have to be already defined in the root filesystem of the image at `/etc/passwd` and `/etc/group` respectively, otherwise the build of the image would fail.

The WORKDIR keyword

The `WORKDIR` keyword defines the working directory or context that is used when a container is run from our custom image. So, if I want to set the context to the `/app/bin` folder inside the image, my expression in the Dockerfile would have to look as follows:

```
WORKDIR /app/bin
```

All activity that happens inside the image after the preceding line will use this directory as the working directory. It is very important to note that the following two snippets from a Dockerfile are not the same:

```
RUN cd /app/bin
RUN touch sample.txt
```

Compare the preceding code with the following code:

```
WORKDIR /app/bin
RUN touch sample.txt
```

The former will create the file in the root of the image filesystem, while the latter will create the file at the expected location in the /app/bin folder. Only the WORKDIR keyword sets the context across the layers of the image. The cd command alone is not persisted across layers.

The CMD and ENTRYPOINT keywords

The CMD and ENTRYPOINT keywords are special. While all other keywords defined for a Dockerfile are executed at the time the image is built by the Docker builder, these two are actually definitions of what will happen when a container is started from the image we define. When the container runtime starts a container, it needs to know what the process or application will be that has to run inside this container. That is exactly what CMD and ENTRYPOINT are used for—to tell Docker what the start process is and how to start that process.

Now, the differences between CMD and ENTRYPOINT are subtle, and honestly most users don't fully understand them or use them in the intended way. Luckily, in most cases, this is not a problem and the container will run anyway; it's just the handling of it that is not as straightforward as it could be.

To better understand how to use the two keywords, let's analyze what a typical Linux command or expression looks like—for example, let's take the ping utility as an example, as follows:

```
$ ping 8.8.8.8 -c 3
```

In the preceding expression, ping is the command and 8.8.8.8 -c 3 are the parameters to this command. Let's look at another expression:

```
$ wget -O - http://example.com/downloads/script.sh
```

Again, in the preceding expression, `wget` is the command and `-O -` `http://example.com/downloads/script.sh` are the parameters.

Now that we have dealt with this, we can get back to `CMD` and `ENTRYPOINT`. `ENTRYPOINT` is used to define the command of the expression while `CMD` is used to define the parameters for the command. Thus, a Dockerfile using `alpine` as the base image and defining `ping` as the process to run in the container could look as follows:

```
FROM alpine:latest
ENTRYPOINT ["ping"]
CMD ["8.8.8.8", "-c", "3"]
```

For both `ENTRYPOINT` and `CMD`, the values are formatted as a JSON array of strings, where the individual items correspond to the tokens of the expression that are separated by whitespace. This the preferred way of defining `CMD` and `ENTRYPOINT`. It is also called the **exec** form.

Alternatively, one can also use what's called the **shell** form, for example:

```
CMD command param1 param2
```

We can now build an image from the preceding Dockerfile, as follows:

```
$ docker image build -t pinger .
```

Then, we can run a container from the `pinger` image we just created:

```
$ docker container run --rm -it pinger
PING 8.8.8.8 (8.8.8.8): 56 data bytes
64 bytes from 8.8.8.8: seq=0 ttl=37 time=19.298 ms
64 bytes from 8.8.8.8: seq=1 ttl=37 time=27.890 ms
64 bytes from 8.8.8.8: seq=2 ttl=37 time=30.702 ms
```

The beauty of this is that I can now override the `CMD` part that I have defined in the Dockerfile (remember, it was `["8.8.8.8", "-c", "3"]`) when I create a new container by adding the new values at the end of the `docker container run` expression:

```
$ docker container run --rm -it pinger -w 5 127.0.0.1
```

This will now cause the container to ping the loopback for 5 seconds.

If we want to override what's defined in the ENTRYPOINT in the Dockerfile, we need to use the --entrypoint parameter in the docker container run expression. Let's say we want to execute a shell in the container instead of the ping command. We could do so by using the following command:

```
$ docker container run --rm -it --entrypoint /bin/sh pinger
```

We will then find ourselves inside the container. Type exit to leave the container.

As I already mentioned, we do not necessarily have to follow best practices and define the command through ENTRYPOINT and the parameters through CMD, but we can instead enter the whole expression as a value of CMD and it will work:

```
FROM alpine:latest
CMD wget -O - http://www.google.com
```

Here, I have even used the **shell** form to define the CMD. But what does really happen in this situation where ENTRYPOINT is undefined? If you leave ENTRYPOINT undefined, then it will have the default value of /bin/sh -c, and whatever is the value of CMD will be passed as a string to the shell command. The preceding definition would thereby result in entering following process to run inside the container:

```
/bin/sh -c "wget -O - http://www.google.com"
```

Consequently, /bin/sh is the main process running inside the container, and it will start a new child process to run the wget utility.

A complex Dockerfile

We have discussed the most important keywords commonly used in Dockerfiles. Let's look at a realistic and somewhat complex example of a Dockerfile. The interested reader might note that it looks very similar to the first Dockerfile that we presented in this chapter. Here is the content:

```
FROM node:9.4
RUN mkdir -p /app
WORKDIR /app
COPY package.json /app/
RUN npm install
COPY . /app
ENTRYPOINT ["npm"]
CMD ["start"]
```

OK, so what is happening here? Evidently, this is a Dockerfile that is used to build an image for a Node.js application; we can deduce this from the fact that the base image node:9.4 is used. Then the second line is an instruction to create a /app folder in the filesystem of the image. The third line defines the working directory or context in the image to be this new /app folder. Then, on line four, we copy a package.json file into the /app folder inside the image. After this, on line five, we execute the npm install command inside the container; remember, our context is the /app folder and thus, npm will find the package.json file there that we copied on line four.

After all Node.js dependencies are installed, we copy the rest of the application files from the current folder of the host into the /app folder of the image.

Finally, on the last two lines, we define what the startup command shall be when a container is run from this image. In our case, it is npm start, which will start the Node application.

Building an image

In your home directory, create a FundamentalsOfDocker folder and navigate to it:

```
$ mkdir ~/FundamentalsOfDocker
$ cd ~/FundamentalsOfDocker
```

In the preceding folder, create a sample1 subfolder and navigate to it:

```
$ mkdir sample1 && cd sample1
```

Use your favorite editor to create a file called Dockerfile inside this sample folder with the following content:

```
FROM centos:7
RUN yum install -y wget
```

Save the file and exit your editor.

Back in the Terminal, we can now build a new container image using the preceding Dockerfile as a manifest or construction plan:

```
$ docker image build -t my-centos .
```

Please note that there is a period at the end of the preceding command. This command means that the Docker builder is creating a new image called `my-centos` using the Dockerfile that is present in the current directory. Here, the period at the end of the command stands for *current directory*. We could also write the preceding command as follows, with the same result:

```
$ docker image build -t my-centos -f Dockerfile .
```

But we can omit the `-f` parameter, since the builder assumes that the Dockerfile is literally called `Dockerfile`. We only ever need the `-f` parameter if our Dockerfile has a different name or is not located in the current directory.

The preceding command gives us this (shortened) output:

```
Sending build context to Docker daemon 2.048kB
Step 1/2 : FROM centos:7
7: Pulling from library/centos
af4b0a2388c6: Pull complete
Digest:
sha256:2671f7a3eea36ce43609e9fe7435ade83094291055f1c96d9d1d1d7c0b986a5d
Status: Downloaded newer image for centos:7
---> ff426288ea90
Step 2/2 : RUN yum install -y wget
---> Running in bb726903820c
Loaded plugins: fastestmirror, ovl
Determining fastest mirrors
* base: mirror.dal10.us.leaseweb.net
* extras: repos-tx.psychz.net
* updates: pubmirrors.dal.corespace.com
Resolving Dependencies
--> Running transaction check
---> Package wget.x86_64 0:1.14-15.el7_4.1 will be installed
...
Installed:
wget.x86_64 0:1.14-15.el7_4.1
Complete!
Removing intermediate container bb726903820c
---> bc070cc81b87
Successfully built bc070cc81b87
Successfully tagged my-centos:latest
```

Let's analyze this output:

- First, we have the following line:

```
Sending build context to Docker daemon 2.048kB
```

  The first thing the builder does is package the files in the current build context, excluding the files and folder mentioned in the `.dockerignore` file, if present, and sends the resulting `.tar` file to the Docker daemon.

- Next, we have the following lines:

```
Step 1/2 : FROM centos:7
7: Pulling from library/centos
af4b0a2388c6: Pull complete
Digest: sha256:2671f7a...
Status: Downloaded newer image for centos:7
---> ff426288ea90
```

  The first line tells us which step of the Dockerfile the builder is currently executing. Here, we only have two statements in the Dockerfile, and we are on step 1 of 2. We can also see what the content of that section is. Here is the declaration of the base image, on top of which we want to build our custom image. What the builder then does is pull this image from Docker Hub if it is not already available in the local cache. The last line of the preceding snippet indicates which ID the just-built layer gets assigned by the builder.

- Now, follows the next step. I have shortened it even more than the preceding one to concentrate on the essential part:

```
Step 2/2 : RUN yum install -y wget
---> Running in bb726903820c
...
...
Removing intermediate container bb726903820c
---> bc070cc81b87
```

  Here, again, the first line indicates to us that we are in step 2 of 2. It also shows us the respective entry from the Dockerfile. On line two, we can see `Running in bb726903820c`, which tells us that the builder has created a container with ID bb726903820c inside, which it executes the `RUN` command. We have omitted the output of the `yum install -y wget` command in the snippet since it is not important in this section. When the command is finished, the builder stops the container, commits it to a new layer, and then removes the container. The new layer has ID `bc070cc81b87`, in this particular case.

- At the very end of the output, we encounter the following two lines:

```
Successfully built bc070cc81b87
Successfully tagged my-centos:latest
```

This tells us that the resulting custom image has been given the ID `bc070cc81b87`, and has been tagged with the name `my-centos:latest`.

So, *how does the builder work, exactly?* It starts with the base image. From this base image, once downloaded into the local cache, it creates a container and runs the first statement of the Dockerfile inside this container. Then, it stops the container and persists the changes made in the container into a new image layer. The builder then creates a new container from the base image and the new layer, and runs the second statement inside this new container. Once again, the result is committed to a new layer. This process is repeated until the very last statement in the Dockerfile is encountered. After having committed the last layer of the new image, the builder creates an ID for this image and tags the image with the name we provided in the `build` command:

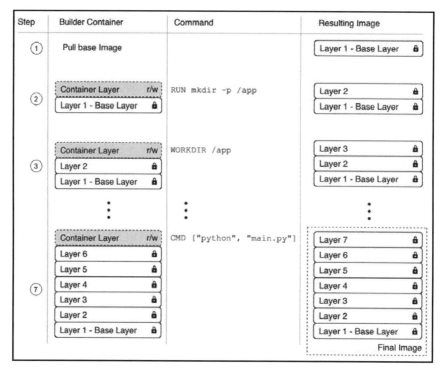

The image build process visualized

Multistep builds

To demonstrate why a Dockerfile with multiple build steps is useful, let's make an example Dockerfile. Let's take a `Hello World` application written in C. Here is the code found inside the `hello.c` file:

```
#include <stdio.h>
int main (void)
{
  printf ("Hello, world!\n");
  return 0;
}
```

Now, we want to containerize this application and write this Dockerfile:

```
FROM alpine:3.7
RUN apk update &&
apk add --update alpine-sdk
RUN mkdir /app
WORKDIR /app
COPY . /app
RUN mkdir bin
RUN gcc -Wall hello.c -o bin/hello
CMD /app/bin/hello
```

Now, let's build this image:

```
$ docker image build -t hello-world .
```

This gives us a fairly long output, since the builder has to install the Alpine SDK, which, among other tools, contains the C++ compiler we need to build the application.

Once the build is done we can list the image and see its size shown as follows:

```
$ docker image ls | grep hello-world
hello-world        latest        e9b...        2 minutes ago        176MB
```

With a size of 176 MB, the resulting image is way too big. In the end, it is just a `Hello World` application. The reason for it being so big is that the image not only contains the `Hello World` binary, but also all the tools to compile and link the application from the source code. But this is really not desirable when running the application, say, in production. Ideally, we only want to have the resulting binary in the image and not a whole SDK.

It is precisely for this reason that we should define Dockerfiles as multistage. We have some stages that are used to build the final artifacts and then a final stage where we use the minimal necessary base image and copy the artifacts into it. This results in very small images. Have a look at this revised Dockerfile:

```
FROM alpine:3.7 AS build
RUN apk update && \
    apk add --update alpine-sdk
RUN mkdir /app
WORKDIR /app
COPY . /app
RUN mkdir bin
RUN gcc hello.c -o bin/hello

FROM alpine:3.7
COPY --from=build /app/bin/hello /app/hello
CMD /app/hello
```

Here, we have a first stage with an alias build that is used to compile the application, and then the second stage uses the same base image `alpine:3.7`, but does not install the SDK, and only copies the binary from the build stage, using the `--from` parameter, into this final image.

Let's build the image again as follows:

```
$ docker image build -t hello-world-small .
```

When we compare the sizes of the images, we get the following output:

```
$ docker image ls | grep hello-world
hello-world-small    latest    f98...    20 seconds ago    4.16MB
hello-world          latest    469...    10 minutes ago    176MB
```

We have been able to reduce the size from 176 MB down to 4 MB. This is reduction in size by a factor of 40. A smaller image size has many advantages, such as a smaller attack surface area for hackers, reduced memory and disk consumption, faster startup times of the corresponding containers, and a reduction of the bandwidth needed to download the image from a registry, such as Docker Hub.

Dockerfile best practices

There are a few recommended best practices to consider when authoring a Dockerfile, which are as follows:

- First and foremost, we need to consider that containers are meant to be ephemeral. By ephemeral, we mean that a container can be stopped and destroyed and a new one built and put in place with an absolute minimum of setup and configuration. That means that we should try hard to keep the time that is needed to initialize the application running inside the container at a minimum, as well as the time needed to terminate or clean up the application.

- The next best practice tells us that we should order the individual commands in the Dockerfile so that we leverage caching as much as possible. Building a layer of an image can take a considerable amount of time, sometimes many seconds or even minutes. While developing an application, we will have to build the container image for our application multiple times. We want to keep the build times at a minimum.

When we're rebuilding a previously built image, the only layers that are rebuilt are the ones that have changed, but if one layer needs to be rebuilt, all subsequent layers also need to be rebuilt. This is very important to remember. Consider the following example:

```
FROM node:9.4
RUN mkdir -p /app
WORKIR /app
COPY . /app
RUN npm install
CMD ["npm", "start"]
```

In this example, the `npm install` command on line five of the Dockerfile usually takes the longest. A classical Node.js application has many external dependencies, and those are all downloaded and installed in this step. This can take minutes until it is done. Therefore, we want to avoid running `npm install` each time we rebuild the image, but a developer changes their source code all the time during development of the application. That means that line four, the result of the `COPY` command, changes all the time and this layer has to be rebuilt each time. But as we discussed previously, that also means that all subsequent layers have to be rebuilt, which in this case includes the `npm install` command. To avoid this, we can slightly modify the Dockerfile and have the following:

```
FROM node:9.4
RUN mkdir -p /app
```

```
WORKIR /app
COPY package.json /app/
RUN npm install
COPY . /app
CMD ["npm", "start"]
```

What we have done here is that, on line four, we only copy the single file that the `npm install` command needs as a source, which is the `package.json` file. This file rarely changes in a typical development process. As a consequence, the `npm install` command also has to be executed only when the `package.json` file changes. All the remaining, frequently changed content is added to the image after the `npm install` command.

- A further best practice is to keep the number of layers that make up your image relatively small. The more layers an image has, the more the graph driver needs to work to consolidate the layers into a single root filesystem for the corresponding container. Of course, this takes time, and thus the fewer layers an image has, the faster the startup time for the container can be.

But *how can we keep our number of layers low?* Remember that in a Dockerfile, each line that starts with a keyword, such as FROM, COPY, or RUN, creates a new layer. The easiest way to reduce the number of layers is to combine multiple individual RUN commands into a single one—for example, say that we had the following in a Dockerfile:

```
RUN apt-get update
RUN apt-get install -y ca-certificates
RUN rm -rf /var/lib/apt/lists/*
```

We could combine these into a single concatenated expression, as follows:

```
RUN apt-get update \
    && apt-get install -y ca-certificates \
    && rm -rf /var/lib/apt/lists/*
```

The former will generate three layers in the resulting image, while the latter only creates a single layer.

The next three best practices all result in smaller images. Why is this important? Smaller images reduce the time and bandwidth needed to download the image from a registry. They also reduce the amount of disk space needed to store a copy locally on the Docker host and the memory needed to load the image. Finally, smaller images also means a smaller attack surface for hackers. Here are the best practices mentioned:

- The first best practice that helps to reduce the image size is to use a .dockerignore file. We want to avoid copying unnecessary files and folders into an image to keep it as lean as possible. A .dockerignore file works in exactly the same way as a .gitignore file, for those who are familiar with Git. In a .dockerignore file, we can configure patterns to exclude certain files or folders from being included in the context when building the image.
- The next best practice is to avoid installing unnecessary packages into the filesystem of the image. Once again, this is to keep the image as lean as possible.
- Last but not least, it is recommended that you use multistage builds so that the resulting image is as small as possible and only contains the absolute minimum needed to run your application or application service.

Saving and loading images

The third way to create a new container image is by importing or loading it from a file. A container image is nothing more than a tarball. To demonstrate this, we can use the docker image save command to export an existing image to a tarball:

```
$ docker image save -o ./backup/my-alpine.tar my-alpine
```

The preceding command takes our my-alpine image that we previously built and exports it into a ./backup/my-alpine.tar file.

If, on the other hand, we have an existing tarball and want to import it as an image into our system, we can use the docker image load command as follows:

```
$ docker image load -i ./backup/my-alpine.tar
```

Sharing or shipping images

To be able to ship our custom image to other environments, we need to first give it a globally unique name. This action is often called tagging an image. We then need to publish the image to a central location from which other interested or entitled parties can pull it. These central locations are called **image registries**.

Tagging an image

Each image has a so-called **tag**. A tag is often used to version images, but it has a broader reach than just being a version number. If we do not explicitly specify a tag when working with images, then Docker automatically assumes we're referring to the *latest* tag. This is relevant when pulling an image from Docker Hub, for example:

```
$ docker image pull alpine
```

The preceding command will pull the `alpine:latest` image from the Hub. If we want to explicitly specify a tag, we do so like this:

```
$ docker image pull alpine:3.5
```

This will now pull the `alpine` image that has been tagged with `3.5`.

Image namespaces

So far, you have been pulling various images and haven't worried so much about where those images originated from. Your Docker environment is configured so that, by default, all images are pulled from Docker Hub. We also only pulled so-called official images from the Docker Hub, such as `alpine` or `busybox`.

Now it is time to widen our horizon a bit and learn about how images are namespaced. The most generic way to define an image is by its fully qualified name, which looks as follows:

```
<registry URL>/<User or Org>/<name>:<tag>
```

Let's look at this in a bit more detail:

- `<registry URL>`: This is the URL to the registry from which we want to pull the image. By default, this is `docker.io`. More generally, this could be `https://registry.acme.com`.

Other than Docker Hub, there are quite a few public registries out there that you could pull images from. The following is a list of some of them, in no particular order:

- Google at `https://cloud.google.com/container-registry`
- Amazon AWS at `https://aws.amazon.com/ecr/`
- Microsoft Azure at `https://azure.microsoft.com/en-us/services/container-registry/`
- Red Hat at `https://access.redhat.com/containers/`
- Artifactory at `https://jfrog.com/integration/artifactory-docker-registry/`

- `<User or Org>`: This is the private Docker ID of either an individual or an organization defined on Docker Hub, or any other registry for that matter, such as `microsoft` or `oracle`.
- `<name>`: This is the name of the image that is often also called a repository.
- `<tag>`: This is the tag of the image.

Let's look at an example:

```
https://registry.acme.com/engineering/web-app:1.0
```

Here, we have an image, `web-app`, that is tagged with version `1.0` and belongs to the `engineering` organization on the private registry at `https://registry.acme.com`.

Now, there are some special conventions:

- If we omit the registry URL, then Docker Hub is automatically taken
- If we omit the tag, then `latest` is taken
- If it is an official image on Docker Hub, then no user or organization namespace is needed

A few samples in tabular form are as follows:

Image	Description
`alpine`	Official `alpine` image on Docker Hub with the `latest` tag.
`ubuntu:16.04`	Official `ubuntu` image on Docker Hub with the `16.04` tag or version.

`microsoft/nanoserver`	`nanoserver` image of Microsoft on Docker Hub with the `latest` tag.
`acme/web-api:12.0`	`web-api` image version `12.0` associated with the `acme` org. The image is on Docker Hub.
`gcr.io/gnschenker/sample-app:1.1`	`sample-app` image with the `1.1` tag belonging to an individual with the `gnschenker` ID on Google's container registry.

Official images

In the preceding table, we mentioned *official image* a few times. This needs an explanation. Images are stored in repositories on the Docker Hub registry. Official repositories are a set of repositories that are hosted on Docker Hub and are curated by individuals or organizations that are also responsible for the software that is packaged inside the image. Let's look at an example of what that means. There is an official organization behind the Ubuntu Linux distro. This team also provides official versions of Docker images that contain their Ubuntu distros.

Official images are meant to provide essential base OS repositories, images for popular programming language runtimes, frequently used data storage, and other important services.

Docker sponsors a team whose task it is to review and publish all those curated images in public repositories on Docker Hub. Furthermore, Docker scans all official images for vulnerabilities.

Pushing images to a registry

Creating custom images is all well and good, but at some point, we want to actually share or ship our images to a target environment, such as a test, QA, or production system. For this, we typically use a container registry. One of the most popular and public registries out there is Docker Hub. It is configured as a default registry in your Docker environment, and it is the registry from which we have pulled all our images so far.

On a registry, one can usually create personal or organizational accounts. For example, my personal account at Docker Hub is `gnschenker`. Personal accounts are good for personal use. If we want to use the registry professionally, then we probably want to create an organizational account, such as `acme`, on Docker Hub. The advantage of the latter is that organizations can have multiple teams. Teams can have differing permissions.

To be able to push an image to my personal account on Docker Hub, I need to tag it accordingly. Let's say I want to push the latest version of `alpine` to my account and give it a tag of `1.0`. I can do this in the following way:

```
$ docker image tag alpine:latest gnschenker/alpine:1.0
```

Now, to be able to push the image, I have to log in to my account:

```
$ docker login -u gnschenker -p <my secret password>
```

After a successful login, I can then push the image:

```
$ docker image push gnschenker/alpine:1.0
```

I will see something similar to this in the terminal:

```
The push refers to repository [docker.io/gnschenker/alpine]
04a094fe844e: Mounted from library/alpine
1.0: digest: sha256:5cb04fce... size: 528
```

For each image that we push to Docker Hub, we automatically create a repository. A repository can be private or public. Everyone can pull an image from a public repository. From a private repository, one can only pull an image if one is logged in to the registry and has the necessary permissions configured.

Summary

In this chapter, we have discussed in detail what container images are and how we can build and ship them. As we have seen, there are three different ways that an image can be created—either manually, automatically, or by importing a tarball into the system. We also learned some of the best practices commonly used when building custom images.

In the next chapter, we're going to introduce Docker volumes that can be used to persist the state of a container, and we will also introduce some helpful system commands that can be used to inspect the Docker host more deeply, work with events generated by the Docker daemon, and clean up unused resources.

Questions

Please try to answer the following questions to assess your learning progress:

1. How will you create a Dockerfile that inherits from Ubuntu version 17.04, and that installs `ping` and runs `ping` when a container starts. The default address to ping will be `127.0.0.1`.

2. How will you create a new container image that uses `alpine:latest` and installs `curl`. Name the new image `my-alpine:1.0`.

3. Create a Dockerfile that uses multiple steps to create an image of a `Hello World` app of minimal size, written in C or Go.

4. Name three essential characteristics of a Docker container image.

5. You want to push an image named `foo:1.0` to your `jdoe` personal account on Docker Hub. Which of the following is the right solution?
    1. `$ docker container push foo:1.0`

    2. `$ docker image tag foo:1.0 jdoe/foo:1.0`
       `$ docker image push jdoe/foo:1.0`

    3. `$ docker login -u jdoe -p <your password>`
       `$ docker image tag foo:1.0 jdoe/foo:1.0`
       `$ docker image push jdoe/foo:1.0`

    4. `$ docker login -u jdoe -p <your password>`
       `$ docker container tag foo:1.0 jdoe/foo:1.0`
       `$ docker container push jdoe/foo:1.0`

    5. `$ docker login -u jdoe -p <your password>`
       `$ docker image push foo:1.0 jdoe/foo:1.0`

Further reading

The following list of references gives you some material that dives more deeply into the topic of authoring and building container images:

- *Best practices for writing Dockerfiles at* `http://dockr.ly/22WiJiO`
- *Using multistage builds at* `http://dockr.ly/2ewcUY3`
- *About Storage drivers at* `http://dockr.ly/1TuWndC`
- *Graphdriver plugins at* `http://dockr.ly/2eIVCab`
- *User-guided caching in Docker for MAC at* `http://dockr.ly/2xKafPf`

Data Volumes and System Management

5

In the last chapter, we learned how to build and share our own container images. Particular focus was put on how to build images that are as small as possible by only containing artifacts that are really needed by the containerized application.

In this chapter, we are going to learn how we can work with stateful containers, that is containers that consume and produce data. We will also learn how to keep our Docker environment clean and free from unused resources. Last but not least, we will be looking into the stream of events that a Docker engine is producing.

Here is a list of the topics we're going to discuss:

- Creating and mounting data volumes
- Sharing data between containers
- Using host volumes
- Defining volumes in images
- Obtaining exhaustive Docker system information
- Listing resource consumption
- Pruning unused resources
- Consuming Docker system events

After working through this chapter, you will be able to:

- Create, delete, and list data volumes
- Mount an existing data volume into a container
- Create durable data from within a container using a data volume

- Share data between multiple containers using data volumes
- Mount any host folder into a container using data volumes
- Define the access mode (read/write or read-only) for a container when accessing data in a data volume
- List the amount of space consumed by Docker resources on a given host, such as images, containers, and volumes
- Free your system from unused Docker resources, such as containers, images, and volumes
- Display Docker system events in a console in real time

Technical requirements

For this chapter, you need either Docker Toolbox installed on your machine or access to a Linux VM running Docker on your laptop or in the cloud. There is no code accompanying this chapter.

Creating and mounting data volumes

All meaningful applications consume or produce data. Yet containers are preferably meant to be stateless. How are we going to deal with this? One way is to use Docker volumes. Volumes allow containers to consume, produce, and modify state. Volumes have a life cycle that goes beyond the life cycle of containers. When a container that uses a volume dies, the volume continues to exist. This is great for the durability of state.

Modifying the container layer

Before we dive into volumes, let's first discuss what's happening if an application in a container changes something in the filesystem of the container. In this case, the changes are all happening in the writable container layer. Let's quickly demonstrate this by running a container and execute a script in it that is creating a new file:

```
$ docker container run --name demo \
    alpine /bin/sh -c 'echo "This is a test" > sample.txt'
```

The preceding command creates a container named demo and inside this container creates a file called sample.txt with the content This is a test. The container exits after this but remains in memory available for us to do our investigations. Let's use the diff command to find out what has changed in the container's filesystem in relation to the filesystem of the image:

```
$ docker container diff demo
```

The output should look like this:

```
A /sample.txt
```

Evidently a new file, A, has been added to the filesystem of the container as expected. Since all layers that stem from the underlying image (alpine in this case) are immutable, the change could only happen in the writeable container layer.

If we now remove the container from memory, its container layer will also be removed and with it all the changes will be irreversibly deleted. If we need our changes to persist even beyond the lifetime of the container, this is not a solution. Luckily, we have better options in the form of Docker volumes. Let's get to know them.

Creating volumes

Since, at this time, when using Docker for Mac or Windows containers are not running natively on OS X or Windows but rather in a (hidden) VM created by Docker for Mac and Windows, it is best we use docker-machine to create and use an explicit VM running Docker. At this point, we assume that you have Docker Toolbox installed on your system. If not, then please go back to Chapter 2, *Setting up a Working Environment*, where we provide detailed instructions on how to install Toolbox.

Use docker-machine to list all VMs currently running in VirtualBox:

```
$ docker-machine ls
```

If you do not have a VM called node-1 listed then create one:

```
$ docker-machine create --driver virtualbox node-1
```

If you have a VM called node-1 but it is not running then please start it:

```
$ docker-machine start node-1
```

Now that everything is ready, SSH into this VM called `node-1`:

```
$ docker-machine ssh node-1
```

You should be greeted by a **boot2docker** welcome image .

To create a new data volume, we can use the `docker volume create` command. This will create a named volume which can then be mounted into a container and be used for persistent data access or storage. The following command creates a volume, `my-data` using the default volume driver:

```
$ docker volume create my-data
```

The default volume driver is the so-called local driver which stores the data locally in the host filesystem. The easiest way to find out where the data is stored on the host is by using the `inspect` command on the volume we just created. The actual location can differ from system to system and so, this is the safest way to find the target folder:

```
$ docker volume inspect my-data
[
    {
        "CreatedAt": "2018-01-28T21:55:41Z",
        "Driver": "local",
        "Labels": {},
        "Mountpoint": "/mnt/sda1/var/lib/docker/volumes/my-data/_data",
        "Name": "my-data",
        "Options": {},
        "Scope": "local"
    }
]
```

The host folder can be found in the output under `Mountpoint`. In our case, when using `docker-machine` with a LinuxKit-based VM running in VirtualBox, the folder is `/mnt/sda1/var/lib/docker/volumes/my-data/_data`.

The target folder often is a protected folder and we thus might need to use `sudo` to navigate to this folder and execute any operations in it. In our case, we do not need to use `sudo`:

```
$ cd /mnt/sda1/var/lib/docker/volumes/my-data/_data
```

If you are using Docker for Mac to create a volume on your laptop and then do a `docker volume inspect` on the volume you just created, the `Mountpoint` is shown as `/var/lib/docker/volumes/my-data/_data`. But you will discover that there is no such folder on the Mac. The reason is that the path is in relation to the hidden VM that Docker for Mac uses to run containers. At this time, containers cannot run natively on OS X. The same applies to volumes created with Docker for Windows.

There are other volume drivers available from third parties in the form of plugins. We can use the `--driver` parameter in the `create` command to select a different volume driver. Other volume drivers use different types of storage systems to back a volume, such as cloud storage, NFS drives, software-defined storage and more.

Mounting a volume

Once we have created a named volume, we can mount it into a container. For this, we can use the `-v` parameter in the `docker container run` command:

```
$ docker container run --name test -it \
    -v my-data:/data alpine /bin/sh
```

The preceding command mounts the `my-data` volume to the `/data` folder inside the container. Inside the container, we can now create files in the `/data` folder and then exit:

```
# / cd /data
# / echo "Some data" > data.txt
# / echo "Some more data" > data2.txt
# / exit
```

If we navigate to the host folder that contains the volume data and list its content, we should see the two files we just created inside the container:

```
$ cd /mnt/sda1/var/lib/docker/volumes/my-data/_data
$ ls -l
total 8
-rw-r--r-- 1 root root 10 Jan 28 22:23 data.txt
-rw-r--r-- 1 root root 15 Jan 28 22:23 data2.txt
```

We can even try to output the content of say, the second file:

```
$ cat data2.txt
```

Let's try to create a file in this folder from the host and then use the volume with another container:

```
$ echo "This file we create on the host" > host-data.txt
```

Now, let's delete the `test` container and run another one based on CentOS. This time we are even mounting our volume to a different container folder, `/app/data`:

```
$ docker container rm test
$ docker container run --name test2 -it \
    -v my-data:/app/data \
    Centos:7 /bin/bash
```

Once inside the CentOS container, we can navigate to the folder `/app/data` where we have mounted the volume to and list its content:

```
# / cd /app/data
# / ls -l
```

As expected, we should see these three files:

```
-rw-r--r-- 1 root root 10 Jan 28 22:23 data.txt
-rw-r--r-- 1 root root 15 Jan 28 22:23 data2.txt
-rw-r--r-- 1 root root 32 Jan 28 22:31 host-data.txt
```

This is the definitive proof that data in a Docker volume persists beyond the lifetime of a container, and also that volumes can be reused by other, even different containers from the one that used it first.

It is important to note that the folder inside the container to which we mount a Docker volume is excluded from the union filesystem. That is, each change inside this folder and any of its subfolders will not be part of the container layer, but persisted in the backing storage provided by the volume driver. This fact is really important since the container layer is deleted when the corresponding container is stopped and removed from the system.

Removing volumes

Volumes can be removed using the `docker volume rm` command. It is important to remember that removing a volume destroys the containing data irreversibly and thus is to be considered a dangerous command. Docker helps us a bit in this regard as it does not allow us to delete a volume that is still in use by a container. Always make sure before you remove or delete a volume that you either have a backup of its data or you really don't need this data anymore.

The following command deletes our `my-data` volume that we created earlier:

```
$ docker volume rm my-data
```

After executing the preceding command, double-check that the folder on the host has been deleted.

To remove all running containers to clean up the system, run the following command:

```
$ docker container rm -f $(docker container ls -aq)
```

Sharing data between containers

Containers are like sandboxes for the applications running inside them. This is mostly beneficial and wanted in order to protect applications running in different containers from each other. That also means that the whole filesystem visible to an application running inside a container is private to this application and no other application running in a different container can interfere with it.

At times though, we want to share data between containers. Say an application running in container A produces some data that will be consumed by another application running in container B. *How can we achieve this?* Well I'm sure you've already guessed it—we can use Docker volumes for this purpose. We can create a volume and mount it to container A as well as to container B. In this way, both applications A and B have access to the same data.

Now, as always when multiple applications or processes concurrently access data, we have to be very careful to avoid inconsistencies. To avoid concurrency problems, such as race conditions, we ideally have only one application or process that is creating or modifying data, while all other processes concurrently accessing this data only read it. We can enforce a process running in a container to only be able to read the data in a volume by mounting this volume as read only. Have a look at the following command:

```
$ docker container run -it --name writer \
    -v shared-data:/data \
    alpine /bin/sh
```

Here we create a container called `writer` which has a volume, `shared-data`, mounted in default read/write mode. Try to create a file inside this container:

```
# / echo "I can create a file" > /data/sample.txt
```

It should succeed. Exit this container and then execute the following command:

```
$ docker container run -it --name reader \
    -v shared-data:/app/data:ro \
    ubuntu:17.04 /bin/bash
```

And we have a container called `reader` that has the same volume mounted as **read-only** (**ro**). Firstly, make sure you can see the file created in the first container:

```
$ ls -l /app/data
total 4
-rw-r--r-- 1 root root 20 Jan 28 22:55 sample.txt
```

And then try to create a file:

```
# / echo "Try to break read/only" > /app/data/data.txt
```

It will fail with the following message:

```
bash: /app/data/data.txt: Read-only file system
```

Let's exit the container by typing `exit` at the Command Prompt. Back on the host, let's clean up all containers and volumes:

```
$ docker container rm -f $(docker container ls -aq)
$ docker volume rm $(docker volume ls -q)
```

Once this is done, exit the `docker-machine` VM by also typing `exit` at the Command Prompt. You should be back on your Docker for Mac or Windows. Use `docker-machine` to stop the VM:

```
$ docker-machine stop node-1
```

Using host volumes

In certain scenarios, such as when developing new containerized applications or when a containerized application needs to consume data from a certain folder produced, say, by a legacy application, it is very useful to use volumes that mount a specific host folder. Let's look at the following example:

```
$ docker container run --rm -it \
    -v $(pwd)/src:/app/src \
    alpine:latest /bin/sh
```

The preceding expression interactively starts an `alpine` container with a shell and mounts the subfolder `src` of the current directory into the container at `/app/src`. We need to use `$(pwd)` (or `'pwd'` for that matter) which is the current directory, as when working with volumes we always need to use absolute paths.

Developers use these techniques all the time when they are working on their application that runs in a container, and want to make sure that the container always contains the latest changes they make to the code, without the need to rebuild the image and rerun the container after each change.

Let's make a sample to demonstrate how that works. Let's say we want to create a simple static website using Nginx as our web server. First, let's create a new folder on the host where we will put our web assets, such as HTML, CSS, and JavaScript files and navigate to it:

```
$ mkdir ~/my-web
$ cd ~/my-web
```

Then we create a simple web page like this:

```
$ echo "<h1>Personal Website</h1>" > index.html
```

Now, we add a Dockerfile which will contain the instructions on how to build the image containing our sample website. Add a file called Dockerfile to the folder with this content:

```
FROM nginx:alpine
COPY . /usr/share/nginx/html
```

The Dockerfile starts with the latest Alpine version of Nginx and then copies all files from the current host directory into the containers folder, `/usr/share/nginx/html`. This is where Nginx expects web assets to be located. Now let's build the image with the following command:

```
$ docker image build -t my-website:1.0 .
```

And finally, we run a container from this image. We will run the container in detached mode:

```
$ docker container run -d \
   -p 8080:80 --name my-site\
   my-website:1.0
```

Note the `-p 8080:80` parameter. We haven't discussed this yet but we will do it in detail in `Chapter 7`, *Single-Host Networking*. At the moment, just know that this maps the container port `80` on which Nginx is listening for incoming requests to port `8080` of your laptop where you can then access the application. Now, open a browser tab and navigate to `http://localhost:8080/index.html` and you should see your website which currently consists only of a title, `Personal Website`.

Now, edit the file `index.html` in your favorite editor to look like this:

```
<h1>Personal Website</h1>
<p>This is some text</p>
```

And save it. Then refresh the browser. OK, that didn't work. The browser still displays the previous version of the `index.html` which consists only of the title. So let's stop and remove the current container, then rebuild the image, and rerun the container:

```
$ docker container rm -f my-site
$ docker image build -t my-website:1.0 .
$ docker container run -d \
    -p 8080:80 --name my-site\
    my-website:1.0
```

This time when you refresh the browser the new content should be shown. Well, it worked, but there is way too much friction involved. Imagine you have to do this each and every time that you make a simple change in your website. That's not sustainable.

Now is the time to use host-mounted volumes. Once again, remove the current container and rerun it with the volume mount:

```
$ docker container rm -f my-site
$ docker container run -d \
    -v $(pwd):/usr/share/nginx/html \
    -p 8080:80 --name my-site\
    my-website:1.0
```

Now, append some more content to the `index.html` and save it. Then refresh your browser. You should see the changes. And this is exactly what we wanted to achieve; we also call this an edit-and-continue experience. You can make as many changes in your web files and always immediately see the result in the browser without having to rebuild the image and restart the container containing your website.

It is important to note that the updates are now propagated bi-directionally. If you make changes on the host they will be propagated to the container and vice versa. Also important is the fact that when you mount the current folder into the container target folder, `/usr/share/nginx/html`, the content that is already there is replaced by the content of the host folder.

Defining volumes in images

If we go for a moment back to what we have learned about containers in `Chapter 3`, *Working with Containers*, then we have this: the filesystem of each container when started is made up of the immutable layers of the underlying image plus a writable container layer specific to this very container. All changes that the processes running inside the container make to the filesystem will be persisted in this container layer. Once the container is stopped and removed from the system, the corresponding container layer is deleted from the system and irreversibly lost.

Some applications, such as databases running in containers, need to persist their data beyond the lifetime of the container. In this case they can use volumes. To make things a bit more explicit let's look at a concrete sample. MongoDB is a popular open source document database. Many developers use MongoDB as a storage service for their applications. The maintainers of MongoDB have created an image and published it on Docker Hub which can be used to run an instance of the database in a container. This database will be producing data that needs to be persisted long term. But the MongoDB maintainers do not know who uses this image and how it is used. So they have no influence over the `docker container run` command with which the users of the database will start this container. *How can they now define volumes?*

Luckily, there is a way of defining volumes in the Dockerfile. The keyword to do so is `VOLUME` and we can either add the absolute path to a single folder or a comma-separated list of paths. These paths represent folders of the container's filesystem. Let's look at a few samples of such volume definitions:

```
VOLUME /app/data
VOLUME /app/data, /app/profiles, /app/config
VOLUME ["/app/data", "/app/profiles", "/app/config"]
```

The first line defines a single volume to be mounted at `/app/data`. The second line defines three volumes as a comma-separated list and the last one defines the same as the second line, but this time the value is formatted as a JSON array.

When a container is started, Docker automatically creates a volume and mounts it to the corresponding target folder of the container for each path defined in the Dockerfile. Since each volume is created automatically by Docker, it will have an SHA-256 as ID.

At container runtime, the folders defined as volumes in the Dockerfile are excluded from the union filesystem and thus any changes in those folders do not change the container layer but are persisted to the respective volume. It is now the responsibility of the operations engineers to make sure that the backing storage of the volumes is properly backed up.

We can use the `docker image inspect` command to get information about the volumes defined in the Dockerfile. Let's see what MongoDB gives us. First, we pull the image with the following command:

```
$ docker image pull mongo:3.7
```

Then we inspect this image and use the `--format` parameter to only extract the essential part from the massive amount of data:

```
$ docker image inspect \
  --format='{{json .ContainerConfig.Volumes}}' \
   mongo:3.7 | jq
```

Which will return the following result:

```
{
"/data/configdb": {},
"/data/db": {}
}
```

Evidently, the Dockerfile for MongoDB defines two volumes at `/data/configdb` and `/data/db`.

Now, let's run an instance of MongoDB as follows:

```
$ docker run --name my-mongo -d mongo:3.7
```

We can now use the `docker container inspect` command to get information about the volumes that have been created, among other things. Use this command to just get the volume information:

```
$ docker inspect --format '{{json .Mounts}}' my-mongo | jq
```

The expression should output something like this:

```
[
  {
    "Type": "volume",
    "Name": "b9ea0158b5...",
    "Source": "/var/lib/docker/volumes/b9ea0158b.../_data",
    "Destination": "/data/configdb",
    "Driver": "local",
    "Mode": "",
    "RW": true,
    "Propagation": ""
  },
  {
    "Type": "volume",
    "Name": "5becf84b1e...",
    "Source": "/var/lib/docker/volumes/5becf84b1.../_data",
    "Destination": "/data/db",
    "Driver": "local",
    "Mode": "",
    "RW": true,
    "Propagation": ""
  }
]
```

Note that the values of the `Name` and `Source` fields have been trimmed for readability. The `Source` field gives us the path to the host directory where the data produced by the MongoDB inside the container will be stored.

Obtaining Docker system information

Whenever we need to troubleshoot our system, the commands presented in this section are essential. They provide us with a lot about the Docker engine installed on the host and about the host operating system. Let's first introduce the `docker version` command. It provides abundant information about the Docker client and server that your current configuration is using. If you enter the command in the CLI, you should see something similar to this:

```
$ docker version
Client:
 Version:       18.04.0-ce
 API version:   1.37
 Go version:    go1.9.4
 Git commit:    3d479c0
 Built: Tue Apr 10 18:13:16 2018
 OS/Arch:       darwin/amd64
 Experimental:  true
 Orchestrator:  swarm

Server:
 Engine:
  Version:      18.04.0-ce
  API version:  1.37 (minimum version 1.12)
  Go version:   go1.9.4
  Git commit:   3d479c0
  Built:        Tue Apr 10 18:23:05 2018
  OS/Arch:      linux/amd64
  Experimental: true
$
```

Version Information about Docker

In my case, I can see that on both client and server, I am using version `18.04.0-ce-rc2` of the Docker engine. I can also see that my orchestrator is Swarm and more.

Now to clarify what the client and what the server is, let's look at the following diagram:

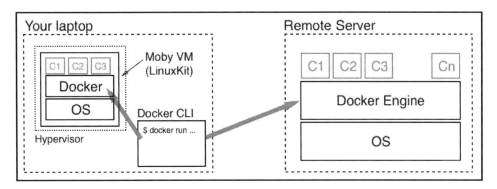

CLI accessing different Docker Hosts

You can see that the client is the little CLI through which we send Docker commands to the remote API of the Docker host. The Docker host is the container runtime which hosts the containers and might run on the same machine as the CLI, or it might run on a remote server, on-premise or in the cloud. We can use the CLI to manage different servers. We do this by setting a bunch of environment variables such as `DOCKER_HOST`, `DOCKER_TLS_VERIFY`, and `DOCKER_CERT_PATH`. If these environment variables are not set on your working machine and you're using Docker for Mac or Windows then that means that you are using the Docker engine that runs on your machine.

The next important command is the `docker system info` command. This command provides information about what mode the Docker engine is operating in (swarm mode or not), what storage driver is used for the union filesystem, what version of the Linux kernel we have on our host, and much more. Please have a careful look at the output generated by your system when running the command. Analyze what kind of information is shown:

```
$ docker system info
Containers: 1
 Running: 0
 Paused: 0
 Stopped: 1
Images: 70
Server Version: 18.04.0-ce
Storage Driver: overlay2
 Backing Filesystem: extfs
 Supports d_type: true
 Native Overlay Diff: true
Logging Driver: json-file
Cgroup Driver: cgroupfs
Plugins:
 Volume: local
 Network: bridge host ipvlan macvlan null overlay
 Log: awslogs fluentd gcplogs gelf journald json-file logentries splunk syslog
Swarm: inactive
Runtimes: runc
Default Runtime: runc
Init Binary: docker-init
containerd version: 773c489c9c1b21a6d78b5c538cd395416ec50f88
runc version: 4fc53a81fb7c994640722ac585fa9ca548971871
init version: 949e6fa
Security Options:
 seccomp
  Profile: default
Kernel Version: 4.9.87-linuxkit-aufs
Operating System: Docker for Mac
OSType: linux
Architecture: x86_64
CPUs: 4
Total Memory: 1.952GiB
Name: linuxkit-025000000001
ID: WV5X:CY7N:LHIP:SWJ2:T55W:P5QM:MEYU:MM3V:55OH:RALF:5ZDN:QH7Y
Docker Root Dir: /var/lib/docker
Debug Mode (client): false
Debug Mode (server): true
 File Descriptors: 22
 Goroutines: 42
 System Time: 2018-04-21T12:08:17.962868Z
 EventsListeners: 2
HTTP Proxy: gateway.docker.internal:3128
HTTPS Proxy: gateway.docker.internal:3129
Registry: https://index.docker.io/v1/
Labels:
Experimental: true
Insecure Registries:
 127.0.0.0/8
Live Restore Enabled: false
```

Output of the Command docker system info

Listing resource consumption

Over time, a Docker host can accumulate quite a bit of resources such as images, containers, and volumes in memory and on disk. As in every good household, we should keep our environment clean and free unused resources to reclaim space. Otherwise, there will come the moment when Docker does not allow us to add any more new resources, meaning actions such as pulling an image can fail due to lack of available space on disk or in memory.

The Docker CLI provides a handy little `system` command that lists how much resources currently are used on our system and how much of this space can possibly be reclaimed. The command is:

```
$ docker system df
```

If you execute this command on your system, you should see an output similar to this:

```
TYPE            TOTAL   ACTIVE   SIZE      RECLAIMABLE
Images          21      9        1.103GB   845.3MB (76%)
Containers      14      11       9.144kB   4.4kB (48%)
Local Volumes   14      14       340.3MB   0B (0%)
Build Cache                      0B        0B
```

The last line in the output, the `Build Cache`, is only displayed on newer versions of Docker. This information has been added recently. The preceding output is explained as follows:

- In my case, the output tells me that on my system I am currently having 21 images locally cached of which 9 are in active use. An image is considered to be in active use if currently at least one running or stopped container is based on it. These images occupy 1.1 GB disk space. Close to 845 MB can technically be reclaimed since the corresponding images are not currently used.
- Further, I have 11 running containers on my system and three stopped ones for a total of 14 containers. I can reclaim the space occupied by the stopped containers which is 4.4 kB in my case.
- I also have 14 active volumes on my host that together consume about 340 MB of disk space. Since all volumes are in use, I cannot reclaim any space at this time.
- Finally, my `Build Cache` is currently empty and thus of course I cannot reclaim any space there too.

If I want even more detailed information about the resource consumption on my system, I can run the same command in verbose mode using the −v flag:

```
$ docker system df -v
```

This will give me a detailed list of all images, containers, and volumes with their respective size. A possible output could look like this:

Verbose output of the system resources consumed by Docker

This verbose output should give us enough detailed information to make an informed decision as to whether or not we need to start cleaning up our system, and which parts we might need to clean up.

Pruning unused resources

Once we have concluded that some clean up is needed Docker provides us with so-called pruning commands. For each resource, such as images, containers, volumes, and networks there exists a `prune` command.

Pruning containers

In this section we want to regain unused system resources by pruning containers. Let's start with this command:

```
$ docker container prune
```

The preceding command will remove all containers from the system that are not in running status. Docker will ask for confirmation before deleting the containers that are currently in exited or created status. If you want to skip this confirmation step you can use the -f (or --force) flag:

```
$ docker container prune -f
```

Under certain circumstances, we might want to remove all containers from our system, even the running ones. We cannot use the prune command for this. Instead we should use a command, such as the following combined expression:

```
$ docker container rm -f $(docker container ls -aq)
```

Please be careful with the preceding command. It removes all containers without warning, even the running ones! Please, before you proceed look at the preceding command again in detail and try to explain what exactly happens and why.

Pruning images

Next in line are images. If we want to free all space occupied by unused image layers we can use the following command:

```
$ docker image prune
```

After we reconfirm to Docker that we indeed want to free space occupied by unused image layers, those get removed. Now I have to specify what we mean when talking about unused image layers. As you recall from the previous chapter, an image is made up of a stack of immutable layers. Now, when we are building a custom image multiple times, each time making some changes in, say, the source code of the application for which we're building the image, then we are recreating layers and previous versions of the same layer become orphaned. *Why is this the case?* The reason is that layers are immutable, as discussed in detail in the previous chapter. Thus, when something in the source that is used to build a layer is changed, the very layer has to be rebuilt and the previous version will be abandoned.

On a system where we often build images, the number of orphaned image layers can increase substantially over time. All these orphaned layers are removed with the preceding `prune` command.

Similar to the `prune` command for containers, we can avoid Docker asking us for a confirmation by using the force flag:

```
$ docker image prune -f
```

There is an even more radical version of the image `prune` command. Sometimes we do not just want to remove orphaned image layers but all images that are not currently in use on our system. For this, we can use the `-a` (or `--all`) flag:

```
$ docker image prune --force --all
```

After execution of the preceding command, only images that are currently used by one or more containers will remain in our local image cache.

Pruning volumes

Docker volumes are used to allow for persistent access of data by containers. This data can be important and thus the commands discussed in this section should be applied with special care.

If you know that you want to reclaim space occupied by volumes and with it irreversibly destroy the underlying data, you can use the following command:

```
$ docker volume prune
```

This command will remove all volumes that are not currently in use by at least one container.

 This is a destructive command and cannot be undone. You should always create a backup of the data associated with the volumes before you delete them except when you're sure that the data has no further value.

To avoid system corruption or malfunctioning applications, Docker does not allow you to remove volumes that are currently in use by at least one container. This applies even to the situation where a volume is used by a stopped container. You always have to remove the containers that use a volume first.

A useful flag when pruning volumes is the `-f` or `--filter` flag which allows us to specify the set of volumes which we're considering for pruning. Look at the following command:

```
$ docker volume prune --filter 'label=demo'
```

This will only apply the command to volumes that have a `label` with the `demo` value. The filtering flag format is `key=value`. If there is more than one filter needed, then we can use multiple flags:

```
$ docker volume prune --filter 'label=demo' --filter 'label=test'
```

The filter flag can also be used when pruning other resources such as containers and images.

Pruning networks

The last resource that can be pruned are networks. We will discuss networks in detail in `Chapter 7`, *Single-Host Networking*. To remove all unused networks, we use the following command:

```
$ docker network prune
```

This will remove the networks on which currently no container or service is attached. Please don't worry about networks too much at this time. We will come back to them and all this will make much more sense to you.

Pruning everything

If we just want to prune everything at once without having to enter multiple commands, we can use the following command:

```
$ docker system prune
```

The Docker CLI will ask us for a confirmation and then remove all unused containers, images, volumes, and networks in one go and in the right order.

Once again, to avoid Docker asking us for a confirmation, we can just use the force flag with the command.

Consuming Docker system events

The Docker engine, when creating, running, stopping, and removing containers and other resources such as volumes or networks, produces a log of events. These events can be consumed by external systems, such as some infrastructure services that use them to make informed decisions. An example of such a service could be a tool that creates an inventory of all containers that are currently running on the system.

We can hook ourselves into this stream of system events and output them, for example in a terminal, by using the following command:

```
$ docker system events
```

This command is a blocking command. Thus, when you execute it in your terminal session the according session is blocked. Therefore, we recommend that you always open an extra window when you want to use this command.

Assuming we have executed the preceding command in an extra terminal window, we can now test it and run a container like this:

```
$ docker container run --rm alpine echo "Hello World"
```

The output produced should look like this:

```
2018-01-28T15:08:57.318341118-06:00 container create
8e074342ef3b20cfa73d17e4ef7796d424aa8801661765ab5024acf166c6ecf3
(image=alpine, name=confident_hopper)

2018-01-28T15:08:57.320934314-06:00 container attach
8e074342ef3b20cfa73d17e4ef7796d424aa8801661765ab5024acf166c6ecf3
(image=alpine, name=confident_hopper)

2018-01-28T15:08:57.354869473-06:00 network connect
c8fd270e1a776c5851c9fa1e79927141a1e1be228880c0aace4d0daebccd190f
(container=8e074342ef3b20cfa73d17e4ef7796d424aa8801661765ab5024acf166c6ecf3
, name=bridge, type=bridge)

2018-01-28T15:08:57.818494970-06:00 container start
8e074342ef3b20cfa73d17e4ef7796d424aa8801661765ab5024acf166c6ecf3
(image=alpine, name=confident_hopper)

2018-01-28T15:08:57.998941548-06:00 container die
8e074342ef3b20cfa73d17e4ef7796d424aa8801661765ab5024acf166c6ecf3
(exitCode=0, image=alpine, name=confident_hopper)

2018-01-28T15:08:58.304784993-06:00 network disconnect
```

```
c8fd270e1a776c5851c9fa1e79927141a1e1be228880c0aace4d0daebccd190f
(container=8e074342ef3b20cfa73d17e4ef7796d424aa8801661765ab5024acf166c6ecf3
, name=bridge, type=bridge)

2018-01-28T15:08:58.412513530-06:00 container destroy
8e074342ef3b20cfa73d17e4ef7796d424aa8801661765ab5024acf166c6ecf3
(image=alpine, name=confident_hopper)
```

In this output, we can follow the exact life cycle of the container. The container is created, started, and then destroyed. If the output generated by this command is not to your liking you can always change it by using the `--format` parameter. The value of the format has to be written using the Go template syntax. The following sample outputs the type, image, and action of the event:

```
$ docker system events --format 'Type={{.Type}}
Image={{.Actor.Attributes.image}} Action={{.Action}}'
```

If we run the exact same container `run` command as before, the output generated now looks like this:

```
Type=container   Image=alpine       Action=create
Type=container   Image=alpine       Action=attach
Type=network     Image=<no value>   Action=connect
Type=container   Image=alpine       Action=start
Type=container   Image=alpine       Action=die
Type=network     Image=<no value>   Action=disconnect
Type=container   Image=alpine       Action=destroy
```

Summary

In this chapter, we have introduced Docker volumes that can be used to persist states produced by containers and make it durable. We can also use volumes to provide containers with data originating from various sources. We have learned how to create, mount and use volumes. We have learned various techniques of defining volumes such as by name, by mounting a host directory, or by defining volumes in a container image.

In this chapter, we have also discussed various system-level commands that either provide us with abundant information to troubleshoot a system, or to manage and prune resources used by Docker. Lastly, we have learned how we can visualize and potentially consume the event stream generated by the container runtime.

In the next chapter, we are going to get an introduction into the fundamentals of container orchestration. There we're going to discuss what's needed when we have to manage and run not just one or a few containers but potentially hundreds of them on many nodes in a cluster. We will see that there are a lot of challenges to solve. This is where orchestration engines come into play.

Questions

Please try to answer the following questions to assess your learning progress:

1. How will you create a named data volume with a name, for example `my-products`, using the default driver?
2. How will you run a container using the image `alpine` and mount the volume `my-products` in read-only mode into the /data container folder?
3. How will you locate the folder which is associated with the volume `my-products` and navigate to it? Also, how will you create a file, `sample.txt` with some content?
4. How will you run another `alpine` container to which you mount the `my-products` volume to the `/app-data` folder, in read/write mode? Inside this container, navigate to the `/app-data` folder and create a `hello.txt` file with some content.
5. How will you mount a host volume, for example `~/my-project`, into a container?
6. How will you remove all unused volumes from your system?
7. How will you determine the exact version of the Linux kernel and of Docker running on your system?

Further reading

The following articles provide more in-depth information:

- Use volumes at `http://dockr.ly/2EUjTml`
- Manage data in Docker at `http://dockr.ly/2EhBpzD`
- Docker volumes on PWD at `http://bit.ly/2sjIfDj`
- Containers—clean up your house at `http://bit.ly/2bVrCBn`
- Docker system events at `http://dockr.ly/2BlZmXY`

6
Distributed Application Architecture

In the previous chapter, we learned how we can use Docker volumes to persist created or modified state, as well as share data between applications running in containers. We also learned how to work with events generated by the Docker daemon and clean up unused resources.

In this chapter, we introduce the concept of a distributed application architecture and discuss the various patterns and best practices that are required to run a distributed application successfully. Finally, we will discuss the additional requirements that need to be fulfilled to run such an application in production.

In this chapter, we will cover the following topics:

- What is a distributed application architecture?
- Patterns and best practices
- Running in production

After finishing this chapter, you will be able to do the following:

- Name at least four characteristics of a distributed application architecture
- Name at least four patterns that need to be implemented for a production-ready distributed application

What is a distributed application architecture?

In this section, we are going to explain in detail what we mean when we talk about a distributed application architecture. First, we need to make sure that all words or acronyms we use have a meaning and that we are all talking the same language.

Defining the terminology

In this and the subsequent chapters, we will talk a lot about concepts that might not be familiar to everyone. To make sure we all talk the same language, let's briefly introduce and describe the most important of these concepts or words:

VM	**Acronym for virtual machine. This is a virtual computer.**
Node	Individual server used to run applications. This can be a physical server, often called **bare metal**, or a VM. A node can be a mainframe, supercomputer, standard business server, or even a Raspberry Pi. Nodes can be computers in a company's own data center or in the cloud. Normally, a node is part of a cluster.
Cluster	Group of nodes connected by a network used to run distributed applications.
Network	Physical and software-defined communication paths between individual nodes of a cluster and programs running on those nodes.
Port	Channel on which an application such a web server listens for incoming requests.
Service	This, unfortunately, is a very overloaded term and its real meaning depends on the context in which it is used. If we use the term *service* in the context of an application such as an application service, then it usually means that this is a piece of software that implements a limited set of functionality which is then used by other parts of the application. As we progress through this book, other types of services that have a slightly different definition will be discussed.

Naively said, a distributed application architecture is the opposite of a monolithic application architecture, but it's not unreasonable to look at this monolithic architecture first. Traditionally, most business applications have been written in such a way that the result can be seen as one single, tightly coupled program that runs on a named server somewhere in a data center. All its code is compiled into a single binary or a few very tightly coupled binaries that need to be co-located when running the application. The fact that the server, or more general host, on which the application is running has a well-defined name or static IP address is also important in this context. Let's look at the following diagram to illustrate this type of application architecture a bit more clearly:

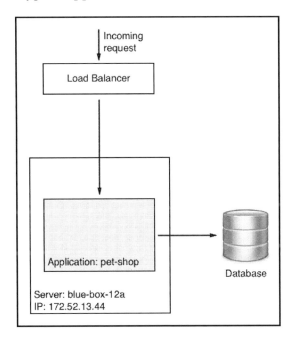

Monolithic application architecture

In the preceding figure, we see a server named **blue-box-12a** with an IP address of 172.52.13.44 running an application called **pet-shop**, which is a monolith consisting of a main module and a few tightly coupled libraries.

Now, let's look at the following figure:

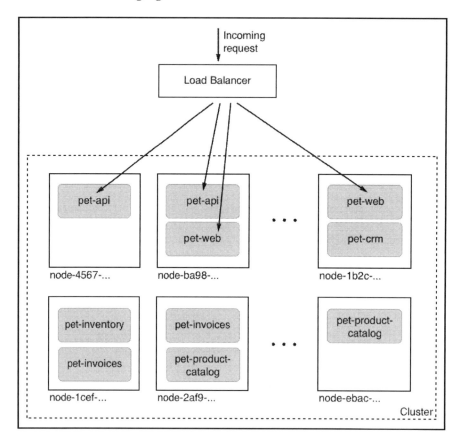

Distributed application architecture

Here, all of a sudden, we don't have only a single named server anymore, but we have a lot of them and they don't have human-friendly names, but rather some unique IDs that can be something like a **universal unique identifier** (**UUID**). The pet shop application, all of a sudden, also does not consist of a single monolithic block anymore but rather of a plethora of interacting yet loosely coupled services such as **pet-api**, **pet-web**, and **pet-inventory**. Furthermore, each service runs in multiple instances in this cluster of servers or hosts.

You might be wondering why we are discussing this in a book about Docker containers, and you are right to ask. While all the topics we're going to investigate apply equally to a world where containers do not (yet) exist, it is important to realize that containers and container orchestration engines help to address all the problems in a much more efficient and straightforward way. Most of the problems that used to be very hard to solve in a distributed application architecture become quite simple in a containerized world.

Patterns and best practices

A distributed application architecture has many compelling benefits, but it has also one very significant drawback compared to a monolithic application architecture - the former is way more complex. To tame this complexity, the industry has come up with some important best practices and patterns. In the following sections, we are going to look into some of the most important ones in more detail.

Loosely coupled components

The best way to address a complex subject has always been to divide it into smaller sub problems that are more manageable. As an example, it would be insanely complex to build a house in one single step. It is much easier to build the house up from simple parts that are then combined into the final result.

The same also applies to software development. It is much easier to develop a very complex application if we divide this application into smaller components that interoperate and together make up the overall application. Now, it is much easier to develop these components individually if they are only loosely coupled to each other. What this means is that component A makes no assumptions about the inner workings of, say, components B and C, but is only interested in how it can communicate with those two components across a well-defined interface. If each component has a well-defined and simple public interface through which communication with the other components in the system and the outside world happens, then this enables us to develop each component individually, without implicit dependencies to other components. During the development process, other components in the system can be replaced by stubs or mocks to allow us to test our component.

Stateful versus stateless

Every meaningful business application creates, modifies, or uses data. Data is also called state. An application service that creates or modifies persistent data is called a stateful component. Typical stateful components are database services or services that create files. On the other hand, application components that do not create or modify persistent data are called stateless components.

In a distributed application architecture, stateless components are much simpler to handle than stateful components. Stateless components can be easily scaled up and scaled down. They can also be quickly and painlessly torn down and restarted on a completely different node of the cluster—all this because they have no persistent data associated with them.

Given that fact, it is helpful to design a system in a way that most of the application services are stateless. It is best to push all the stateful components to the boundary of the application and limit their number. Managing stateful components is hard.

Service discovery

As we build applications that consist of many individual components or services that communicate with each other, we need a mechanism that allows the individual components to find each other in the cluster. Finding each other usually means that one needs to know on which node the target component is running and on which port it is listening for communication. Most often, nodes are identified by an IP address and a port, which is just a number in a well-defined range.

Technically, we could tell **Service A**, which wants to communicate with a target, **Service B**, what the IP address and port of the target are. This could happen, for example, through an entry in a configuration file:

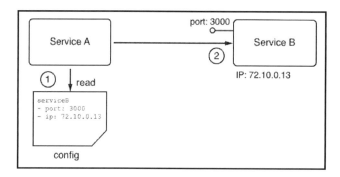

Components are hardwired

While this might work very well in the context of a monolithic application that runs on one or only a few well-known and curated servers, it totally falls apart in a distributed application architecture. First of all, in this scenario, we have many components, and keeping track of them manually becomes a nightmare. It is definitely not scalable. Furthermore, Service A typically should or will never know on which node of the cluster the other components run. Their location may not even be stable as component B could be moved from node X to another node Y, due to various reasons external to the application. Thus, we need another way in which Service A can locate Service B, or any other service for that matter. What is most commonly used is an external authority that is aware of the topology of the system at any given time. This external authority or service knows all the nodes and their IP addresses that currently pertain to the cluster; it knows all services that are running and where they are running. Often, this kind of service is called a **DNS service**, where **DNS** stands for **Domain Name System**. As we will see, Docker has a DNS service implemented as part of the underlying engine. Kubernetes also uses a DNS service to facilitate communication between components running in the cluster:

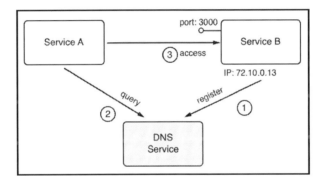

Components consult an external locator service

In the preceding figure, we see how Service A wants to communicate with Service B. But it can't do this directly; it has to first query the external authority, a registry service, here called a **DNS Service**, about the whereabouts of Service B. The registry service will answer with the requested information and hand out the IP address and port number with which Service A can reach Service B. Service A then uses this information and establishes communication with Service B. Of course, this is a naive picture of what's really happening on a low level, but it is a good picture to understand the architectural pattern of service discovery.

Routing

Routing is the mechanism of sending packets of data from a source component to a target component. Routing is categorized into different types. One uses the so-called OSI model (see reference in the *Further reading* section of this chapter) to distinguish between different types of routing. In the context of containers and container orchestration, routing at layers 2, 3, 4, and 7 is relevant. We will dive into more detail about routing in the subsequent chapters. Here, let's just say that layer 2 routing is the most low-level type of routing, which connects a MAC address to a MAC address, while layer 7 routing, which is also called application-level routing, is the most high-level one. The latter is, for example, used to route requests having a target identifier that is a URL such as `example.com/pets` to the appropriate target component in our system.

Load balancing

Load balancing is used whenever Service A requests a service from Service B, but the latter is running in more than one instance, as shown in the following figure:

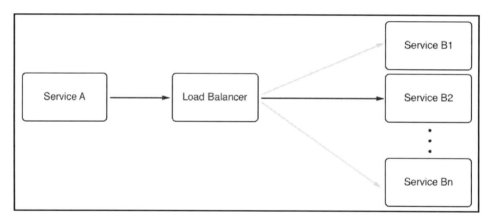

Request of Service A load balanced to Service B

If we have multiple instances of a service such as Service B running in our system, we want to make sure that every, of those instances gets an equal amount of workload assigned to it. This task is a generic one, which means that we don't want the caller to have to do the load balancing, but rather an external service that intercepts the call and takes over the part of deciding to which of the target service instances to forward the call. This external service is called a **load balancer**. Load balancers can use different algorithms to decide how to distribute the incoming calls to the target service instances. The most common algorithm used is called round robin. This algorithm just assigns requests in a repetitive way, starting with instance 1 then 2 until instance n. After the last instance has been served, the load balancer starts over with instance number 1.

Defensive programming

When developing a service for a distributed application, it is important to remember that this service is not going to be standalone, but is dependent on other application services or even on external services provided by third parties, such as credit card validation services or stock information services, to just name two. All these other services are external to the service we are developing. We have no control over their correctness or their availability at any given time. Thus, when coding, we always need to assume the worst and hope for the best. Assuming the worst means that we have to deal with potential failures explicitly.

Retries

When there is a possibility that an external service might be temporarily unavailable or not responsive enough, then the following procedure can be used. When the call to the other service fails or times out, the calling code should be structured in such a way that the same call is repeated after a short wait time. If the call fails again, the wait should be a bit longer before the next trial. The calls should be repeated up until a maximum number of times, each time increasing the wait time. After that, the service should give up and provide a degraded service, which could mean to return some stale cached data or no data at all, depending on the situation.

Logging

Important operations in a service should always be logged. Logging information needs to be categorized to be of a real value. A common list of categories is debug, info, warning, error, and fatal. Logging information should be collected by a central log aggregation service and not be stored on an individual node of the cluster. Aggregated logs are easy to parse and filter for relevant information.

Error handling

As mentioned earlier, each application service in a distributed application is dependent on other services. As developers, we should always expect the worst and have appropriate error handling in place. One of the most important best practices is to fail fast. Code the service in such a way that unrecoverable errors are discovered as early as possible and, if such an error is detected, have the service fail immediately. But don't forget to log meaningful information to STDERR or STDOUT, which can be used by developers or system operators later to track malfunctions of the system. Also, return a helpful error to the caller, indicating as precisely as possible why the call failed.

One sample of fail fast is to always check the input values provided by the caller. *Are the values in the expected ranges and complete?* If not, then do not try to continue processing, but immediately abort the operation.

Redundancy

A mission-critical system has to be available all the time, around the clock, 365 days a year. Downtime is not acceptable, since it might result in a huge loss of opportunities or reputation for the company. In a highly distributed application, the likelihood of a failure of at least one of the many involved components is non-neglectable. One can say that the question is not whether a component will fail, but rather when a failure will occur.

To avoid downtime when one of the many components in the system fails, each individual part of the system needs to be redundant. This includes the application components as well as all infrastructure parts. What that means is that if we, say, have a payment service as part of our application, then we need to run this service redundantly. The easiest way to do that is to run multiple instances of this very service on different nodes of our cluster. The same applies, say, for an edge router or a load balancer. We cannot afford for this to ever go down. Thus the router or load balancer must be redundant.

Health checks

We have mentioned various times that in a distributed application architecture, with its many parts, failure of an individual component is highly likely and it is only a matter of time until it happens. For that reason, we run every single component of the system redundantly. Proxy services then load balance the traffic across the individual instances of a service.

But now there is another problem. *How does the proxy or router know whether a certain service instance is available or not?* It could have crashed or it could be unresponsive. To solve this problem, one uses so-called health checks. The proxy, or some other system service on behalf of the proxy, periodically polls all the service instances and checks their health. The questions are basically *Are you still there? Are you healthy?* The answer of each service is either *Yes* or *No*, or the health check times out if the instance is not responsive anymore.

If the component answers with *No* or a timeout occurs, then the system kills the corresponding instance and spins up a new instance in its place. If all this happens in a fully automated way, then we say that we have an auto-healing system in place.

Circuit breaker pattern

A **circuit breaker** is a mechanism that is used to avoid a distributed application going down due to a cascading failure of many essential components. Circuit breakers help to avoid one failing component tearing down other dependent services in a domino effect. Like circuit breakers in an electrical system, which protect a house from burning down due to the failure of a malfunctioning plugged-in appliance by interrupting the power line, circuit breakers in a distributed application interrupt the connection from Service A to Service B if the latter is not responding or is malfunctioning.

This can be achieved by wrapping a protected service call in a circuit breaker object. This object monitors for failures. Once the number of failures reaches a certain threshold, the circuit breaker trips. All subsequent calls to the circuit breaker will return with an error, without the protected call being made at all:

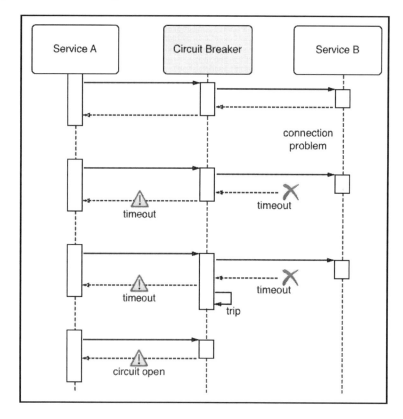

Circuit breaker pattern

Running in production

To successfully run a distributed application in production, we need to consider a few more aspects beyond the best practices and patterns presented in the preceding sections. One specific area that comes to mind is introspection and monitoring. Let's go through the most important aspects in detail.

Logging

Once a distributed application is in production, it is not possible to debug it. But how can we then find out *what exactly is the root cause of a malfunction of the application that has been reported by a user?* The solution to this problem is to produce abundant and meaningful logging information. Developers need to instrument their application services in such a way that they output helpful information, such as when an error happens or a potentially unexpected or unwanted situation is encountered. Often, this information is output to STDOUT and STDERR, from where it is then collected by system daemons that write the information to local files or forward it to a central log aggregation service.

If there is sufficient information in the logs, developers can use those logs to track down the root cause of errors in the system that have been reported.

In a distributed application architecture, with its many components, logging is even more important than in a monolithic application. The paths of execution of a single request through all the components of the application can be very complex. Also, remember that the components are distributed across a cluster of nodes. Thus, it makes sense to log everything of importance and to each log entry add things such as the exact time when it happened, the component in which it happened, and the node on which the component ran, to name just a few. Furthermore, the logging information should be aggregated in a central location so that it is readily available for developers and system operators to analyze.

Tracing

Tracing is used to find out how an individual request is funneled through a distributed application and how much time is spent overall for the request and in every individual component. This information, if collected, can be used as one of the sources for dashboards that show the behavior and health of the system.

Monitoring

Operators like to have dashboards showing live key metrics of the system, which show them the overall health of the application in one glance. These metrics can be non-functional metrics such as memory and CPU usage, number of crashes of a system or application component, health of a node, and so on, as well as functional and thus application-specific metrics such as the number of checkouts in an ordering system or the number of items out of stock in an inventory service.

Most often, the base data used to aggregate the numbers that are used for a dashboard are extracted from logging information. This can either be system logs, which will mostly be used for non-functional metrics, and application-level logs, for functional metrics.

Application updates

One of the competitive advantages for a company is to be able to react in a timely manner to changing market situations. Part of this is to be able to quickly adjust an application to fulfill new and changed needs or to add new functionality. The faster we can update our applications, the better. Many companies these days roll out new or changed features multiple times per day.

Since application updates are so frequent, these updates have to be non-disruptive. We cannot allow the system to go down for maintenance when upgrading. It all has to happen seamlessly and transparently.

Rolling updates

One way of updating an application or an application service is to use rolling updates. The assumption here is that the particular piece of software that has to be updated runs in multiple instances. Only then can we use this type of update.

What happens is that the system stops one instance of the current service and replaces it with an instance of the new service. As soon as the new instance is ready, it will be served traffic. Usually, the new instance is monitored for some time to see whether or not it works as expected and, if it does, the next instance of the current service is taken down and replaced by a new instance. This pattern is repeated until all service instances have been replaced.

Since there are always a few instances running at any given time, current or new, the application is operational all the time. No downtime is needed.

Blue-green deployments

In blue-green deployments, the current version of the application service, called *blue*, handles all the application traffic. We then install the new version of the application service, called *green*, on the production system. The new service is not yet wired with the rest of the application.

Once green is installed, one can execute smoke tests against this new service and, if those succeed, the router can be configured to funnel all traffic that previously went to blue to the new service, green. The behavior of green is then observed closely and, if all success criteria are met, blue can be decommissioned. But if, for some reason, green shows some unexpected or unwanted behavior, the router can be reconfigured to return all traffic to blue. Green can then be removed and fixed, and a new blue-green deployment can be executed with the corrected version:

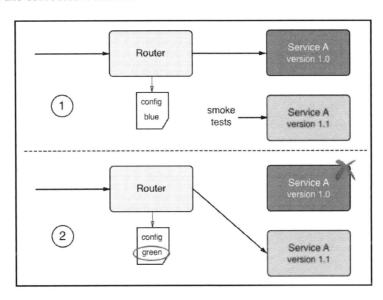

Blue-green deployment

Canary releases

Canary releases are releases where we have the current version of the application service and the new version installed on the system in parallel. As such, they resemble blue-green deployments. At first, all traffic is still routed through the current version. We then configure a router so that it funnels a small percentage, say 1%, of the overall traffic to the new version of the application service. The behavior of the new service is then monitored closely to find out whether or not it works as expected. If all the criteria for success are met, then the router is configured to funnel more traffic, say 5% this time, through the new service. Again, the behavior of the new service is closely monitored and, if it is successful, more and more traffic is routed to it until we reach 100%. Once all traffic is routed to the new service and it has been stable for some time, the old version of the service can be decommissioned.

Why do we call this a canary release? It is named after the coal miners who would use canary birds as an early warning system in the mines. Canary birds are particularly sensitive to toxic gas and if such a canary bird died, the miners knew they had to abandon the mine immediately.

Irreversible data changes

If part of our update process is to execute an irreversible change in our state, such as an irreversible schema change in a backing relational database, then we need to address this with special care. It is possible to execute such changes without downtime if one uses the right approach. It is important to recognize that, in such a situation, one cannot deploy the code changes that require the new data structure in the data store at the same time as the changes to the data. Rather, the whole update has to be separated into three distinct steps. In the first step, one rolls out a backward-compatible schema and data change. If this is successful, then one rolls out the new code in the second step. Again, if that is successful, one cleans up the schema in the third step and removes the backwards-compatibility:

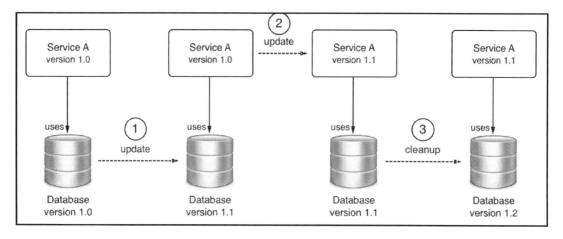

Rolling out an irreversible data or schema change

Rollback

If we have frequent updates to our application services that run in production, sooner or later there will be a problem with one of those updates. Maybe a developer, while fixing a bug, introduced a new one, which was not caught by all the automated, and maybe manual, tests, so the application is misbehaving and it is imperative that we roll back the service to the previous good version. In this regard, a rollback is a recovery from a disaster.

Again, in a distributed application architecture, it is not a question of whether a rollback will ever be needed, but rather when a rollback will have to occur. Thus we need to absolutely be sure that we can always roll back to a previous version of any service that makes up our application. Rollbacks cannot be an afterthought but have to be a tested and proven part of our deployment process.

If we are using blue-green deployments to update our services, then rollbacks should be fairly simple. All we need to do is switch the router from the new green version of the service back to the previous blue version.

Summary

In this chapter, we learned what a distributed application architecture is and what patterns and best practices are helpful or needed to successfully run a distributed application. Lastly, we discussed what is needed in addition to run such an application in production.

In the next chapter, we will dive into networking limited to a single host. We're going to discuss in detail how containers living on the same host can communicate with each other and how external clients can access containerized applications if necessary.

Questions

Please answer the following questions to assess your understanding of this chapter's content.

1. When and why does every part in a distributed application architecture have to be redundant? Explain in a few short sentences.
2. Why do we need DNS services? Explain in 3 to 5 sentences.
3. What is a circuit breaker and why is it needed?
4. What are some important differences between a monolithic application and a distributed or multi-service application?
5. What is a blue-green deployment?

Further reading

The following articles provide more in-depth information:

- *CircuitBreaker* at `http://bit.ly/1NU1sgW`
- *The OSI model explained* at `http://bit.ly/1UCcvMt`
- *BlueGreenDeployment* at `http://bit.ly/2r2IxNJ`

Single-Host Networking

7

In the last chapter, we learned about the most important architectural patterns and best practices that are used when dealing with a distributed application architecture.

In this chapter, we will introduce the Docker container networking model and its single-host implementation in the form of the bridge network. This chapter also introduces the concept of software-defined networks and how they are used to secure containerized applications. Finally, it demonstrates how container ports can be opened to the public and thus make containerized components accessible to the outside world.

This chapter will contain the following topics:

- The container network model
- Network firewalling
- The bridge network
- The host network
- The null network
- Running in an existing network namespace
- Port management

After completing this module, you will be able to do the following:

- Draft the container networking model—along with all the essential components onto a whiteboard
- Create and delete a custom bridge network
- Run a container attached to a custom bridge network
- Inspect a bridge network
- Isolate containers from each other by running them on different bridge networks
- Publish a container port to a host port of your choice

Technical requirements

For this chapter, the only thing you will need is a Docker host that is able to run Linux containers. You can use your laptop with either Docker for Mac or Windows or Docker Toolbox installed.

The container network model

So far, we have worked with single containers. But in reality, a containerized business application consists of several containers that need to collaborate to achieve a goal. Therefore, we need a way for individual containers to communicate with each other. This is achieved by establishing pathways that we can use to send data packets back and forth between containers. These pathways are called **networks**. Docker has defined a very simple networking model, the so-called **container network model** (**CNM**), to specify the requirements that any software that implements a container network has to fulfill. The following is a graphical representation of the CNM:

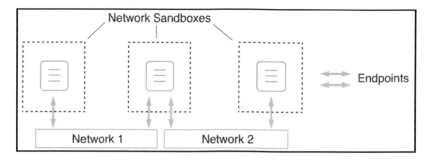

The Docker container network model

The CNM has three elements—sandbox, endpoint, and network:

- **Sandbox:** The sandbox perfectly isolates a container from the outside world. No inbound network connection is allowed into the sandboxed container. Yet, it is very unlikely that a container will be of any value in a system if absolutely no communication with it is possible. To work around this, we have element number two, which is the endpoint.
- **Endpoint:** An endpoint is a controlled gateway from the outside world into the network's sandbox that shields the container. The endpoint connects the network sandbox (but not the container) to the third element of the model, which is the network.

- **Network:** The network is the pathway that transports the data packets of an instance of communication from endpoint to endpoint, or ultimately from container to container.

It is important to note that a network sandbox can have zero to many endpoints, or, said differently, each container living in a network sandbox can either be attached to no network at all or it can be attached to multiple different networks at the same time. In the preceding image, the middle of the three network sandboxes is attached to both networks 1 and 2 through a respective endpoint.

This networking model is very generic and does not specify where the individual containers that communicate with each other run over a network. All containers could, for example, run on one and the same host (local) or they could be distributed across a cluster of hosts (global).

Of course, the CNM is just a model describing how networking works among containers. To be able to use networking with our containers, we need real implementations of the CNM. For both local and global scope, we have multiple implementations of the CNM. In the following table, we give a short overview of the existing implementations and their main characteristics. The list is in no particular order:

Network	Company	Scope	Description
Bridge	Docker	Local	Simple network based on Linux bridges allowing networking on a single host
Macvlan	Docker	Local	Configures multiple layer 2 (that is, MAC) addresses on a single physical host interface
Overlay	Docker	Global	Multinode-capable container network based on **Virtual Extensible LAN (VXLan)**
Weave Net	Weaveworks	Global	Simple, resilient, multihost Docker networking
Contiv Network Plugin	Cisco	Global	Open source container networking

All network types not directly provided by Docker can be added to a Docker host as a plugin.

Network firewalling

Docker has always had the mantra of security first. This philosophy had a direct influence on how networking in a single and multihost Docker environment was designed and implemented. Software-defined networks are easy and cheap to create, yet they perfectly firewall containers that are attached to this network from other non-attached containers, and from the outside world. All containers that belong to the same network can freely communicate with each other, while others have no means to do so:

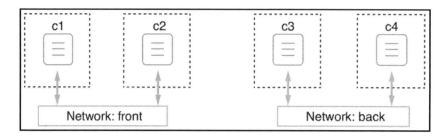

Docker networks

In the preceding image, we have two networks called **front** and **back**. Attached to the front network, we have containers **c1** and **c2**, and attached to the back network, we have containers **c3** and **c4**. **c1** and **c2** can freely communicate with each other, as can **c3** and **c4**. But **c1** and **c2** have no way to communicate with either **c3** or **c4**, and vice versa.

Now what about the situation where we have an application consisting of three services, **webAPI**, **productCatalog**, and **database**? We want webAPI to be able to communicate with productCatalog, but not with the database, and we want productCatalog to be able to communicate with the database service. We can solve this situation by placing webAPI and the database on different networks and attach productCatalog to both of these networks, as shown in the following image:

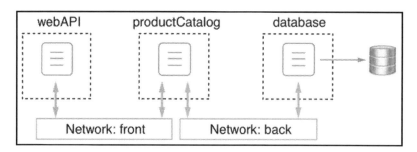

Container attached to multiple networks

Since creating SDNs is cheap, and each network provides added security by isolating resources from unauthorized access, it is highly recommended that you design and run applications so that they use multiple networks and run only services on the same network that absolutely need to communicate with each other. In the preceding example, there is absolutely no need for the web API component to ever communicate directly with the database service, so we have put them on different networks. If the worst-case scenario happens and a hacker compromises the web API, they have no ability to access the database from there without first also hacking the product catalog service.

The bridge network

The Docker bridge network is the first implementation of the container network model that we're going to look at in detail. This network implementation is based on the Linux bridge. When the Docker daemon runs for the first time, it creates a Linux bridge and calls it docker0. This is the default behavior, and can be changed by changing the configuration. Docker then creates a network with this Linux bridge and calls the network bridge. All the containers that we create on a Docker host and that we do not explicitly bind to another network leads to Docker automatically attaching to this bridge network.

To verify that we indeed have a network called bridge of type bridge defined on our host, we can list all networks on the host with the following command:

```
$ docker network ls
```

This should provide an output similar to the following:

```
$ docker network ls
NETWORK ID       NAME       DRIVER       SCOPE
928c8ce47bf2     bridge     bridge       local
bdb36adcf70c     host       host         local
af82006f2f2d     none       null         local
$
```

Listing of all Docker networks available by default

In your case, the IDs will be different, but the rest of the output should look the same. We do indeed have a first network called bridge using the driver bridge. The scope being local just means that this type of network is restricted to a single host and cannot span across multiple hosts. In a later chapter, we will also discuss other types of networks that have a global scope, meaning they can span whole clusters of hosts.

Now, let's look a little bit deeper into what this bridge network is all about. For this, we are going to use the Docker `inspect` command:

```
$ docker network inspect bridge
```

When executed, this outputs a big chunk of detailed information about the network in question. This information should look like the following:

```
C:\Users\admin>docker network inspect bridge
[
    {
        "Name": "bridge",
        "Id": "3b08c1c711ada84ae859c4bed48b5af1f45b68db89356ca5045dc7ee8672e946",
        "Created": "2018-04-09T09:47:29.9424652Z",
        "Scope": "local",
        "Driver": "bridge",
        "EnableIPv6": false,
        "IPAM": {
            "Driver": "default",
            "Options": null,
            "Config": [
                {
                    "Subnet": "172.17.0.0/16",
                    "Gateway": "172.17.0.1"
                }
            ]
        },
        "Internal": false,
        "Attachable": false,
        "Ingress": false,
        "ConfigFrom": {
            "Network": ""
        },
        "ConfigOnly": false,
        "Containers": {},
        "Options": {
            "com.docker.network.bridge.default_bridge": "true",
            "com.docker.network.bridge.enable_icc": "true",
            "com.docker.network.bridge.enable_ip_masquerade": "true",
            "com.docker.network.bridge.host_binding_ipv4": "0.0.0.0",
            "com.docker.network.bridge.name": "docker0",
            "com.docker.network.driver.mtu": "1500"
        },
        "Labels": {}
    }
]
```

Output generated when inspecting the Docker bridge network

We have already seen the ID, Name, Driver, and Scope values when we listed all the networks, so that is nothing new. But let's have a look at the **IP address management (IPAM)** block. IPAM is software that is used to track IP addresses that are used on a computer. The important part in the IPAM block is the Config node with its values for Subnet and Gateway. The subnet for the bridge network is defined by default as 172.17.0.0/16. This means that all containers attached to this network will get an IP address assigned by Docker that is taken from the given range, which is 172.17.0.2 to 172.17.255.255. The 172.17.0.1 address is reserved for the router of this network whose role in this type of network is taken by the Linux bridge. One can expect that the very first container that will be attached to this network by Docker will get the 172.17.0.2 address. All subsequent containers will get a higher number; the following image illustrates this fact:

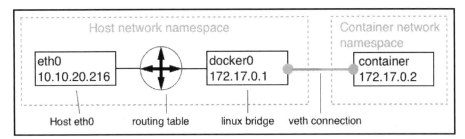

The bridge network

In the preceding image, we can see the network namespace of the host, which includes the host's eth0 endpoint, which is typically a NIC if the Docker host runs on bare metal or a virtual NIC if the Docker host is a VM. All traffic to the host comes through eth0. The Linux bridge is responsible for the routing of the network traffic between the host's network and the subnet of the bridge network.

By default, only traffic from the egress is allowed, and all ingress is blocked. What this means is that while containerized applications can reach the internet, they cannot be reached by any outside traffic. Each container attached to the network gets its own **virtual ethernet (veth)** connection with the bridge. This is illustrated in the following image:

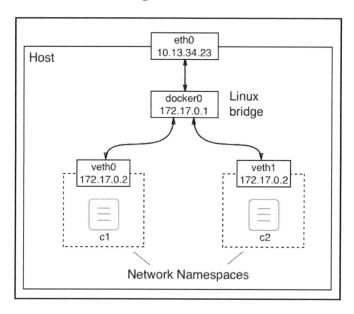

Details of the bridge network

The preceding image shows us the world from the perspective of the host. We will explore how the situation looks from within a container later on in this section.

We are not limited to just the `bridge` network, as Docker allows us to define our own custom bridge networks. This is not just a feature that is nice to have, but it is a recommended best practice to not run all containers on the same network, but to use additional bridge networks to further isolate containers that have no need to communicate with each other. To create a custom bridge network called `sample-net`, use the following command:

```
$ docker network create --driver bridge sample-net
```

If we do this, we can then inspect what subnet Docker has created for this new custom network as follows:

```
$ docker network inspect sample-net | grep Subnet
```

This returns the following value:

```
"Subnet": "172.18.0.0/16",
```

Evidently, Docker has just assigned the next free block of IP addresses to our new custom bridge network. If, for some reason, we want to specify our own subnet range when creating a network, we can do so by using the `--subnet` parameter:

```
$ docker network create --driver bridge --subnet "10.1.0.0/16" test-net
```

To avoid conflicts due to duplicate IP addresses, make sure you avoid creating networks with overlapping subnets.

Now that we have discussed what a bridge network is and how one can create a custom bridge network, we want to understand how we can attach containers to these networks. First, let's interactively run an Alpine container without specifying the network to be attached:

```
$ docker container run --name c1 -it --rm alpine:latest /bin/sh
```

In another Terminal window, let's inspect the `c1` container:

```
$ docker container inspect c1
```

In the vast output, let's concentrate for a moment on the part that provides network-related information. It can be found under the `NetworkSettings` node. I have it listed in the following output:

```
},
"NetworkSettings": {
    "Bridge": "",
    "SandboxID": "ae53496fba49de3d0a4727105cc0799b7fbd30746d76700238cb47c611f3eb68",
    "HairpinMode": false,
    "LinkLocalIPv6Address": "",
    "LinkLocalIPv6PrefixLen": 0,
    "Ports": {},
    "SandboxKey": "/var/run/docker/netns/ae53496fba49",
    "SecondaryIPAddresses": null,
    "SecondaryIPv6Addresses": null,
    "EndpointID": "c063a725d1f66e867b5769a80d1477cc88d07618860655fa3033a97478e55713",
    "Gateway": "172.17.0.1",
    "GlobalIPv6Address": "",
    "GlobalIPv6PrefixLen": 0,
    "IPAddress": "172.17.0.4",
    "IPPrefixLen": 16,
    "IPv6Gateway": "",
    "MacAddress": "02:42:ac:11:00:04",
    "Networks": {
        "bridge": {
            "IPAMConfig": null,
            "Links": null,
            "Aliases": null,
            "NetworkID": "026e653c2504e464748b4ce9b25cce69d29bc82a52105a25920f2b796663e635",
            "EndpointID": "c063a725d1f66e867b5769a80d1477cc88d07618860655fa3033a97478e55713",
            "Gateway": "172.17.0.1",
            "IPAddress": "172.17.0.4",
            "IPPrefixLen": 16,
            "IPv6Gateway": "",
            "GlobalIPv6Address": "",
            "GlobalIPv6PrefixLen": 0,
            "MacAddress": "02:42:ac:11:00:04",
            "DriverOpts": null
        }
    }
}
}
```

Network settings section of the container metadata

In the preceding output, we can see that the container is indeed attached to the `bridge` network since the `NetworkID` is equal to `026e65...`, which we can see from the preceding code is the ID of the `bridge` network. We can also see that the container got the IP address of `172.17.0.4` assigned as expected and that the gateway is at `172.17.0.1`. Please note that the container also had a `MacAddress` associated with it. This is important as the Linux bridge uses the Mac address for routing.

So far, we have approached this from the outside of the container's network namespace. Now, let's see how the situation looks when we're not only inside the container, but inside the container's network namespace. Inside the `c1` container, let's use the `ip` tool to inspect what's going on. Run the `ip addr` command and observe the output that is generated as follows:

```
/ # ip addr
1: lo: <LOOPBACK,UP,LOWER_UP> mtu 65536 qdisc noqueue state UNKNOWN qlen 1
    link/loopback 00:00:00:00:00:00 brd 00:00:00:00:00:00
    inet 127.0.0.1/8 scope host lo
       valid_lft forever preferred_lft forever
2: tunl0@NONE: <NOARP> mtu 1480 qdisc noop state DOWN qlen 1
    link/ipip 0.0.0.0 brd 0.0.0.0
3: ip6tnl0@NONE: <NOARP> mtu 1452 qdisc noop state DOWN qlen 1
    link/tunnel6 00:00:00:00:00:00:00:00:00:00:00:00:00:00:00:00 brd 00:00:00:00:00:00:00:00:00:00:00:00:00:00:00:00
19: eth0@if20: <BROADCAST,MULTICAST,UP,LOWER_UP,M-DOWN> mtu 1500 qdisc noqueue state UP
    link/ether 02:42:ac:11:00:04 brd ff:ff:ff:ff:ff:ff
    inet 172.17.0.4/16 brd 172.17.255.255 scope global eth0
       valid_lft forever preferred_lft forever
/ #
```

Container namespace as seen by the IP tool

The interesting part of the preceding output is the number `19`, the `eth0` endpoint. The `veth0` endpoint that the Linux bridge created outside of the container namespace is mapped to `eth0` inside the container. Docker always maps the first endpoint of a container network namespace to `eth0`, as seen from inside the namespace. If the network namespace is attached to an additional network, then that endpoint will be mapped to `eth1`, and so on.

Since at this point we're not really interested in any endpoint other than `eth0`, we could have used a more specific variant of the command, which would have given us the following:

```
/ # ip addr show eth0
195: eth0@if196: <BROADCAST,MULTICAST,UP,LOWER_UP,M-DOWN> mtu 1500 qdisc
noqueue state UP
    link/ether 02:42:ac:11:00:02 brd ff:ff:ff:ff:ff:ff
    inet 172.17.0.2/16 brd 172.17.255.255 scope global eth0
       valid_lft forever preferred_lft forever
```

In the output, we can also see what MAC address (`02:42:ac:11:00:02`) and what IP (`172.17.0.2`) have been associated with this container network namespace by Docker.

We can also get some information about how requests are routed by using the `ip route` command:

```
/ # ip route
default via 172.17.0.1 dev eth0
172.17.0.0/16 dev eth0 scope link src 172.17.0.2
```

This output tells us that all traffic to the gateway at `172.17.0.1` is routed through the `eth0` device.

Now, let's run another container called `c2` on the same network:

```
$ docker container run --name c2 -d alpine:latest ping 127.0.0.1
```

The `c2` container will also be attached to the `bridge` network, since we have not specified any other network. Its IP address will be the next free one from the subnet, which is `172.17.0.3`, as we can readily test:

```
$ docker container inspect --format "{{.NetworkSettings.IPAddress}}" c2
172.17.0.3
```

Now, we have two containers attached to the `bridge` network. We can try to inspect this network once again to find a list of all containers attached to it in the output.:

```
$ docker network inspect bridge
```

The information is found under the `Containers` node:

```
"ConfigOnly": false,
"Containers": {
    "27b96de70b58cd918d35c235a7c180f56f71df58cf4cec50b8f0103dd529b95f": {
        "Name": "c2",
        "EndpointID": "8883649774c5c4c53063da02598c8d09fe7ee427145b348b1d1703f31213e9ca",
        "MacAddress": "02:42:ac:11:00:03",
        "IPv4Address": "172.17.0.3/16",
        "IPv6Address": ""
    },
    "35b8dd512acb985647833e1cc52625e129c15e903fd8a0c0ab247932bc910166": {
        "Name": "c1",
        "EndpointID": "28269a9cc630135ab287052fa69c72f28c57a10bd5e7523c451bf2d0976fd1b5",
        "MacAddress": "02:42:ac:11:00:02",
        "IPv4Address": "172.17.0.2/16",
        "IPv6Address": ""
    }
},
"Options": {
```

The containers section of the output of docker network inspect bridge

Once again, we have shortened the output to the essentials for readability.

Now, let's create two additional containers, c3 and c4, and attach them to the test-net. For this, we use the --network parameter:

```
$ docker container run --name c3 -d --network test-net \
    alpine:latest ping 127.0.0.1
$ docker container run --name c4 -d --network test-net \
    alpine:latest ping 127.0.0.1
```

Let's inspect network test-net and confirm that the containers c3 and c4 are indeed attached to it:

```
$ docker network inspect test-net
```

This will give us the following output for the Containers section:

```
"Containers": {
    "134295caa6012df5dc7d541436954af1a5264c6f69d5b8012e88f9c12faf40f1": {
        "Name": "c3",
        "EndpointID": "5693cd9329437a9ecec1d27f439887bb0258837b9342a1c32204fa4571298457",
        "MacAddress": "02:42:0a:01:00:02",
        "IPv4Address": "10.1.0.2/16",
        "IPv6Address": ""
    },
    "4a277d33ebfb74f00d31be272d2d74cbfec4b17666e44d88e26cfe83b0a790cc": {
        "Name": "c4",
        "EndpointID": "a1e9ecafebdcf816261883c171434273d9973832d43255b5aa224b081853ed0f",
        "MacAddress": "02:42:0a:01:00:03",
        "IPv4Address": "10.1.0.3/16",
        "IPv6Address": ""
    }
}
```

Containers section of the command docker network inspect test-net

The next question we're going to ask ourselves is whether the two c3 and c4 containers can freely communicate with each other. To demonstrate that this is indeed the case, we can exec into the container c3:

```
$ docker container exec -it c3 /bin/sh
```

Once inside the container, we can try to ping container c4 by name and by IP address:

```
/ # ping c4
PING c4 (10.1.0.3): 56 data bytes
64 bytes from 10.1.0.3: seq=0 ttl=64 time=0.192 ms
64 bytes from 10.1.0.3: seq=1 ttl=64 time=0.148 ms
. . .
```

The following is the result of the ping using the IP address of the container c4:

```
/ # ping 10.1.0.3
PING 10.1.0.3 (10.1.0.3): 56 data bytes
64 bytes from 10.1.0.3: seq=0 ttl=64 time=0.200 ms
64 bytes from 10.1.0.3: seq=1 ttl=64 time=0.172 ms
. . .
```

The answer in both cases confirms to us that the communication between containers attached to the same network is working as expected. The fact that we can even use the name of the container we want to connect to shows us that the name resolution provided by the Docker DNS service works inside this network.

Now we want to make sure that the `bridge` and the `test-net` networks are firewalled from each other. To demonstrate this, we can try to ping the c2 container from the c3 container, either by its name or by its IP address:

```
/ # ping c2
ping: bad address 'c2'
```

The following is the result of the ping using the IP address of the target container c2 instead:

```
/ # ping 172.17.0.3
PING 172.17.0.3 (172.17.0.3): 56 data bytes
^C
--- 172.17.0.3 ping statistics ---
43 packets transmitted, 0 packets received, 100% packet loss
```

The preceding command remained hanging and I had to terminate the command with *Ctrl+C*. From the answer to pinging c2, we can also see that the name resolution does not work across networks. This is the expected behavior. Networks provide an extra layer of isolation, and thus security, to containers.

Earlier, we learned that a container can be attached to multiple networks. Let's attach a `c5` container to the `sample-net` and `test-net` networks at the same time:

```
$ docker container run --name c5 -d \
    --network sample-net \
    --network test-net \
    alpine:latest ping 127.0.0.1
```

We can then test that `c5` is reachable from the `c2` container similar to when we tested the same for containers `c4` and `c2`. The result will show that the connection indeed works.

If we want to remove an existing network, we can use the `docker network rm` command, but note that one cannot accidentally delete a network that has containers attached to it:

```
$ docker network rm test-net
Error response from daemon: network test-net id 863192... has active
endpoints
```

Before we continue, let's clean up and remove all containers:

```
$ docker container rm -f $(docker container ls -aq)
```

Then we remove the two custom networks that we created:

```
$ docker network rm sample-net
$ docker network rm test-net
```

The host network

There exist occasions where we want to run a container in the network namespace of the host. This can be necessary when we need to run some software in a container that is used to analyze or debug the host network's traffic. But keep in mind that these are very specific scenarios. When running business software in containers, there is no good reason to ever run the respective containers attached to the host's network. For security reasons, it is strongly recommended that you do not run any such container attached to the host network on a production or production-like environment.

That said, *how can we run a container inside the network namespace of the host?* Simply by attaching the container to the `host` network:

```
$ docker container run --rm -it --network host alpine:latest /bin/sh
```

If we now use the `ip` tool to analyze the network namespace from within the container, we will see that we get exactly the same picture as we would if we were running the `ip` tool directly on the host. For example, if I inspect the `eth0` device on my host, I get this:

```
/ # ip addr show eth0
2: eth0: <BROADCAST,MULTICAST,UP,LOWER_UP> mtu 1500 qdisc pfifo_fast state
UP qlen 1000
    link/ether 02:50:00:00:00:01 brd ff:ff:ff:ff:ff:ff
    inet 192.168.65.3/24 brd 192.168.65.255 scope global eth0
       valid_lft forever preferred_lft forever
    inet6 fe80::c90b:4219:ddbd:92bf/64 scope link
       valid_lft forever preferred_lft forever
```

Here, I find that `192.168.65.3` is the IP address that the host has been assigned and that the MAC address shown here also corresponds to that of the host.

We can also inspect the routes to get the following (shortened):

```
/ # ip route
default via 192.168.65.1 dev eth0 src 192.168.65.3 metric 202
10.1.0.0/16 dev cni0 scope link src 10.1.0.1
127.0.0.0/8 dev lo scope host
172.17.0.0/16 dev docker0 scope link src 172.17.0.1
...
192.168.65.0/24 dev eth0 scope link src 192.168.65.3 metric 202
```

Before I let you go on to the next section of this chapter, I want to once more point out that the use of the `host` network is dangerous and needs to be avoided if possible.

The null network

Sometimes, we need to run a few application services or jobs that do not need any network connection at all to execute the task. It is strongly advised that you run those applications in a container that is attached to the `none` network. This container will be completely isolated, and thus safe from any outside access. Let's run such a container:

```
$ docker container run --rm -it --network none alpine:latest /bin/sh
```

Once inside the container, we can verify that there is no `eth0` network endpoint available:

```
/ # ip addr show eth0
ip: can't find device 'eth0'
```

There is also no routing information available, as we can demonstrate by using the following command:

```
/ # ip route
```

This returns nothing.

Running in an existing network namespace

Normally, Docker creates a new network namespace for each container we run. The network namespace of the container corresponds to the sandbox of the container network model we described earlier on. As we attach the container to a network, we define an endpoint that connects the container network namespace with the actual network. This way, we have one container per network namespace.

Docker provides an additional way to define the network namespace in which a container runs. When creating a new container, we can specify that it should be attached to or maybe we should say included in the network namespace of an existing container. With this technique, we can run multiple containers in a single network namespace:

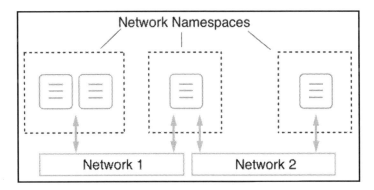

Multiple containers running in a single network namespace

In the preceding image, we can see that in the leftmost network namespace, we have two containers. The two containers, since they share the same namespace, can communicate on localhost with each other. The network namespace (and not the individual containers) is then attached to **Network 1**.

This is useful when we want to debug the network of an existing container without running additional processes inside that container. We can just attach a special utility container to the network namespace of the container to inspect. This feature is also used by Kubernetes when it creates a pod. We will hear more about Kubernetes and pods in subsequent chapters of this book.

Now, let's demonstrate how this works. First, we create a new bridge network:

```
$ docker network create --driver bridge test-net
```

Next, we run a container attached to this network:

```
$ docker container run --name web -d --network test-net nginx:alpine
```

Finally, we run another container and attach it to the network of our web container:

```
$ docker container run -it --rm --network container:web alpine:latest
/bin/sh
```

Specifically, note how we define the network: `--network container:web`. This tells Docker that our new container shall use the same network namespace as the container called `web`.

Since the new container is in the same network namespace as the web container running Nginx, we're now able to access Nginx on localhost! We can prove this by using the `wget` tool, which is part of the Alpine container, to connect to Nginx. We should see the following:

```
/ # wget -qO - localhost
<!DOCTYPE html>
<html>
<head>
<title>Welcome to nginx!</title>
...
</html>
```

Note that we have shortened the output for readability. Please also note that there is an important difference between running two containers attached to the same network and two containers running in the same network namespace. In both cases, the containers can freely communicate with each other, but in the latter case, the communication happens over localhost.

To clean up the container and network we can use the following command:

```
$ docker container rm --force web
$ docker network rm test-net
```

Port management

Now that we know how we can isolate or firewall containers from each other by placing them on different networks, and that we can have a container attached to more than one network, we have one problem that remains unsolved. *How can we expose an application service to the outside world?* Imagine a container running a web server hosting our webAPI from before. We want customers from the internet to be able to access this API. We have designed it to be a publicly accessible API. To achieve this, we have to, figuratively speaking, open a gate in our firewall through which we can funnel external traffic to our API. For security reasons, we don't just want to open the doors wide, but to have only a single controlled gate through which traffic flows.

We can create such a gate by mapping a container port to an available port on the host. We're also calling this container port to publish a port. Remember, the container has its own virtual network stack, as does the host. Therefore, container ports and host ports exist completely independently, and by default have nothing in common at all. But we can now wire a container port with a free host port and funnel external traffic through this link, as illustrated in the following image:

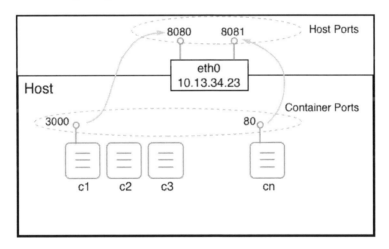

Mapping container ports to host ports

But now it is time to demonstrate how one can actually map a container port to a host port. This is done when creating a container. We have different ways of doing so:

- First, we can let Docker decide which host port our container port shall be mapped to. Docker will then select one of the free host ports in the range of 32xxx. This automatic mapping is done by using the -P parameter:

```
$ docker container run --name web -P -d nginx:alpine
```

The preceding command runs an Nginx server in a container. Nginx is listening at port 80 inside the container. With the -P parameter, we're telling Docker to map all the exposed container ports to a free port in the 32xxx range. We can find out which host port Docker is using by using the docker container port command:

```
$ docker container port web
80/tcp -> 0.0.0.0:32768
```

The Nginx container only exposes port 80, and we can see that it has been mapped to the host port 32768. If we open a new browser window and navigate to localhost:32768, we should see the following screenshot:

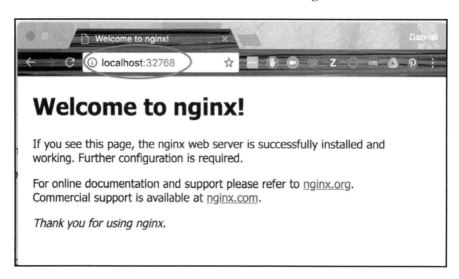

The welcome page of Nginx

- An alternative way to find out which host port Docker is using for our container is to inspect it. The host port is part of the `NetworkSettings` node:

```
$ docker container inspect web | grep HostPort
32768
```

- Finally, the third way of getting this information is to list the container:

```
$ docker container ls
CONTAINER ID      IMAGE              ...      PORTS
NAMES
56e46a14b6f7      nginx:alpine   ...      0.0.0.0:32768->80/tcp   web
```

Please note that in the preceding output, the `/tcp` part tells us that the port has been opened for communication with the TCP protocol, but not for the UDP protocol. TCP is the default, and if we want to specify that we want to open the port for UDP, then we have to specify this explicitly. The `0.0.0.0` in the mapping tells us that traffic from any host IP address can now reach the container port `80` of the `web` container.

Sometimes, we want to map a container port to a very specific host port. We can do this by using the parameter`-p` (or `--publish`). Let's look at how this is done with the following command:

```
$ docker container run --name web2 -p 8080:80 -d nginx:alpine
```

The value of the `-p` parameter is in the form of `<host port>:<container port>`. Therefore, in the preceding case, we map container port `80` to host port `8080`. Once the `web2` container runs, we can test it in the browser by navigating to `localhost:8080`, and we should be greeted by the same Nginx welcome page that we saw in the previous example that dealt with automatic port mapping.

When using the UDP protocol for communication over a certain port, then the `publish` parameter will look like `-p 3000:4321/udp`. Note that if we want to allow communication with both TCP and UDP protocols over the same port, then we have to map each protocol separately.

Summary

In this chapter, we have learned about how containers running on a single host can communicate with each other. First, we looked at the CNM that defines the requirements of a container network and then we looked at several implementations of the CNM, such as the bridge network. We then looked at how the bridge network functions in detail and also what kind of information Docker provides us with about the networks and the containers attached to those networks. We also learned about adopting two different perspectives, from both outside and inside the container.

In the next chapter, we're going to introduce Docker Compose. We will learn about creating an application that consists of multiple services, each running in a container, and how Docker Compose allows us to easily build, run, and scale such an application using a declarative approach.

Questions

To assess your skills, please try to answer the following questions:

1. Name the three core elements of the **container network model** (**CNM**).
2. How will you create a custom bridge network called for example, frontend?
3. How will you run two nginx:alpine containers attached to the frontend network.
4. For the frontend network, get the following:
    1. IPs of all attached containers.
    2. The subnet associated with the network.
5. What is the purpose of the host network?
6. Name one or two scenarios where the use of the host network is appropriate.
7. What is the purpose of the none network?
8. In what scenarios should the none network be used?

Further reading

Here are some articles that describe the topics presented in this chapter in more detail:

- *Docker networking overview* at `http://dockr.ly/2sXGzQn`
- *Container networking* at `http://dockr.ly/2HJfQKn`
- **What is a Bridge** at `https://bit.ly/2HyC3Od`
- *Use bridge networks* at `http://dockr.ly/2BNxjRr`
- *Use Macvlan networks* at `http://dockr.ly/2ETjy2x`
- *Networking using the host network* at `http://dockr.ly/2F4aI59`

8
Docker Compose

In the previous chapter, we learned a lot about how container networking works on a single Docker host. We introduced the **Container Network Model (CNM)**, which forms the basis of all networking between Docker containers, and then we dove deep into different implementations of the CNM, specifically the bridge network.

This chapter introduces the concept of an application consisting of multiple services, each running in a container, and how Docker Compose allows us to easily build, run, and scale such an application using a declarative approach.

The chapter covers the following topics:

- Demystifying declarative versus imperative
- Running a multi-service application
- Scaling a service
- Building and pushing an application

After completing this chapter, the reader will be able to do the following:

- Explain in a few short sentences the main differences between an imperative and declarative approach for defining and running an application
- Describe in their own words the difference between a container and a Docker Compose service
- Author a Docker Compose YAML file for a simple multi-service application
- Build, push, deploy, and tear down a simple multi-service application using Docker Compose
- Use Docker Compose to scale an application service up and down

Technical requirements

The code accompanying this chapter can be found at `https://github.com/fundamentalsofdocker/labs/tree/master/ch08`.

Demystifying declarative versus imperative

Docker Compose is a tool provided by Docker that is mainly used where one needs to run and orchestrate containers running on a single Docker host. This includes but is not limited to development, **continuous integration (CI)**, automated testing, and manual QA.

Docker Compose uses files formatted in YAML as input. By default, Docker Compose expects these files to be called `docker-compose.yml`, but other names are possible. The content of a `docker-compose.yml` is said to be a *declarative* way of describing and running a containerized application potentially consisting of more than a single container.

So, *what is the meaning of declarative?*

First of all, *declarative* is the antonym of *imperative*. Well, that doesn't help much. Now that I have introduced another definition, I need to explain both of them:

- **Imperative:** It's a way in which we can solve problems by specifying the exact procedure which has to be followed by the system.

  If I tell a system such as the Docker daemon imperatively how to run an application then that means that I have to describe step by step what the system has to do and how it has to react if some unexpected situation occurs. I have to be very explicit and precise in my instructions. I need to cover all edge cases and how they need to be treated.

- **Declarative:** It's a way in which we can solve problems without requiring the programmer to specify an exact procedure to be followed.

  A declarative approach means that I tell the Docker engine what my desired state for an application is and it has to figure out on its own how to achieve this desired state and how to reconcile it if the system deviates from it.

Docker clearly recommends the declarative approach when dealing with containerized applications. Consequently, the Docker Compose tool uses this approach.

Running a multi-service app

In most cases, applications do not consist of only one monolithic block, but rather of several application services that work together. When using Docker containers, each application service runs in its own container. When we want to run such a multi-service application, we can of course start all the participating containers with the well-known `docker container run` command. But this is inefficient at best. With the Docker Compose tool, we are given a way to define the application in a declarative way in a file that uses the YAML format.

Let's have a look at the content of a simple `docker-compose.yml` file:

```
version: "3.5"
services:
  web:
    image: fundamentalsofdocker/ch08-web:1.0
    ports:
      - 3000:3000
  db:
    image: fundamentalsofdocker/ch08-db:1.0
    volumes:
      - pets-data:/var/lib/postgresql/data

volumes:
  pets-data:
```

The lines in the file are explained as follows:

- `version`: In this line, we specify the version of the Docker Compose format we want to use. At the time of writing, this is version 3.5.
- `services`: In this section, we specify the services that make up our application in the `services` block. In our sample, we have two application services and we call them `web` and `db`:
  - web: The `web` service is using the image `fundamentalsofdocker/ch08-web:1.0` from the Docker Hub and is publishing container port `3000` to the host port, also `3000`.
  - db: The `db` service, on the other hand, is using the image `fundamentalsofdocker/ch08-db:1.0`, which is a customized PostgreSQL database. We are mounting a volume called `pets-data` into the container of the `db` service.

- `volumes`: The volumes used by any of the services have to be declared in this section. In our sample, this is the last section of the file. The first time the application is run, a volume called `pets-data` will be created by Docker and then, in subsequent runs, if the volume is still there, it will be reused. This could be important when the application, for some reason, crashes and has to be restarted. Then, the previous data is still around and ready to be used by the restarted database service.

Navigate to the subfolder `ch08` of the `labs` folder and start the application using Docker Compose:

```
$ docker-compose up
```

If we enter the preceding command, then the tool will assume that there must be a file in the current directory called `docker-compose.yml` and it will use that one to run. In our case, this is indeed the case and the application will start. We should see the output as follows:

```
$ docker-compose up
Creating network "ch08_default" with the default driver
Creating volume "ch08_pets-data" with default driver
Pulling web (fundamentalsofdocker/ch08-web:1.0)...
1.0: Pulling from fundamentalsofdocker/ch08-web
605ce1bd3f31: Pull complete
d9c1bb40879c: Pull complete
d610e8516793: Pull complete
bf3a86e46185: Pull complete
f082b7c3a97c: Pull complete
188ade417c9f: Pull complete
ad8771290e5e: Pull complete
Digest: sha256:d7978627352813340e8f9bbf700ecb39bece12873956e5b77dc5e6431e9126a8
Status: Downloaded newer image for fundamentalsofdocker/ch08-web:1.0
Pulling db (fundamentalsofdocker/ch08-db:1.0)...
1.0: Pulling from fundamentalsofdocker/ch08-db
ff3a5c916c92: Pull complete
a503b44e1ce0: Pull complete
211706713093: Pull complete
8df57d533e71: Pull complete
7858f71c02fb: Pull complete
55a8ef17ba59: Pull complete
3fb44f23d323: Pull complete
65cad41156b3: Pull complete
5492a5bead70: Pull complete
ac3385cd756f: Pull complete
Digest: sha256:eb5364a418bf7072de3e992517cad4ce8c55725a1cdfcd18e1c04ea2ec2a7356
Status: Downloaded newer image for fundamentalsofdocker/ch08-db:1.0
Creating ch08_db_1  ... done
Creating ch08_web_1 ... done
Attaching to ch08_db_1, ch08_web_1
```

Running the sample application, part 1

```
db_1    |   done
db_1    | server started
web_1   | Listening at 0.0.0.0:3000
db_1    | CREATE DATABASE
db_1    |
db_1    | CREATE ROLE
db_1    |
db_1    |
db_1    | /usr/local/bin/docker-entrypoint.sh: running /docker-entrypoint-initdb.d/init-db.sql
db_1    | CREATE TABLE
db_1    | ALTER TABLE
db_1    | ALTER ROLE
db_1    | INSERT 0 1
db_1    | INSERT 0 1
db_1    | INSERT 0 1
db_1    | INSERT 0 1
db_1    | INSERT 0 1
db_1    | INSERT 0 1
db_1    | INSERT 0 1
db_1    | INSERT 0 1
db_1    | INSERT 0 1
db_1    | INSERT 0 1
db_1    | INSERT 0 1
db_1    | INSERT 0 1
db_1    |
db_1    |
db_1    | waiting for server to shut down....2018-03-21 12:52:40.709 UTC [34] LOG:  received fast shutdown
 request
db_1    | 2018-03-21 12:52:40.711 UTC [34] LOG:  aborting any active transactions
db_1    | 2018-03-21 12:52:40.712 UTC [34] LOG:  worker process: logical replication launcher (PID 41) exi
ted with exit code 1
db_1    | 2018-03-21 12:52:40.712 UTC [36] LOG:  shutting down
db_1    | 2018-03-21 12:52:40.737 UTC [34] LOG:  database system is shut down
db_1    |   done
db_1    | server stopped
db_1    |
db_1    | PostgreSQL init process complete; ready for start up.
db_1    |
db_1    | 2018-03-21 12:52:40.817 UTC [1] LOG:  listening on IPv4 address "0.0.0.0", port 5432
db_1    | 2018-03-21 12:52:40.817 UTC [1] LOG:  listening on IPv6 address "::", port 5432
db_1    | 2018-03-21 12:52:40.821 UTC [1] LOG:  listening on Unix socket "/var/run/postgresql/.s.PGSQL.543
2"
db_1    | 2018-03-21 12:52:40.832 UTC [49] LOG:  database system was shut down at 2018-03-21 12:52:40 UTC
db_1    | 2018-03-21 12:52:40.835 UTC [1] LOG:  database system is ready to accept connections
```

Running the sample application, part 2

The preceding output is explained as follows:

- In the first part of the output, we can see how Docker Compose pulls the two images that constitute our application. This is followed by the creation of a network ch08_default and a volume ch08_pets-data, followed by the two containers ch08_web_1 and ch08_db_1, one for each service, web and db. All the names are automatically prefixed by Docker Compose with the name of the parent directory, which in this case is called ch08.
- After that, we see the logs produced by the two containers. Each line of the output is conveniently prefixed with the name of the service, and each service's output is in a different color. Here, the lion's share is produced by the database and only one line is from the web service.

We can now open a browser tab and navigate to localhost:3000/pet. We should be greeted by a nice cat image and some additional information about the container it came from, as shown in the following screenshot:

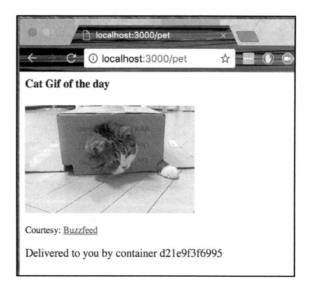

The sample application in the browser

Refresh the browser a few times to see other cat images. The application selects the current image randomly from a set of 12 images whose URLs are stored in the database.

As the application is running in interactive mode and thus the Terminal where we ran Docker Compose is blocked, we can cancel the application by pressing *Ctrl+C*. If we do so, we will see the following:

```
^CGracefully stopping... (press Ctrl+C again to force)
Stopping ch08_web_1 ... done
Stopping ch08_db_1 ... done
```

We will notice that the database service stops immediately while the web service takes about 10 seconds to do so. The reason for this being that the database service listens to and reacts to the SIGTERM signal sent by Docker while the web service doesn't, and thus Docker kills it after 10 seconds.

If we run the application again, the output will be much shorter:

```
$ docker-compose up
Creating network "ch08_default" with the default driver
Creating ch08_web_1 ... done
Creating ch08_db_1  ... done
Attaching to ch08_web_1, ch08_db_1
db_1   | 2018-03-02 01:25:35.874 UTC [1] LOG:  listening on IPv4 address "0.0.0.0", port 5432
db_1   | 2018-03-02 01:25:35.875 UTC [1] LOG:  listening on IPv6 address "::", port 5432
db_1   | 2018-03-02 01:25:35.877 UTC [1] LOG:  listening on Unix socket "/var/run/postgresql/.s.PGSQL.5432"
db_1   | 2018-03-02 01:25:35.890 UTC [19] LOG:  database system was shut down at 2018-03-02 01:25:23 UTC
db_1   | 2018-03-02 01:25:35.894 UTC [1] LOG:  database system is ready to accept connections
web_1  | Listening at 0.0.0.0:3000
```

Output of docker-compose up

This time, we didn't have to download the images and the database didn't have to initialize from scratch, but it was just reusing the data that was already present in the volume pets-data from the previous run.

We can also run the application in the background. All containers will run as daemons. For this, we just need to use the -d parameter, as shown in the following code:

```
$ docker-compose up -d
```

Docker Compose offers us many more commands than just up. We can use it to list all services that are part of the application:

Output of docker-compose ps

This command is similar to docker container ls, with the only difference being that it only lists containers that are part of the application.

To stop and clean up the application, we use the docker-compose down command:

```
$ docker-compose down
Stopping ch08_web_1 ... done
Stopping ch08_db_1 ... done
Removing ch08_web_1 ... done
Removing ch08_db_1 ... done
Removing network ch08_default
```

If we also want to remove the volume for the database, then we can use the following command:

```
$ docker volume rm ch08_pets-data
```

Why is there a ch08 *prefix in the name of the volume?* In the docker-compose.yml file, we have called the volume to use pets-data. But as we have already mentioned, Docker Compose prefixes all names with the name of the parent folder of the docker-compose.yml file plus an underscore. In this case, the parent folder is called ch08.

Scaling a service

Now, let's, for a moment, assume that our sample application has been live on the web and become very successful. Loads of people want to see our cute animal images. So now we're facing a problem since our application has started to slow down. To counteract this problem, we want to run multiple instances of the web service. With Docker Compose, this is readily done.

Running more instances is also called scaling up. We can use this tool to scale our web service up to, say, three instances:

```
$ docker-compose up --scale web=3
```

If we do this, we are in for a surprise. The output will look similar to the following screenshot:

```
$ docker-compose up --scale web=3
WARNING: The "web" service specifies a port on the host. If multiple containers for this
service are created on a single host, the port will clash.
Starting ch08_web_3 ...
Starting ch08_web_3 ... error

ERROR: for ch08_web_3  Cannot start service web: driver failed programming external conne
ctivity on endpoint ch08_web_3 (534216cc36e0284b775e48c6450e25ff21fe90ff6d7b8b9716f421cb9
8560351): Bind for 0.0.0.0:3000 failed: port is already allocated

ERROR: for web  Cannot start service web: driver failed programming external connectivity
 on endpoint ch08_web_3 (534216cc36e0284b775e48c6450e25ff21fe90ff6d7b8b9716f421cb98560351
): Bind for 0.0.0.0:3000 failed: port is already allocated
ERROR: Encountered errors while bringing up the project.
$
```

Output of docker-compose --scale

The second and third instances of the web service fail to start. The error message tells us why: we cannot use the same host port more than once. When instances 2 and 3 try to start, Docker realizes that port 3000 is already taken by the first instance. *What can we do?* Well, we can just let Docker decide which host port to use for each instance.

If, in the ports section of the compose file, we only specify the container port and leave out the host port, then Docker automatically selects an ephemeral port. Let's do exactly this:

1. First, let's tear down the application:

   ```
   $ docker-compose down
   ```

2. Then, we modify the docker-compose.yml file to look as follows:

   ```
   version: "3.5"
   services:
     web:
       image: fundamentalsofdocker/ch08-web:1.0
       ports:
         - 3000
     db:
       image: fundamentalsofdocker/ch08-db:1.0
   ```

```
            volumes:
              - pets-data:/var/lib/postgresql/data

            volumes:
              pets-data:
```

3. Now, we can start the application again and scale it up immediately after that:

```
$ docker-compose up -d
$ docker-compose scale web=3
Starting ch08_web_1 ... done
Creating ch08_web_2 ... done
Creating ch08_web_3 ... done
```

4. If we now do a docker-compose ps, we should see the following screenshot:

```
$ docker-compose ps
    Name            Command              State           Ports

ch08_db_1      docker-entrypoint.sh postgres   Up      5432/tcp
ch08_web_1     /bin/sh -c node src/server.js   Up      0.0.0.0:32769->3000/tcp
ch08_web_2     /bin/sh -c node src/server.js   Up      0.0.0.0:32771->3000/tcp
ch08_web_3     /bin/sh -c node src/server.js   Up      0.0.0.0:32770->3000/tcp
$
```

Output of docker-compose ps

5. As we can see, each service has been associated to a different host port. We can try to see whether they work, for example, using curl. Let's test the third instance, ch08_web_3:

```
$ curl -4 localhost:32770
Pets Demo Application
```

The answer, Pets Demo Application, tells us that, indeed, our application is still working as expected. Try it out for the other two instances to be sure.

Building and pushing an application

We can also use the `docker-compose build` command to just build the images of an application defined in the underlying `compose` file. But to make this work, we'll have to add the build information to the `docker-compose` file. In the folder, we have a file, `docker-compose.dev.yml`, which has those instructions already added:

```
version: "3.5"
services:
  web:
    build: web
    image: fundamentalsofdocker/ch08-web:1.0
    ports:
      - 3000:3000
  db:
    build: database
    image: fundamentalsofdocker/ch08-db:1.0
    volumes:
      - pets-data:/var/lib/postgresql/data

volumes:
  pets-data:
```

Please note the `build` key for each service. The value of that key indicates the context or folder where Docker is expecting to find the Dockerfile to build the corresponding image.

Let's use that file now:

```
$ docker-compose -f docker-compose.dev.yml build
```

The `-f` parameter will tell the Docker Compose application which compose file to use.

To push all images to Docker Hub, we can use `docker-compose push`. We need to be logged in to Docker Hub so that this succeeds, otherwise we get an authentication error while pushing. Thus, in my case, I do the following:

```
$ docker login -u fundamentalsofdocker -p <password>
```

Assuming the login succeeds, I can then push the following code:

```
$ docker-compose -f docker-compose.dev.yml push
```

The preceding command pushes the two images to the account `fundamentalsofdocker` on Docker Hub. You can find these two images at the URL: `https://hub.docker.com/u/fundamentalsofdocker/`.

Summary

In this chapter, we introduced the tool `docker-compose`. This tool is mostly used to run and scale multi-service applications on a single Docker host. Typically, developers and CI servers work with single hosts and those two are the main users of Docker Compose. The tool is using YAML files as input that contain the description of the application in a declarative way.

The tool can also be used to build and push images among many other helpful tasks. The code accompanying this chapter can be found in `labs/ch08`.

In the next chapter, we are going to introduce orchestrators. An **orchestrator** is an infrastructure software that is used to run and manage containerized applications in a cluster and it makes sure that these applications are in their desired state at all the time.

Questions

To assess your learning progress please answer the following questions:

1. How will you use `docker-compose` to run an application in daemon mode?
2. How will you use `docker-compose` to display the details of the running service?
3. How will you scale up a particular web service to say, three instances?

Further reading

The following links provide additional information on the topics discussed in this chapter:

- *The official YAML website* at `http://www.yaml.org/`
- *Docker Compose documentation* at `http://dockr.ly/1FL2VQ6`
- *Compose file version 3 reference* at `http://dockr.ly/2iHUpeX`

9
Orchestrators

In the previous chapter, we introduced Docker Compose, a tool that allows us to work with multi-service applications that are defined in a declarative way on a single Docker host.

This chapter introduces the concept of orchestrators. It teaches why orchestrators are needed and how they work conceptually. This chapter will also provide an overview of the most popular orchestrators and names a few of their pros and cons.

In this chapter, we will cover the following topics:

- What are orchestrators and why do we need them?
- The tasks of an orchestrator
- Overview of popular orchestrators

After finishing this chapter you will be able to:

- Name three to four tasks an orchestrator is responsible for
- List two to three of the most popular orchestrators
- Explain to an interested layman in your own words and with appropriate analogies why we need container orchestrators

What are orchestrators and why do we need them?

In Chapter 6, *Distributed Application Architecture*, we learned which patterns and best practices are commonly used to successfully build, ship, and run a highly distributed application. Now, if our highly distributed application is containerized, then we're facing the exact same problems or challenges that a non-containerized distributed application faces. Some of these challenges are those discussed in Chapter 6, *Distributed Application Architecture*, service discovery, load balancing, scaling, and so on.

Similar to what Docker did with containers—standardizing the packaging and shipping of software with the introduction of containers—we would like to have some tool or infrastructure software that handles all or most of the challenges mentioned. This software turns out to be what we call orchestrators or, as we also call them, orchestration engines.

If what I just said doesn't make much sense to you yet, then let's look at it from a different angle. Take an artist who plays an instrument. They can play wonderful music to an audience all on their own, just the artist and their instrument. But now take an orchestra of musicians. Put them all in a room, give them the notes of a symphony, ask them to play it, and leave the room. Without any director, this group of very talented musicians would not be able to play this piece in harmony; it would more or less sound like a cacophony. Only if the orchestra has a conductor who orchestrates the group of musicians will the resulting music of the orchestra be enjoyable to our ears:

A container orchestrator is like the conductor of an orchestra

Instead of musicians, we now have containers, and instead of different instruments, we have containers that have different requirements to the container hosts to run. And instead of the music being played in varying tempi, we have containers that communicate with each other in particular ways and have to scale up and scale down. In this regard, a container orchestrator has very much the same role as a conductor in an orchestra. It makes sure that the containers and other resources in a cluster play together in harmony.

I hope you can now see more clearly what a container orchestrator is and why we need one. Assuming that you confirm this question, we can now ask ourselves how the orchestrator is going to achieve the expected outcome, namely to make sure all the containers in the cluster play with each other in harmony. Well, the answer is, the orchestrator has to execute very specific tasks, similar to the way in which the conductor of an orchestra also has a set of tasks they execute in order to tame and at the same time elevate the orchestra.

The tasks of an orchestrator

So, what are the tasks that we expect an orchestrator worth its money to execute for us? Let's look at them in detail. The following list shows the most important tasks that, at the time of writing, enterprise users typically expect from their orchestrator.

Reconciling the desired state

When using an orchestrator, one tells it in a declarative way how one wants it to run a given application or application service. We learned what *declarative* versus *imperative* means in `Chapter 8`, *Docker Compose*. Part of this declarative way of describing the application service we want to run is elements such as which container image to use, how many instances to run of this service, which ports to open, and more. This declaration of the properties of our application service is what we call the *desired state*.

So, when we now tell the orchestrator the first time to create such a new application service based on the declaration, then the orchestrator makes sure to schedule as many containers in the cluster as requested. If the container image is not yet available on the target nodes of the cluster where the containers are supposed to run, then the scheduler makes sure they're downloaded from the image registry first. Next, the containers are started with all the settings, such as networks to which to attach, or ports to expose. The orchestrator works as hard as it can to exactly match in reality in the cluster what it got in our declaration.

Once our service is up and running as requested, that is, it is running in the desired state, then the orchestrator continues to monitor it. Each time the orchestrator discovers a discrepancy between the actual state of the service and its desired state, it again tries its best to reconcile the desired state.

What could such a discrepancy between the actual and desired states of an application service be? Well, let's say one of the replicas of the service, that is, one of the containers, crashes due to, say, a bug, then the orchestrator will discover that the actual state differs from the desired state in the number of replicas: there is one replica missing. The orchestrator will immediately schedule a new instance to another cluster node, which replaces the crashed instance. Another discrepancy could be that there are too many instances of the application service running, if the service has been scaled down. In this case, the orchestrator will just randomly kill as many instances as needed to achieve parity between the actual and the desired number of instances. Another discrepancy could be when the orchestrator discovers that there is an instance of the application service running a wrong (maybe old) version of the underlying container image. By now, you should get the picture, right?

Thus, instead of us actively monitoring our application's services running in the cluster and correcting any deviation from the desired state, we delegate this tedious task to the orchestrator. This works very well, if we use a declarative and not an imperative way of describing the desired state of our application services.

Replicated and global services

There are two quite different types of services that we might want to run in a cluster managed by an orchestrator. They are **replicated** and **global** services. A replicated service is a service which is required to run in a specific number of instances, say 10. A global service, in turn, is a service that is required to have an instance running on every single worker node of the cluster. I have used the term *worker node* here. In a cluster managed by an orchestrator, we typically have two types of nodes, **managers** and **workers**. A manager node is usually exclusively used by the orchestrator to manage the cluster and does not run any other workload. Worker nodes, in turn, run the actual applications.

So, the orchestrator makes sure that, for a global service, an instance of it is running on every single worker node, no matter how many there are. We do not need to care about the number of instances, but only that on each node it is guaranteed to run a single instance of the service.

Once again, we can fully rely on the orchestrator to take care of this feat. In a replicated service, we will always be guaranteed to find the exact desired number of instances, while for a global service, we can be assured that on every worker node, there will always run exactly one instance of the service. The orchestrator will always work as hard as it can to guarantee this desired state.

 In Kubernetes, a global service is also called a daemon set.

Service discovery

When we describe an application service in a declarative way, we are never supposed to tell the orchestrator on which cluster nodes the different instances of the service have to run. We leave it up to the orchestrator to decide which nodes best fit this task.

It is, of course, technically possible to instruct the orchestrator to use very deterministic placement rules, but this would be an anti-pattern and is not recommended at all.

So, if we now assume that the orchestration engine has complete and free will as to where to place individual instances of the application service and, furthermore, that instances can crash and be rescheduled by the orchestrator to different nodes, then we will realize that it is a futile task for us to keep track of where the individual instances are running at any given time. Even better, we shouldn't even try to know this since it is not important.

OK, you might say, but what about if I have two services, A and B, and Service A relies on Service B; *shouldn't any given instance of Service A know where it can find an instance of Service B?*

There I have to say loudly and clearly—no, it shouldn't. This kind of knowledge is not desirable in a highly distributed and scalable application. Rather, we should rely on the orchestrator to provide us the information we need to reach other service instances we depend on. It is a bit like in the old days of telephony, when we could not directly call our friends but had to call the phone company's central office, where some operator would then route us to the correct destination. In our case, the orchestrator plays the role of the operator, routing a request coming from an instance of Service A to an available instance of Service B. This whole process is called **service discovery**.

Routing

We have learned so far that in a distributed application, we have many interacting services. When Service A interacts with Service B, it happens through the exchange of data packets. These data packets need to somehow be funneled from Service A to Service B. This process of funneling the data packets from a source to a destination is also called **routing**. As authors or operators of an application, we do expect the orchestrator to take over this task of routing. As we will see in later chapters, routing can happen on different levels. It is like in real life. Suppose you're working in a big company in one of their office buildings. Now, you have a document that needs to be forwarded to another employee of the company. The internal post service will pick up the document from your outbox and take it to the post office located in the same building. If the target person works in the same building, the document can then be directly forwarded to that person. If, on the other hand, the person works in another building of the same block, the document will be forwarded to the post office in that target building, from where it is then distributed to the receiver through the internal post service. Thirdly, if the document is targeted at an employee working in another branch of the company located in a different city or even country, then the document is forwarded to an external postal service such as UPS, which will transport it to the target location, from where, once again, the internal post service takes over and delivers it to the recipient.

Similar things happen when routing data packets between application services running in containers. The source and target containers can be located on the same cluster node, which corresponds to the situation where both employees work in the same building. The target container can be running on a different cluster node, which corresponds to the situation where the two employees work in different buildings of the same block. Finally, the third situation is when a data packet comes from outside of the cluster and has to be routed to the target container running inside the cluster.

All these situations and more have to be handled by the orchestrator.

Load balancing

In a highly available distributed application, all components have to be redundant. That means that every application service has to be run in multiple instances so that if one instance fails, the service as a whole is still operational.

To make sure that all instances of a service are actually doing work and not just sitting around idle, one has to make sure that the requests for service are distributed equally to all the instances. This process of distributing workload among service instances is called **load balancing**. Various algorithms exist for how the workload can be distributed. Usually, a load balancer works using the so-called round robin algorithm, which makes sure that the workload is distributed equally to the instances using a cyclic algorithm.

Once again, we expect the orchestrator to take care of load balancing requests from one service to another or from external sources to internal services.

Scaling

When running our containerized, distributed application in a cluster managed by an orchestrator, we also want an easy way to handle expected or unexpected increases in workload. To handle an increased workload, we usually just schedule additional instances of a service that is experiencing this increased load. Load balancers will then automatically be configured to distribute the workload over more available target instances.

But in real-life scenarios, the workload varies over time. If we look at a shopping site such as Amazon, it might have a high load during peak hours in the evening, when everyone is at home and shopping online; it may experience extreme loads during special days such as Black Friday; and it may experience very little traffic early in the morning. Thus, services need to not just be able to scale up, but also to scale down when the workload goes down.

We also expect orchestrators to distribute the instances of a service in a meaningful way when scaling up or down. It would not be wise to schedule all instances of the service on the same cluster node, since if that node goes down, the whole service goes down. The scheduler of the orchestrator, which is responsible for the placement of the containers, needs to also consider not placing all instances into the same rack of computers, since if the power supply of the rack fails, again the whole service is affected. Furthermore, service instances of critical services should even be distributed across data centers to avoid outages. All these decisions and many more are the responsibility of the orchestrator.

Self-healing

These days, orchestrators are very sophisticated and can do a lot for us to maintain a healthy system. Orchestrators monitor all containers running in the cluster and they automatically replace crashed or unresponsive ones with new instances. Orchestrators monitor the health of cluster nodes and take them out of the scheduler loop if a node becomes unhealthy or is down. A workload that was located on those nodes is automatically rescheduled to different available nodes.

All these activities where the orchestrator monitors the current state and automatically repairs the damage or reconciles the desired state lead to a so-called **self-healing** system. We do not, in most cases, have to actively engage and repair damage. The orchestrator will do this for us automatically.

But there are a few situations that the orchestrator cannot handle without our help. Imagine a situation where we have a service instance running in a container. The container is up and running and, from the outside, looks perfectly healthy. But the application inside is in an unhealthy state. The application did not crash, it just is not able to work as designed anymore. *How could the orchestrator possibly know about this without us giving it a hint?* It can't! Being in an unhealthy or invalid state means something completely different for each application service. In other words, the health status is service dependent. Only the authors of the service or its operators know what health means in the context of a service.

Now, orchestrators define seams or probes, over which an application service can communicate to the orchestrator in what state it is. Two fundamental types of probe exist:

- The service can tell the orchestrator that it is healthy or not
- The service can tell the orchestrator that it is ready or temporarily unavailable

How the service determines either of the preceding answers is totally up to the service. The orchestrator only defines how it is going to ask, for example, through an HTTP GET request, or what type of answers it is expecting, for example, OK or NOT OK.

If our services implement logic to answer the preceding health or availability questions, then we have a truly self-healing system, since the orchestrator can kill unhealthy service instances and replace them with new healthy ones, and it can take service instances that are temporarily unavailable out of the load balancer's round robin.

Zero downtime deployments

These days, it gets harder and harder to justify a complete downtime for a mission-critical application that needs to be updated. Not only does that mean missed opportunities, but it can also result in a damaged reputation for the company. Customers using the application are just not ready to accept such an inconvenience anymore and will turn away quickly. Furthermore, our release cycles get shorter and shorter. Where, in the past, we would have one or two new releases per year, these days, a lot of companies update their applications multiple times a week or even multiple times per day.

The solution to that problem is to come up with a zero downtime application update strategy. The orchestrator needs to be able to update individual application services batch-wise. This is also called **rolling updates**. At any given time, only one or a few of the total number of instances of a given service are taken down and replaced by the new version of the service. Only if the new instances are operational and do not produce any unexpected errors or show any misbehavior will the next batch of instances be updated. This is repeated until all instances are replaced with their new version. If, for some reason, the update fails, we expect the orchestrator to automatically roll the updated instances back to their previous version.

Other possible zero downtime deployments are so-called canary releases and blue-green deployments. In both cases, the new version of a service is installed in parallel with the current, active version. But initially, the new version is only accessible internally. Operations can then run smoke tests against the new version and when the new version seems to be running just fine, then, in the case of blue-green deployment, the router is switched from the current blue to the new green version. For some time, the new green version of the service is closely monitored and, if everything is fine, the old blue version can be decommissioned. If, on the other hand, the new green version does not work as expected, then it is only a matter of setting the router back to the old blue version to achieve a complete rollback.

In the case of a canary release, the router is configured in such a way that it funnels a tiny percentage, say 1%, of the overall traffic through the new version of the service, while 99% of the traffic is still routed through the old version. The behavior of the new version is closely monitored and compared to the behavior of the old version. If everything looks good, then the percentage of the traffic funneled through the new service is slightly increased. This process is repeated until 100% of the traffic is routed through the new service. If the new service has run for a while and everything looks good, then the old service can be decommissioned.

Most orchestrators support at least the rolling update type of zero downtime deployment out of the box. Blue-green and canary releases are often quite easy to implement.

Affinity and location awareness

Sometimes, certain application services require the availability of dedicated hardware on the nodes they run on. For example I/O-bound services require cluster nodes with an attached high-performance **solid-state drive (SSD)**, or some services require an **Accelerated Processing Unit (APU)**. Orchestrators allow us to define node affinities per application service. The orchestrator will then make sure that its scheduler only schedules containers on cluster nodes that fulfill the required criteria.

Defining an affinity to a particular node should be avoided; this would introduce a single point of failure and thus compromise high availability. Always define a set of multiple cluster nodes as the target for an application service.

Some orchestration engines also support what is called **location awareness** or **geo-awareness**. What this means is that one can request the orchestrator to equally distribute instances of a service over a set of different locations. One could, for example, define a label `datacenter` with the possible values `west`, `center`, and `east` and apply the label to all cluster nodes with the value that corresponds to the geographical region in which the respective node is located. Then, one instructs the orchestrator to use this label for geo-awareness of a certain application service. In this case, if one requests nine replicas of the service, the orchestrator would make sure that three instances are deployed to nodes in each of the three data centers, west, center, and east.

Geo-awareness can even be defined hierarchically; for example, one can have a data center as the top-level discriminator, followed by the availability zone and then the server rack.

Geo-awareness or location awareness is used to decrease the probability of outages due to power supply failures or data center outages. If the application instances are distributed across server racks, availability zones, or even data centers, it is extremely unlikely that everything goes down at once. One region will always be available.

Security

These days, security in IT is a very hot topic. Cyberwarfare is at an all-time high. Most high-profile companies have been victims of hacker attacks, with very costly consequences. One of the worst nightmares of each **chief information officer (CIO)** or **chief technology officer (CTO)** is to wake up in the morning and hear in the news that their company has become a victim of a hacker attack and that sensitive information has been stolen or compromised.

To counter most of these security threats, we need to establish a secure software supply chain and enforce security defense in depth. Let's look at some of the tasks one can expect from an enterprise-grade orchestrator.

Secure communication and cryptographic node identity

First and foremost, we want to make sure that our cluster managed by the orchestrator is secure. Only trusted nodes can join the cluster. Each node that joins the cluster gets a cryptographic node identity, and all communication between the nodes must be encrypted. For this, nodes can use **mutual transport layer security** (MTLS). To authenticate nodes of the cluster with each other, certificates are used. These certificates are automatically rotated periodically or on request to protect the system in case a certificate is leaked.

The communication that happens in a cluster can be separated into three types. One talks about communication planes. There are **management**, **control**, and **data** planes:

- The management plane is used by the cluster managers or masters to, for example, schedule service instances, execute health checks, or create and modify any other resources in the cluster, such as data volumes, secrets, or networks.
- The control plane is used to exchange important state information between all nodes of the cluster. This kind of information is, for example, used to update the local IP tables on clusters which are used for routing purposes.
- The data plane is where the application services communicate with each other and exchange data.

Normally, orchestrators mainly care about securing the management and control plane. Securing the data plane is left to the user, yet the orchestrator may facilitate this task.

Secure networks and network policies

When running application services, not every service needs to communicate with every other service in the cluster. Thus, we want the ability to sandbox services from each other and only run those services in the same networking sandbox that absolutely need to communicate with each other. All other services and all network traffic coming from outside of the cluster should have no possibility of accessing the sandboxed services.

There are at least two ways in which this network-based sandboxing can happen. We can either use a **software-defined network** (SDN) to group application services or we can have one flat network and use network policies to control who does and does not have access to a particular service or group of services.

Role-based access control (RBAC)

One of the most important tasks, next to security, an orchestrator must fulfill to make it enterprise ready is to provide role-based access to the cluster and its resources. RBAC defines how subjects, users, or groups of users of the system, organized into teams and so on, can access and manipulate the system. It makes sure that unauthorized personnel cannot do any harm to the system nor see any resources available in the system they're not supposed to know of or see.

A typical enterprise might have user groups such as Development, QA, and Prod, and each of those groups can have one to many users associated with it. John Doe, the developer, is a member of the Development group and, as such, can access resources dedicated to the development team, but he cannot access, for example, the resources of the Prod team, of which Ann Harbor is a member. She, in turn, cannot interfere with the Development team's resources.

One way of implementing RBAC is through the definition of **grants**. A grant is an association between a subject, a role, and a resource collection. Here, a role is comprised of a set of access permissions to a resource. Such permissions can be to create, stop, remove, list, or view containers; to deploy a new application service; to list cluster nodes or view the details of a cluster node; and many more.

A resource collection is a group of logically related resources of the cluster, such as application services, secrets, data volumes, or containers.

Secrets

In our daily life, we have loads of secrets. Secrets are information that is not meant to be publicly known, such as the username and password combination you use to access your online bank account, or the code to your cell phone or your locker at the gym.

When writing software, we often need to use secrets, too. For example, we need some certificate to authenticate our application service with some external service we want to access, or we need a token to authenticate and authorize our service when accessing some other API. In the past, developers, for convenience, have just hardcoded those values or put them in clear text in some external configuration files. There, this very sensitive information has been accessible to a broad audience that in reality should never have had the opportunity to see those secrets.

Luckily, these days, orchestrators offer what's called secrets to deal with such sensitive information in a highly secure way. Secrets can be created by authorized or trusted personnel. The values of those secrets are then encrypted and stored in the highly available cluster state database. The secrets, since they are encrypted, are now secure at rest. Once a secret is requested by an authorized application service, the secret is only forwarded to the cluster nodes that actually run an instance of that particular service, and the secret value is never stored on the node but mounted into the container in a `tmpfs` RAM-based volume. Only inside the respective container is the secret value available in clear text.

We already mentioned that the secrets are secure at rest. Once they are requested by a service, the cluster manager or master decrypts the secret and sends it over the wire to the target nodes. *So, what about the secrets being secure in transit?* Well, we learned earlier that the cluster nodes use MTLS for their communication, thus the secret, although transmitted in clear text, is still secure since data packets will be encrypted by MTLS. Thus, secrets are secure at rest and in transit. Only services that are authorized to use secrets will ever have access to those secret values.

Content trust

For added security, we want to make sure that only trusted images run in our production cluster. Some orchestrators allow us to configure a cluster so that it can only ever run signed images. Content trust and signing images is all about making sure that the authors of the image are the ones that we expect them to be, namely our trusted developers or, even better, our trusted CI server. Furthermore, with content trust, we want to guarantee that the image we get is fresh and not an old and maybe vulnerable image. And finally, we want to make sure that the image cannot be compromised by malicious hackers in transit. The latter is often called a **man-in-the-middle (MITM)** attack.

By signing images at the source and validating the signature at the target, we can guarantee that the images we want to run are not compromised.

Reverse uptime

The last point I want to discuss in the context of security is reverse uptime. *What do we mean by that?* Imagine that you have configured and secured a production cluster. On this cluster, you're running a few mission-critical applications of your company. Now, a hacker has managed to find a security hole in one your software stacks and has gained root access to one of your cluster nodes. That alone is already bad enough but, even worse, this hacker could now mask their presence on this node they are root on the machine, after all, and then use it as a base to attack further nodes of your cluster.

Root access in Linux or any Unix-type operating system means that one can do anything on this system. It is the highest level of access that someone can have. In Windows, the equivalent role is that of an Administrator.

But *what if we leverage the fact that containers are ephemeral and cluster nodes are quickly provisioned, usually in a matter of minutes if fully automated?* We just kill each cluster node after a certain uptime of, say, 1 day. The orchestrator is instructed to drain the node and then exclude it from the cluster. Once the node is out of the cluster, it is torn down and replaced by a freshly provisioned node.

That way, the hacker has lost their base and the problem has been eliminated. This concept is not yet broadly available, though, but to me it seems to be a huge step towards increased security and, as far as I have discussed it with engineers working in this area, it is not difficult to implement.

Introspection

So far, we have discussed a lot of tasks that the orchestrator is responsible for and that it can execute in a completely autonomous way. But there is also the need for human operators to be able to see and analyze what's currently running on the cluster and in what state or health the individual applications are. For all this, we need the possibility of introspection. The orchestrator needs to surface crucial information in a way that is easily consumable and understandable.

The orchestrator should collect system metrics from all the cluster nodes and make it accessible to the operators. Metrics include CPU, memory and disk usage, network bandwidth consumption, and more. The information should be easily available on a node-per-node basis, as well in an aggregated form.

We also want the orchestrator to give us access to logs produced by service instances or containers. Even more, the orchestrator should provide us exec access to each and every container if we have the correct authorization to do so. With exec access to containers, one can then debug misbehaving containers.

In highly distributed applications, where each request to the application goes through numerous services until it is completely handled, tracing requests is really important task. Ideally, the orchestrator supports us in implementing a tracing strategy or gives us some good guidelines to follow.

Finally, human operators can best monitor a system when working with a graphical representation of all the collected metrics and logging and tracing information. Here, we are speaking about dashboards. Every decent orchestrator should offer at least some basic dashboard with a graphical representation of the most critical system parameters.

But human operators are not all that concerned about introspection. We also need to be able to connect external systems with the orchestrator to consume this information. There needs to be an API available, over which external systems can access data such as cluster state, metrics, and logs and use this information to make automated decisions, such as creating pager or phone alerts, sending out emails, or triggering an alarm siren if some thresholds are exceeded by the system.

Overview of popular orchestrators

At the time of writing, there are many orchestration engines out there and in use. But there are a few clear winners. The number one spot is clearly held by Kubernetes, which reigns supreme. A distant second is Docker's own SwarmKit, followed by others such as Apache Mesos, AWS **Elastic Container Service (ECS)**, or Microsoft **Azure Container Service (ACS)**.

Kubernetes

Kubernetes was originally designed by Google and later donated to the **Cloud Native Computing Foundation (CNCF)**. Kubernetes was modeled after Google's proprietary Borg system, which has been running containers on supermassive scale for years. Kubernetes was Google's attempt to go back to the drawing board and completely start over and design a system that incorporates all the lessons learned with Borg.

Contrary to Borg, which is proprietary technology, Kubernetes was open sourced early on. This was a very wise choice by Google, since it attracted a huge number of contributors from outside of the company and, over only a couple of years, an even more massive ecosystem evolved around Kubernetes. One can rightfully say that Kubernetes is the darling of the community in the container orchestration space. No other orchestrator has been able to produce so much hype and attract so many talented people willing to contribute in a meaningful way to the success of the project as a contributor or an early adopter.

In that regard, Kubernetes in the container orchestration space to me looks very much like what Linux has become in the server operating system space. Linux has become the de facto standard of server operating systems. All relevant companies, such as Microsoft, IBM, Amazon, RedHat, and even Docker, have embraced Kubernetes.

And there is one thing that cannot be denied: Kubernetes was designed from the very beginning for massive scalability. After all, it was designed with Google Borg in mind.

One negative aspect that one could voice against Kubernetes is that it is complex to set up and manage, at least at the time of writing. There is a significant hurdle to overcome for newcomers. The first step is steep. But once one has worked with this orchestrator for a while, it all makes sense. The overall design is carefully thought through and executed very well.

In the newest release of Kubernetes, 1.10, whose **general availability (GA)** was in March 2018, most of the initial shortcomings compared to other orchestrators such as Docker Swarm have been eliminated. For example, security and confidentiality is now not only an afterthought, but an integral part of the system.

New features are implemented at a tremendous speed. New releases are happening every 3 months or so, more precisely, about every 100 days. Most of the new features are demand-driven, that is, companies using Kubernetes to orchestrate their mission-critical applications can voice their needs. This makes Kubernetes enterprise ready. It would be wrong to assume that this orchestrator is only for start-ups and not for risk-averse enterprises. The contrary is the case. *On what do I base this claim?* Well, my claim is justified by the fact that companies such as Microsoft, Docker, and RedHat, whose clients are mostly big enterprises, have fully embraced Kubernetes and provide enterprise-grade support for it if it is used and integrated into their enterprise offerings.

Kubernetes supports both Linux and Windows containers.

Docker Swarm

It is well-known that Docker popularized and commoditized software containers. Docker did not invent containers, but standardized them and made them broadly available, not least by offering the free image registry Docker Hub. Initially, Docker focused mainly on the developer and the development life cycle. But companies that started to use and love containers soon also wanted to use containers, not just during development or testing of new applications, but also to run those applications in production.

Initially, Docker had nothing to offer in that space, so other companies jumped into that vacuum and offered help to the users. But it didn't take long and Docker recognized that there was a huge demand for a simple yet powerful orchestrator. Docker's first attempt was a product called classic Swarm. It was a standalone product that enabled users to create a cluster of Docker host machines that could be used to run and scale their containerized applications in a highly available and self-healing way.

The setup of a classic Docker Swarm, though, was hard. A lot of complicated manual steps were involved. Customers loved the product but struggled with its complexity. So Docker decided it could do better. It went back to the drawing board and came up with SwarmKit. SwarmKit was introduced at DockerCon 2016 in Seattle and was an integral part of the newest version of the Docker engine. Yes, you got that right, SwarmKit was and still is to this day an integral part of the Docker engine. Thus, if you install a Docker host, you automatically have SwarmKit available with it.

SwarmKit was designed with simplicity and security in mind. The mantra was and still is that it has to be almost trivial to set up a swarm, and the swarm has to be highly secure out of the box. Docker Swarm operates on the assumption of least privilege.

Installing a complete, highly available Docker Swarm is literally as simple as starting with a `docker swarm init` on the first node in the cluster, which becomes the so-called leader, and then a `docker swarm join <join-token>` on all other nodes. The `join-token` is generated by the leader during initialization. The whole process takes less that 5 minutes on a Swarm with up to 10 nodes. If it is automated, it takes even less time.

As I already mentioned, security was top on the list of must-haves when Docker designed and developed SwarmKit. Containers provide security by relying on Linux kernel namespaces and cgroups as well as Linux syscall whitelisting (seccomp) and the support of Linux capabilities and the **Linux security module (LSM)**. Now, on top of that, SwarmKit adds MTLS and secrets that are encrypted at rest and in transit. Furthermore, Swarm defines the so-called **container network model (CNM)**, which allows for SDNs that provide sandboxing for application services running on the swarm.

Docker SwarmKit supports both Linux and Windows containers.

Apache Mesos and Marathon

Apache **Mesos** is an open source project and was originally designed to make a cluster of servers or nodes look like one single big server from the outside. Mesos is software that makes the management of computer clusters simple. Users of Mesos should not have to care about individual servers, but just assume they have a gigantic pool of resources to their disposal, which corresponds to the aggregate of all the resources of all the nodes in the cluster.

Mesos, in IT terms, is already pretty old, at least compared to the other orchestrators. It was first publicly presented in 2009. But at that time, of course, it wasn't designed to run containers since Docker didn't even exist yet. Similar to what Docker does with containers, Mesos uses Linux cgroups to isolate resources such as CPU, memory, or disk I/O for individual applications or services.

Mesos is really the underlying infrastructure for other interesting services built on top of it. From the perspective of containers specifically, **Marathon** is important. Marathon is a container orchestrator running on top of Mesos which is able to scale to thousands of nodes.

Marathon supports multiple container runtimes, such as Docker or its own Mesos containers. It supports not only stateless but also stateful application services, for example, databases such as PostgreSQL or MongoDB. Similar to Kubernetes and Docker SwarmKit, it supports many of the features described earlier in this chapter, such as high availability, health checks, service discovery, load balancing, and location awareness, to just name some of the most important ones.

Although Mesos and, to a certain extent, Marathon are rather mature projects, their reach is relatively limited. It seems to be most popular in the area of big data, that is, to run data crunching services such as Spark or Hadoop.

Amazon ECS

If you are looking for a simple orchestrator and have already heavily bought into the AWS ecosystem, then Amazon's ECS might be the right choice for you. It is important to point out one very important limitation of ECS: if you buy into this container orchestrator, then you lock yourself into AWS. You will not be able to easily port an application running on ECS to another platform or cloud.

Amazon promotes its ECS service as a highly scalable, fast container management service that makes it easy to run, stop, and manage Docker containers on a cluster. Next to running containers, ECS gives direct access to many other AWS services from the application services running inside the containers. This tight and seamless integration with many popular AWS services is what makes ECS compelling for users who are looking for an easy way to get their containerized applications up and running in a robust and highly scalable environment. Amazon also provides its own private image registry.

With AWS ECS, you can use Fargate to have it fully manage the underlying infrastructure so that you can concentrate exclusively on deploying containerized applications and do not have to care about how to create and manage a cluster of nodes. ECS supports both Linux and Windows containers.

In summary, ECS is simple to use, highly scalable, and well-integrated with other popular AWS services, but it is not as powerful as, say, Kubernetes or Docker SwarmKit and it is only available on Amazon AWS.

Microsoft ACS

Similar to what we said about ECS, we can claim the same for Microsoft's ACS. It is a simple container orchestration service that makes sense if you are already heavily invested in the Azure ecosystem. I should say the same as I have pointed out for Amazon ECS: if you buy into ACS, then you lock yourself in to the offerings of Microsoft. It will not be easy to move your containerized applications from ACS to any other platform or cloud.

ACS is Microsoft's container service, which supports multiple orchestrators such as Kubernetes, Docker Swarm, and Mesos DC/OS. With Kubernetes becoming more and more popular, the focus of Microsoft has clearly shifted to that orchestrator. Microsoft has even rebranded its service and called it **Azure Kubernetes Service (AKS)** to put the focus on Kubernetes.

AKS manages, for you, a hosted Kubernetes or Docker Swarm or DC/OS environment in Azure, so you can concentrate on the applications you want to deploy and don't have to care about configuring infrastructure. Microsoft, in its own words, claims the following:

> *AKS makes it quick and easy to deploy and manage containerized applications without container orchestration expertise. It also eliminates the burden of ongoing operations and maintenance by provisioning, upgrading, and scaling resources on demand, without taking your applications offline.*

Summary

This chapter demonstrated why orchestrators are needed in the first place and how they conceptually work. It pointed out which orchestrators are the most prominent ones at the time of writing and discussed the main commonalities and differences between the various orchestrators.

The next chapter will introduce Docker's native orchestrator, called SwarmKit. It will elaborate on all the concepts and objects SwarmKit uses to deploy and run a distributed, resilient, robust, and highly available application in a cluster on-premises or in the cloud.

Questions

Answer the following questions to assess your learning progress:

1. Why do we need an orchestrator? Name two to three reasons.
2. Name three to four typical responsibilities of an orchestrator.
3. Name at least two container orchestrators, as well as the main sponsor behind them.

Further reading

The following links provide some deeper insight to orchestration-related topics:

- *Kubernetes - production-grade orchestration at* https://kubernetes.io/
- *Docker Swarm Mode overview at* https://docs.docker.com/engine/swarm/
- *Mesosphere - container orchestration services at* http://bit.ly/2GMpko3
- *Containers and orchestration explained at* http://bit.ly/2DFoQgx

Introduction to Docker Swarm 10

In the last chapter, we introduced orchestrators. Like a conductor in an orchestra, an orchestrator makes sure that all our containerized application services play together nicely and contribute harmoniously to a common goal. Such orchestrators have quite a few responsibilities, which we have discussed in detail. Finally, we have provided a short overview of the most important container orchestrators on the market.

This chapter introduces Docker's native orchestrator, **SwarmKit**. It elaborates on all the concepts and objects SwarmKit uses to deploy and run a distributed, resilient, robust, and highly available application in a cluster on-premise or in the cloud. The chapter also introduces how SwarmKit ensures secure applications by using a **software defined network (SDN)** to isolate containers. Additionally, this chapter demonstrates how to install a highly available Docker Swarm in the cloud. It introduces the routing mesh which provides layer-4 routing and load balancing. Finally, it demonstrates how to deploy a first application consisting of multiple services onto the swarm.

These are the topics we are going to discuss in this chapter:

- Architecture
- Swarm nodes
- Stacks, services, and tasks
- Multi-host networking
- Creating a Docker Swarm
- Deploying a first application
- The swarm routing mesh

After completing this chapter, you will be able to:

- Sketch the essential parts of a highly available Docker Swarm on a whiteboard
- Explain in two or three simple sentences to an interested layman what a (swarm) service is
- Create a highly available Docker Swarm in AWS consisting of three manager and two worker nodes
- Successfully deploy a replicated service such as Nginx on a Docker Swarm
- Scale up and down a running Docker Swarm service
- Retrieve the aggregated log of a replicated Docker Swarm service
- Write a simple stack file for a sample application consisting of at least two interacting services
- Deploy a stack into a Docker Swarm

Architecture

The architecture of a Docker Swarm from a 30,000-foot view consists of two main parts—a raft consensus group of an odd number of manager nodes, and a group of worker nodes that communicate with each other over a gossip network, also called the **control plane**. The following figure illustrates this architecture:

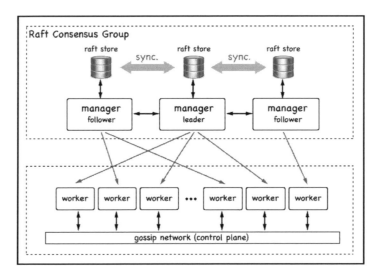

High-level architecture of a Docker Swarm

The manager nodes manage the swarm whilst the worker nodes execute the applications deployed into the swarm. Each manager has a complete copy of the full state of the swarm in its local raft store. Managers communicate with each other in a synchronous way and the raft stores are always in sync.

The workers, on the other hand, communicate with each other asynchronously for scalability reasons. There can be hundreds if not thousands of worker nodes in a swarm. Now that we have a high-level overview of what a Docker Swarm is, let's describe all the individual elements of a Docker Swarm in more detail.

Swarm nodes

A swarm is a collection of nodes. We can classify a node as a physical computer or **virtual machine (VM)**. Physical computers these days are often referred to as *bare metal*. People say *we're running on bare metal* to distinguish from running on a VM.

When we install Docker on such a node, we call this node a **Docker host**. The following figure illustrates a bit better what a node and what a Docker host is:

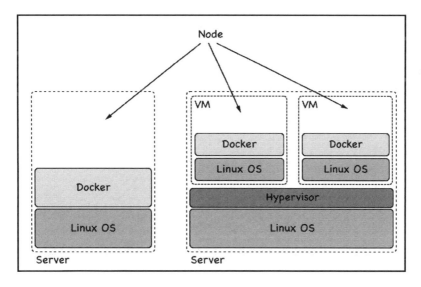

Bare metal and VM type Docker Swarm nodes

To become a member of a Docker Swarm, a node must also be a Docker host. A node in a Docker Swarm can have one of two roles. It can be a manager or it can be a worker. Manager nodes do what their name implies; they manage the swarm. The worker nodes in turn execute application workload.

Technically, a manager node can also be a worker node and thus run application workload, although that is not recommended, especially if the swarm is a production system running mission critical applications.

Swarm managers

Each Docker Swarm needs to have at least one manager node. For high availability reasons we should have more than one manager node in a swarm. This is especially true for production or production-like environments. If we have more than one manager node then these nodes work together using the **Raft consensus protocol**. The Raft consensus protocol is a standard protocol that is often used when multiple entities need to work together and always need to agree with each other as to which activity to execute next.

To work well, the Raft consensus protocol asks for an odd number of members in what is called the **consensus group**. Thus we should always have 1, 3, 5, 7, and so on manager nodes. In such a consensus group there is always a leader. In the case of Docker Swarm, the first node that starts the swarm initially becomes the leader. If the leader goes away then the remaining manager nodes elect a new leader. The other nodes in the consensus group are called **followers**.

Now let's assume that we shut down the current leader node for maintenance reasons. The remaining manager nodes will elect a new leader. When the previous leader node comes back online he will now become a follower. The new leader remains the leader.

All the members of the consensus group communicate in a synchronous way with each other. Whenever the consensus group needs to make a decision, the leader asks all followers for agreement. If a majority of the manager nodes give a positive answer then the leader executes the task. That means if we have three manager nodes then at least one of the followers has to agree with the leader. If we have five manager nodes then at least two followers have to agree.

Since all manager follower nodes have to communicate synchronously with the leader node to make a decision in the cluster, the decision-making process gets slower and slower the more manager nodes we have forming the consensus group. The recommendation of Docker is to use one manager for development, demo, or test environments. Use three manager nodes in small to medium size swarms, and use five managers in large to extra large swarms. To use more than five managers in a swarm is hardly ever justified.

Manager nodes are not only responsible for managing the swarm but also for maintaining the state of the swarm. *What do we mean by that?* When we talk about the state of the swarm we mean all the information about it—for example, *how many nodes are in the swarm, what are the properties of each node, such as name or IP address.* We also mean what containers are running on which node in the swarm and more. What, on the other hand, is not included in the state of the swarm is data produced by the application services running in containers on the swarm. This is called application data and is definitely not part of the state that is managed by the manager nodes:

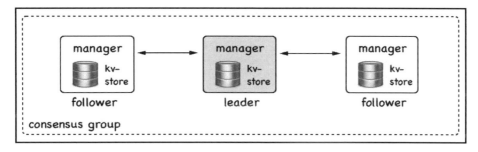

A swarm manager consensus group

All the swarm state is stored in a high performance key-value store (**kv-store**) on each manager node. That's right, each manager node stores a complete replica of the whole swarm state. This redundancy makes the swarm highly available. If a manager node goes down, the remaining managers all have the complete state at hand.

If a new manager joins the consensus group then it synchronizes the swarm state with the existing members of the group until it has a complete replica. This replication is usually pretty fast in typical swarms but can take a while if the swarm is big and many applications are running on it.

Swarm workers

As we mentioned earlier, a swarm worker node is meant to host and run containers that contain the actual application services we're interested in running on our cluster. They are the workhorses of the swarm. In theory, a manager node can also be a worker. But, as we already said, this is not recommended on a production system. On a production system we should let managers be managers.

Worker nodes communicate with each other over the so-called control plane. They use the gossip protocol for their communication. This communication is asynchronous, which means that at any given time not all worker nodes must be in perfect sync.

Now you might ask—*what information do worker nodes exchange?* It is mostly information that is needed for service discovery and routing, that is, information about which containers are running on with nodes and more:

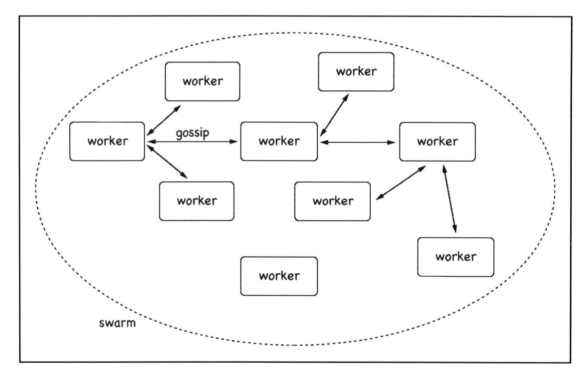

Worker nodes communicating with each other

In the preceding figure, you can see how workers communicate with each other. To make sure the gossiping scales well in a large swarm, each worker node only synchronizes its own state with three random neighbors. For those who are familiar with the Big-O notation, that means that the synchronization of the worker nodes using the gossip protocol scales with O(0).

Worker nodes are kind of passive. They never actively do something other than run the workloads that they get assigned by the manager nodes. The worker makes sure, though, that it runs these workloads to the best of its capabilities. Further down in this chapter we will get to know more about exactly what workloads the worker nodes are assigned by the manager nodes.

Stacks, services, and tasks

When using a Docker Swarm versus a single Docker host, there is a paradigm change. Instead of talking of individual containers that run processes, we are abstracting away to services that represent a set of replicas of each process, and like through become highly available. We also do not speak anymore of individual Docker hosts with well known names and IP addresses to which we deploy containers; we'll now be referring to clusters of hosts to which we deploy services. We don't care about an individual host or node anymore. We don't give it a meaningful name; each node rather becomes a number to us. We also don't care about individual containers and where they are deployed anymore—we just care about having a desired state defined through a service. We can try to depict that as shown in the following figure:

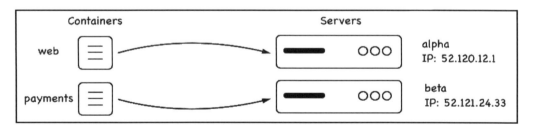

Containers are deployed to well known servers

Instead of deploying individual containers to well known servers like the preceding one, where we deploy container **web** to server **alpha** with IP address 52.120.12.1, and container **payments** to server **beta** with IP 52.121.24.33, we switch to this new paradigm of services and swarms (or, more generally, clusters):

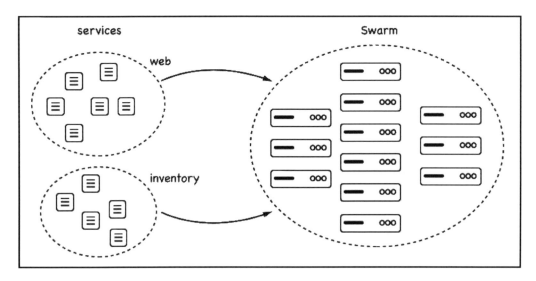

Services are deployed to swarms

In the preceding figure, we see that a service **web** and a service **inventory** are both deployed to a swarm that consists of many nodes. Each of the services has a certain number of replicas; six for web and five for inventory. We don't really care on which node the replicas will run, we only care that the requested number of replicas is always running on whatever nodes the swarm scheduler decides to put them on.

Services

A swarm service is an abstract thing. It is a description of the desired state of an application or application service that we want to run in a swarm. The swarm service is like a manifest describing such things as the:

- Name of the service
- Image from which to create the containers
- Number of replicas to run
- Network(s) that the containers of the service are attached to
- Ports that should be mapped

Having this service manifest the swarm manager, then, makes sure that the described desired state is always reconciled if ever the actual state should deviate from it. So, if for example one instance of the service crashes, then the scheduler on the swarm manager schedules a new instance of the service on a node with free resources so that the desired state is reestablished.

Task

We have learned that a service corresponds to a description of the desired state in which an application service should be at all times. Part of that description was the number of replicas the service should be running. Each replica is represented by a task. In this regard, a swarm service contains a collection of tasks. On Docker Swarm, a task is the atomic unit of deployment. Each task of a service is deployed by the swarm scheduler to a worker node. The task contains all the necessary information that the worker node needs to run a container based off the image, which is part of the service description. Between a task and a container there is a one-to-one relation. The container is the instance that runs on the worker node, while the task is the description of this container as a part of a swarm service.

Stack

Now that we have a good idea about what a swarm service is and what tasks are, we can introduce the stack. A stack is used to describe a collection of swarm services that are related, most probably because they are part of the same application. In that sense, we could also say that a stack describes an application that consists of one to many services that we want to run on the swarm.

Typically, we describe a stack declaratively in a text file that is formatted using YAML and that uses the same syntax as the already-known Docker compose file. This leads to the situation where people sometimes say that a stack is described by a `docker-compose` file. A better wording would be—a stack is described in a stack file that uses similar syntax to a `docker-compose` file.

Let's try to illustrate the relationship between stack, services, and tasks in the following figure and connect it with the typical content of a stack file:

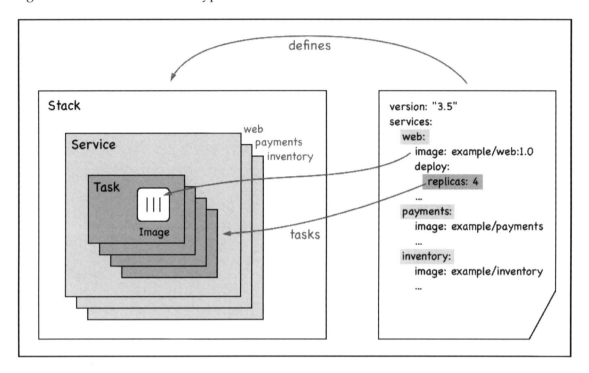

Diagram showing the relationship between stack, services and tasks

In the preceding figure, we see on the right-hand side a declarative description of a sample stack. The stack consists of three services called **web**, **payments**, and **inventory**. We also see that the service **web** uses the image **example/web:1.0** and has four replicas.

On the left-hand side of the figure, we see that the stack embraces the three services mentioned. Each service in turn contains a collection of tasks, as many as there are replicas. In the case of the service **web** we have a collection of four tasks. Each task contains the name of the image from which it will instantiate a container once the task is scheduled on a swarm node.

Multi-host networking

In Chapter 7, *Single-Host Networking*, we discussed how containers communicate on a single Docker host. Now, we have a swarm that consists of a cluster of nodes or Docker hosts. Containers that are located on different nodes need to be able to communicate with each other. There are many techniques that can help one achieve this goal. Docker has chosen to implement an overlay network driver for Docker Swarm. This overlay network allows containers attached to the same **overlay network** to discover each other and freely communicate with each other. The following is a schema for how an overlay network works:

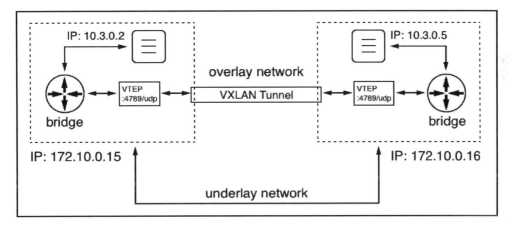

Overlay network

We have two nodes or Docker hosts with the IP addresses 172.10.0.15 and 172.10.0.16. The values we have chosen for the IP addresses are not important; what is important is that both hosts have a distinct IP address and are connected by a physical network (a network cable), which is called the underlay network.

On the node on the left-hand side we have a container running with the IP address 10.3.0.2 and on the node on the right-hand side another container with the IP address 10.3.0.5. Now, the former container wants to communicate with the latter. *How can this happen?* In Chapter 7, *Single-Host Networking*, we saw how this works when both containers are located on the same node; by using a Linux bridge. But Linux bridges only operate locally and cannot span across nodes. So, we need another mechanism. Linux VXLAN comes to the rescue. VXLAN has been available on Linux since way before containers were a thing.

When the left-hand container sends a data packet, the bridge realises that the target of the packet is not on this host. Now, each node participating in an overlay network gets a so-called **VXLAN Tunnel Endpoint** (**VTEP**) object, which intercepts the packet (the packet at that moment is an OSI layer 2 data packet), wraps it with a header containing the target IP address of the host that runs the target container (this makes it now an OSI layer 3 data packet), and sends it over the VXLAN tunnel. The VTEP on the other side of the tunnel unpacks the data packet and forwards it to the local bridge, which in turn forwards it to the target container.

The overlay driver is included in the SwarmKit and is in most cases the recommended network driver for Docker Swarm. There are other multi-node-capable network drivers available from third-parties that can be installed as plugins to each participating Docker host. Certified network plugins are available from the Docker store.

Creating a Docker Swarm

Creating a Docker Swarm is almost trivial. It is so easy that it seems unreal if one knows what an orchestrator is all about. But it is true, Docker has done a fantastic job in making swarms simple and elegant to use. At the same time, Docker Swarm has been proven in use by large enterprises to be very robust and scalable.

Creating a local single node swarm

So, enough fancying, let's demonstrate how one can create a swarm. In its most simple form, a fully functioning Docker Swarm consists only of a single node. If you're using Docker for Mac or Windows, or even if you're using Docker Toolbox, then your personal computer or laptop is such a node. Thus, we can start right there and demonstrate some of the most important features of a swarm.

Let's initialize a swarm. On the command-line, just enter the following command:

```
$ docker swarm init
```

And after an incredibly short time you should see something like the following screenshot:

```
$ docker swarm init
Swarm initialized: current node (mc07c43kp8v8d4ofnl5i9skb2) is now a manager.

To add a worker to this swarm, run the following command:

    docker swarm join --token SWMTKN-1-1ynzcy7z2tze0zhrbw7h855biywspmg9mjewknn5hwg6g10b5m-7h98rot6dfi5723ftkitsb1vt 192.168.65.3:2377

To add a manager to this swarm, run 'docker swarm join-token manager' and follow the instructions.
```

Output of the docker swarm init command

Our computer is now a swarm node. Its role is that of a manager and it is the leader (of the managers, which makes sense since there is only one manager at this time). Although it took only a very short time to finish the `docker swarm init`, the command did a lot of things during that time, some of them are:

- It created a root **certificate authority (CA)**
- It created a key-value store that is used to store the state of the whole swarm

Now, in the preceding output, we can see a command that can be used to join other nodes to the swarm that we just created. The command is as follows:

```
$ docker swarm join --token <join-token> <IP address>:2377
```

Here:

- `<join-token>` is a token generated by the swarm leader at the time the swarm was initialized
- `<IP address>` is the IP address of the leader

Although our cluster remains simple, as it consists of only one member, we can still ask the Docker CLI to list all the nodes of the swarm. This will look similar to the following screenshot:

```
$ docker node ls
ID                           HOSTNAME              STATUS    AVAILABILITY    MANAGER STATUS    ENGINE VERSION
mc07c43kp8v8d4ofnl5i9skb2 *  linuxkit-025000000001 Ready     Active          Leader            18.03.0-ce-rc1
$ ▮
```

Listing the nodes of the Docker Swarm

In this output we first see the ID that was given to the node. The star (*) that follows the ID indicates that this is the node on which the `docker node ls` was executed; basically, saying that this is the active node. Then we have the (human-readable) name of the node, its status, availability, and manager status. As mentioned earlier, this very first node of the swarm automatically became the leader, which is indicated in the preceding screenshot. Lastly, we see which version of the Docker engine we're using.

To get even more information about a node we can use the `docker node inspect` command, as shown in the following screenshot:

```
$ docker node inspect mc07c43kp8v8d4ofnl5i9skb2
[
    {
        "ID": "mc07c43kp8v8d4ofnl5i9skb2",
        "Version": {
            "Index": 9
        },
        "CreatedAt": "2018-03-06T01:48:57.625002327",
        "UpdatedAt": "2018-03-06T01:48:58.235847341Z",
        "Spec": {
            "Labels": {},
            "Role": "manager",
            "Availability": "active"
        },
        "Description": {
            "Hostname": "linuxkit-025000000001",
            "Platform": {
                "Architecture": "x86_64",
                "OS": "linux"
            },
            "Resources": {
                "NanoCPUs": 4000000000,
                "MemoryBytes": 2095788032
            },
            "Engine": {
                "EngineVersion": "18.03.0-ce-rc1",
                "Plugins": [
                    {
                        "Type": "Log",
                        "Name": "awslogs"
                    },
```

Truncated output of the command docker node inspect

There is a lot of information generated by this command, so we only present a truncated version of the output. This output can be useful, for example, when one needs to troubleshoot a misbehaving cluster node.

Creating a local swarm in VirtualBox or Hyper-V

Sometimes a single node swarm is not enough, but we don't have or don't want to use an account to create a swarm in the cloud. In this case, we can create a local swarm in either VirtualBox or Hyper-V. Creating the swarm in VirtualBox is slightly easier than creating it in Hyper-V, but if you're using Windows 10 and have Docker for Windows running then you cannot use VirtualBox at the same time. The two hypervisors are mutually exclusive.

Let's assume we have VirtualBox and `docker-machine` installed on our laptop. We can then use `docker-machine` to list all Docker hosts that are currently defined and may be running in VirtualBox:

```
$ docker-machine ls
NAME       ACTIVE    DRIVER       STATE      URL    SWARM    DOCKER     ERRORS
default    -         virtualbox   Stopped                    Unknown
```

In my case, I have one VM called `default` defined, which is currently stopped. I can easily start the VM by issuing the `docker-machine start default` command. This command takes a while and will result in the following (shortened) output:

```
$ docker-machine start default
Starting "default"...
(default) Check network to re-create if needed...
(default) Waiting for an IP...
Machine "default" was started.
Waiting for SSH to be available...
Detecting the provisioner...
Started machines may have new IP addresses. You may need to re-run the
`docker-machine env` command.
```

Now, if I list my VMs again I should see the following screenshot:

List of all VMs running in VirtualBox

If we do not have a VM called `default` yet, we can easily create one using the `create` command:

```
docker-machine create --driver virtualbox default
```

This results in the following output:

```
$ docker-machine create --driver virtualbox default
Running pre-create checks...
Creating machine...
(default) Copying /Users/gabriel/.docker/machine/cache/boot2docker.iso to /Users/gabriel/.docker/n
(default) Creating VirtualBox VM...
(default) Creating SSH key...
(default) Starting the VM...
(default) Check network to re-create if needed...
(default) Waiting for an IP...
Waiting for machine to be running, this may take a few minutes...
Detecting operating system of created instance...
Waiting for SSH to be available...
Detecting the provisioner...
Provisioning with boot2docker...
Copying certs to the local machine directory...
Copying certs to the remote machine...
Setting Docker configuration on the remote daemon...
Checking connection to Docker...
Docker is up and running!
To see how to connect your Docker Client to the Docker Engine running on this virtual machine, run
$ 
```

Output of docker-machine create

We can see in the preceding output how `docker-machine` creates the VM from an ISO image, defines SSH keys and certificates, and copies them to the VM and to the local `~/.docker/machine` directory, where we will use it later when we want to remotely access this VM through the Docker CLI. It also provisions an IP address for the new VM.

We're using the `docker-machine create` command with the parameter `--driver virtualbox`. Docker machine can also work with other drivers such as Hyper-V, AWS, Azure, DigitalOcean, and many more. Please see the documentation of docker-machine for more information. By default, a new VM gets 1 GB of memory associated, which is enough to use this VM as a node for a development or test swarm.

Now let's create five VMs for a five-node swarm. We can use a bit of scripting to reduce the manual work:

```
$ for NODE in `seq 1 5`; do
  docker-machine create --driver virtualbox "node-${NODE}"
done
```

Docker machine will now create five VMs with the names `node-1` to `node-5`. This might take a few moments, so this is a good time to get yourself a hot cup of tea. After the VMs are created we can list them:

```
$ docker-machine ls
NAME      ACTIVE   DRIVER       STATE     URL                          SWARM   DOCKER        ERRORS
default   -        virtualbox   Running   tcp://192.168.99.100:2376            v17.12.1-ce
node-1    -        virtualbox   Running   tcp://192.168.99.101:2376            v17.12.1-ce
node-2    -        virtualbox   Running   tcp://192.168.99.102:2376            v17.12.1-ce
node-3    -        virtualbox   Running   tcp://192.168.99.103:2376            v17.12.1-ce
node-4    -        virtualbox   Running   tcp://192.168.99.104:2376            v17.12.1-ce
node-5    -        virtualbox   Running   tcp://192.168.99.105:2376            v17.12.1-ce
$
```

List of all VMs we need for the swarm

Now we're ready to build a swarm. Technically, we could SSH into the first VM `node-1` and initialize a swarm and then SSH into all the other VMs and join them to the swarm leader. But this is not efficient. Let's again use a script that does all the hard work:

```
# get IP of Swarm leader
$ export IP=$(docker-machine ip node-1)
# init the Swarm
$ docker-machine ssh node-1 docker swarm init --advertise-addr $IP
# Get the Swarm join-token
$ export JOIN_TOKEN=$(docker-machine ssh node-1 \
    docker swarm join-token worker -q)
```

Now that we have the join token and the IP address of the swarm leader, we can ask the other nodes to join the swarm as follows:

```
$ for NODE in `seq 2 5`; do
  NODE_NAME="node-${NODE}"
  docker-machine ssh $NODE_NAME docker swarm join \
      --token $JOIN_TOKEN $IP:2377
done
```

To make the swarm highly available we can now promote, for example, `node-2` and `node-3` to become managers:

```
$ docker-machine ssh node-1 docker node promote node-2 node-3
Node node-2 promoted to a manager in the swarm.
Node node-3 promoted to a manager in the swarm.
```

Finally, we can list all the nodes of the swarm:

```
$ docker-machine ssh node-1 docker node ls
```

We should see the following screenshot:

```
$ docker-machine ssh node-1 docker node ls
ID                              HOSTNAME    STATUS    AVAILABILITY    MANAGER STATUS
kgvj80vupkw9ucdkxw853dejt *     node-1      Ready     Active          Leader
m2bel1iye6szjqs5nghfpcmzv       node-2      Ready     Active          Reachable
ij0yjtlrd7mzr4jq5mn9fwyky       node-3      Ready     Active          Reachable
ys3cg84plfu6krz4pskebhcg7       node-4      Ready     Active
esm46efplk769rel3q2tebz8b       node-5      Ready     Active
$
```

List of all the nodes of the Docker Swarm on VirtualBox

This is the proof that we have just created a highly available Docker Swarm locally on our laptop or workstation. Let's pull all our code snippets together and make the whole thing a bit more robust. The script will look as follows:

```
alias dm="docker-machine"
for NODE in `seq 1 5`; do
  NODE_NAME=node-${NODE}
  dm rm --force $NODE_NAME
  dm create --driver virtualbox $NODE_NAME
done
alias dms="docker-machine ssh"
export IP=$(docker-machine ip node-1)
dms node-1 docker swarm init --advertise-addr $IP;
export JOIN_TOKEN=$(dms node-1 docker swarm join-token worker -q);
for NODE in `seq 2 5`; do
  NODE_NAME="node-${NODE}"
  dms $NODE_NAME docker swarm join --token $JOIN_TOKEN $IP:2377
done;
dms node-1 docker node promote node-2 node-3
```

The preceding script first deletes (if present) and then recreates five VMs called node-1 to node-5, and then initializes a Swarm on node-1. After that, the remaining four VMs are added to the swarm, and finally, node-2 and node-3 are promoted to manager status to make the swarm highly available. The whole script will take less than 5 minutes to execute and can be repeated as many times as desired. The complete script can be found in the repository, in the subfolder docker-swarm; it is called create-swarm.sh

It is a highly recommended best practice to always script and thus automate operations.

Using Play with Docker (PWD) to generate a Swarm

To experiment with Docker Swarm without having to install or configure anything locally on our computer, we can use PWD. PWD is a website that can be accessed with a browser and which offers us the ability to create a Docker Swarm consisting of up to five nodes. It is definitely a playground, as the name implies, and the time for which we can use it is limited to four hours per session. We can open as many sessions as we want, but each session automatically ends after four hours. Other than that, it is a fully functional Docker environment that is ideal for tinkering with Docker or to demonstrate some features.

Let's access the site now. In your browser, navigate to the website `https://labs.play-with-docker.com`. You will be presented a welcome and login screen. Use your Docker ID to log in. After successfully logging in you will be presented with a screen that looks like the following screenshot:

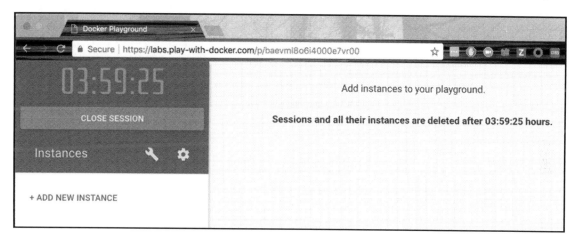

Play with Docker window

As we can see immediately, there is a big timer counting down from four hours. That's how much time we have left to play in this session. Furthermore, we see an **+ ADD NEW INSTANCE** link. Click it to create a new Docker host. When you do that, your screen should look like the following screenshot:

PWD with one new node

On the left-hand side we see the newly-created node with its IP address (192.168.0.53) and its name (node1). On the right-hand side, we have some additional information about this new node in the upper half of the screen and a terminal in the lower half. Yes, this terminal is used to execute commands on this node that we just created. This node has the Docker CLI installed, and thus we can execute all the familiar Docker commands on it such as docker version. Try it out.

But now we want to create a Docker Swarm. Execute the following command in the terminal in your browser:

```
$ docker swarm init --advertise-addr=eth0
```

The output generated by the preceding command corresponds to what we already know from our previous trials with the one-node cluster on our workstation and the local cluster using VirtualBox or Hyper-V. The important information, once again, is the join command that we want to use to join additional nodes to the cluster we just created.

You might have noted that this time we specified the parameter `--advertise-addr` in the swarm `init` command. *Why is that necessary here?* The reason is that the nodes generated by PWD have more than one IP address associated with them. One can easily verify that by executing the command `ip a` on the node. This command will show us that there are indeed two endpoints, `eth0` and `eth1`, present. We thus have to specify explicitly to the new to-be-swarm manager which one we want to use. In our case, it is `eth0`.

Create four additional nodes in PWD by clicking four times on the **+ ADD NEW INSTANCE** link. The new nodes will be called `node2`, `node3`, `node4`, and `node5` and will all be listed on the left-hand side. If you click on one of the nodes on the left-hand side, then the right-hand side shows the details of the respective node and a terminal window for that node.

Select each node (2 to 5) and execute the `docker swarm join` command that you have copied from the leader node (`node1`) in the respective terminal:

Joining a node to the swarm in PWD

Once you have joined all four nodes to the swarm, switch back to `node1` and list all nodes, which, unsurprisingly, results in this:

```
[node1 /]$ docker node ls
ID                            HOSTNAME    STATUS    AVAILABILITY    MANAGER STATUS
8mwcohdn2khf936s0xadkjlcy     node4       Ready     Active
fmr85luxuoryn6i5kgvqqsgqi     node5       Ready     Active
gtwxqt6j614kh1yixvfsckrra     node3       Ready     Active
n0xrvrq2wjbdgbm2nsbjqka06     node2       Ready     Active
rkmkkjt90j4xd9y3m4xyhk32f *   node1       Ready     Active          Leader
[node1 /]$
```

List of all the nodes of the swarm in PWD

Still on `node1`, we can now promote, say, `node2` and `node3`, to make the swarm highly available:

```
$ docker node promote node2 node3
Node node2 promoted to a manager in the swarm.
Node node3 promoted to a manager in the swarm.
```

With this, our swarm on PWD is ready to accept a workload. We have created a highly available Docker Swarm with three manager nodes that form a Raft consensus group and two worker nodes.

Creating a Docker Swarm in the cloud

All the Docker Swarms we have created so far are wonderful to use in development or to experiment or for demonstration purposes. If we want to create a swarm that can be used as a production environment where we run our mission critical applications, though, then we need to create a, I'm tempted to say, real swarm in the cloud or on-premise. In this book, we are going to demonstrate how to create a Docker Swarm in Amazon AWS.

One way to create a swarm is by using **Docker machine (DM)**. DM has a driver for Amazon AWS. If we have an account on AWS, we need the AWS access key ID and the AWS secret access key. We can add those two values to a file called `~/.aws/configuration`. It should look like the following:

```
[default]
aws_access_key_id = AKID1234567890
aws_secret_access_key = MY-SECRET-KEY
```

Every time we run `docker-machine create`, DM will look up those values in that file. For more in-depth information on how to get an AWS account and how to obtain the two secret keys, please consult this link: `http://dockr.ly/2FFelyT`.

Once we have an AWS account in place and have stored the access keys in the configuration file, we can start building our swarm. The necessary code looks exactly the same as the one we used to create a swarm on our local machine in VirtualBox. Let's start with the first node:

```
$ docker-machine create --driver amazonec2 \
    --amazonec2-region us-east-1 aws-node-1
```

This will create an EC2 instance called `aws-node-1` in the requested region (`us-east-1` in my case). The output of the preceding command looks like the following screenshot:

```
~ docker-machine create --driver amazonec2 aws-node-1
Running pre-create checks...
Creating machine...
(aws-node-1) Launching instance...
Waiting for machine to be running, this may take a few minutes...
Detecting operating system of created instance...
Waiting for SSH to be available...
Detecting the provisioner...
Provisioning with ubuntu(systemd)...
Installing Docker...
Copying certs to the local machine directory...
Copying certs to the remote machine...
Setting Docker configuration on the remote daemon...
Checking connection to Docker...
Docker is up and running!
To see how to connect your Docker Client to the Docker Engine running on this virtual machine, run: docker-machine env aws-node-1
~
```

Creating a swarm node on AWS with Docker machine

It looks very similar to the output we already know from working with VirtualBox. We can now configure our terminal for remote access to that EC2 instance:

```
$ eval $(docker-machine env aws-node-1)
```

This will configure the environment variables used by the Docker CLI accordingly:

```
┣→ ~ export | grep DOCKER
DOCKER_CERT_PATH=/Users/gabriel/.docker/machine/machines/aws-node-1
DOCKER_HOST=tcp://35.172.240.127:2376
DOCKER_MACHINE_NAME=aws-node-1
DOCKER_TLS_VERIFY=1
┣→ ~ ▮
```

Environment variables used by Docker to enable remote access to the AWS EC2 node

For security reasons, **transport layer security (TLS)** is used for the communication between our CLI and the remote node. The certificates necessary for that were copied by DM to the path we assigned to the environment variable `DOCKER_CERT_PATH`.

All Docker commands that we now execute in our Terminal will be remotely executed in Amazon AWS on our EC2 instance. Let's try to run Nginx on this node:

```
$ docker container run –d –p 8000:80 nginx:alpine
```

We can use `docker container ls` to verify that the container is running. If so, then let's test it using `curl`:

```
$ curl –4 <IP address>:8000
```

Here, `<IP address>` is the public IP address of the AWS node; in my case it would be `35.172.240.127`. Sadly this doesn't work; the preceding command times out:

```
┣→ ~ curl -4 35.172.240.127:8000
curl: (7) Failed to connect to 35.172.240.127 port 8000: Operation timed out
┣→ ~ ▮
```

Accessing Nginx on the AWS node times out

The reason for this is that our node is part of an AWS **security group (SG)**. By default, access to objects inside this SG is denied. Thus, we have to find out to which SG our instance belongs and configure access explicitly. For this, we typically use the AWS console. Go to the EC2 dashboard and select instances on the left-hand side. Locate the EC2 instance called `aws-node-1` and select it. In the details view, under **Security groups,** click on the link **docker-machine** as shown in the following screenshot:

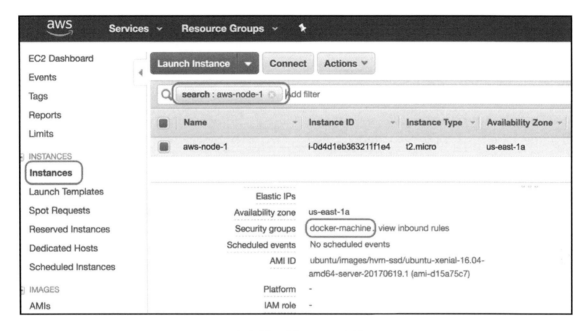

Locating the SG to which our swarm node belongs

This will lead us to the SG page with the SG `docker-machine` pre-selected. In the details section under the tab **Inbound**, add a new rule for your IP address (the IP address of workstation):

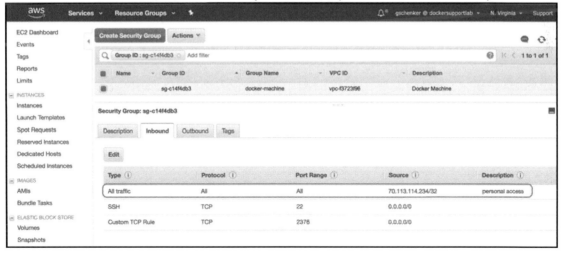

Open access to SG for our computer

In the preceding screenshot, the IP address `70.113.114.234` happens to be the one assigned to my personal workstation. I have enabled all inbound traffic coming from this IP address to the `docker-machine` SG. Note that in a production system you should be very careful about which ports of the SG to open to the public. Usually, it is ports `80` and `443` for HTTP and HTTPS access. Everything else is a potential invitation to hackers.

You can get your own IP address through a service like `https://www.whatismyip.com/`. Now, if we execute the `curl` command again, the greeting page of Nginx is returned.

Before we leave the SG we should add another rule to it. The swarm nodes need to be able to freely communicate on ports `7946` and `4789` through TCP and UDP and on port `2377` through TCP. We could now add five rules with these requirements where the source is the SG itself, or we just define a more crud rule that allows all inbound traffic inside the SG (`sg-c14f4db3` in my case):

Type ⓘ	Protocol ⓘ	Port Range ⓘ	Source ⓘ	Description ⓘ
All traffic	All	All	70.113.114.234/32	personal access
All traffic	All	All	sg-c14f4db3 (docker-machine)	intra swarm commun...
SSH	TCP	22	0.0.0.0/0	
Custom TCP Rule	TCP	2376	0.0.0.0/0	

SG rule to enable intra-swarm communication

Now, let's continue with the creation of the remaining four nodes. Once again, we can use a script to ease the process:

```
$ for NODE in `seq 2 5`; do
    docker-machine create --driver amazonec2 \
        --amazonec2-region us-east-1 aws-node-${NODE}
  done
```

After the provisioning of the nodes is done we can list all nodes with DM. In my case, I see this:

```
 ↦  ~ docker-machine ls
NAME          ACTIVE   DRIVER       STATE     URL                              SWARM   DOCKER        ERRORS
aws-node-1    *        amazonec2    Running   tcp://35.172.240.127:2376                v18.02.0-ce
aws-node-2    -        amazonec2    Running   tcp://54.236.40.1:2376                   v18.02.0-ce
aws-node-3    -        amazonec2    Running   tcp://34.205.171.56:2376                 v18.02.0-ce
aws-node-4    -        amazonec2    Running   tcp://34.239.93.22:2376                  v18.02.0-ce
aws-node-5    -        amazonec2    Running   tcp://52.205.26.218:2376                 v18.02.0-ce
node-1        -        virtualbox   Running   tcp://192.168.99.100:2376                v17.12.1-ce
node-2        -        virtualbox   Running   tcp://192.168.99.101:2376                v17.12.1-ce
node-3        -        virtualbox   Running   tcp://192.168.99.102:2376                v17.12.1-ce
node-4        -        virtualbox   Running   tcp://192.168.99.103:2376                v17.12.1-ce
node-5        -        virtualbox   Running   tcp://192.168.99.104:2376                v17.12.1-ce
 ↦  ~ █
```

List of all the nodes created by Docker Machine

In the preceding screenshot, we can see the five nodes that we originally created in VirtualBox and the five new nodes that we have created in AWS. Apparently, the nodes on AWS are using a new version of Docker; here the version is 18.02.0-ce. The IP addresses we see in the column URL are the public IP addresses of my EC2 instances.

Due to the fact that our CLI is still configured for remote access to the node aws-node-1, we can just run the swarm init command as follows:

```
$ docker swarm init
```

We then need the join-token:

```
$ export JOIN_TOKEN=$(docker swarm join-token -q worker)
```

The address of the leader with the following command:

```
$ export LEADER_ADDR=$(docker node inspect \
    --format "{{.ManagerStatus.Addr}}" self)
```

With this information, we can now join the other four nodes to the swarm leader:

```
$ for NODE in `seq 2 5`; do
    docker-machine ssh aws-node-${NODE} \
      sudo docker swarm join --token ${JOIN_TOKEN} ${LEADER_ADDR}
  done
```

An alternative way to achieve the same without needing to SSH into the individual nodes would be to reconfigure our client CLI every time we want to access a different node:

```
$ for NODE in `seq 2 5`; do
    eval $(docker-machine env aws-node-${NODE})
    docker swarm join --token ${JOIN_TOKEN} ${LEADER_ADDR}
  done
```

As a last step, we want to promote nodes 2 and 3 to manager:

```
$ eval $(docker-machine env node-1)
$ docker node promote aws-node-2 aws-node-3
```

We can then list all the swarm nodes, as shown in the following screenshot:

```
$ docker node ls
ID                              HOSTNAME     STATUS    AVAILABILITY    MANAGER STATUS    ENGINE VERSION
jcjv5id54tp6laevnvjdqktl6 *     aws-node-1   Ready     Active          Leader            18.04.0-ce
i9y6iiyclv9o23x86i5qfyh2a       aws-node-2   Ready     Active          Reachable         18.04.0-ce
zetk7ntzqyf75mk8n39y2o7Zv       aws-node-3   Ready     Active          Reachable         18.04.0-ce
h38drhf7fg50h2n4tc1vc49ko       aws-node-4   Ready     Active                            18.04.0-ce
ofbxw724dvu84dak974s64ocv       aws-node-5   Ready     Active                            18.04.0-ce
$
```

List of all nodes of our swarm in the cloud

And thus do we have a highly available Docker Swarm running in the cloud. To clean up the swarm in the cloud and avoid incurring unnecessary costs, we can use the following command:

```
$ for NODE in `seq 1 5`; do
    docker-machine rm -f aws-node-${NODE}
  done
```

Deploying a first application

We have created a few Docker Swarms on various platforms. Once created, a swarm behaves the same way on any platform. The way we deploy and update applications on a swarm is not platform-dependent. It has been one of Docker's main goals to avoid a vendor lock-in when using a swarm. Swarm-ready applications can be effortlessly migrated from, say, a swarm running on-premise to a cloud based swarm. It is even technically possible to run part of a swarm on-premise and another part in the cloud. It works, yet one has of course to consider possible side effects due to the higher latency between nodes in geographically distant areas.

Now that we have a highly available Docker Swarm up and running, it is time to run some workloads on it. I'm using a local swarm created with Docker Machine. We'll start by first creating a single service. For this we need to SSH into one of the manager nodes. I select node-1:

```
$ docker-machine ssh node-1
```

Creating a service

A service can be either created as part of a stack, or directly using the Docker CLI. Let's first look at a sample stack file that defines a single service:

```
version: "3.5"
services:
  whoami:
    image: training/whoami:latest
    networks:
      - test-net
    ports:
      - 81:8000
    deploy:
      replicas: 6
      update_config:
        parallelism: 2
        delay: 10s
      labels:
        app: sample-app
        environment: prod-south

networks:
  test-net:
    driver: overlay
```

In the preceding example we see what the desired state of a service called whoami is:

- It is based on the image training/whoami:latest
- Containers of the service are attached to the network test-net
- The container port 8000 is published to port 81
- It is running with six replicas (or tasks)

- During a rolling update, the individual tasks are updated in batches of two, with a delay of 10 seconds between each successful batch
- The service (and its tasks and containers) is assigned the two labels `app` and `environment`, with the values `sample-app` and `prod-south` respectively

There are many more settings that we could define for a service, but the preceding ones are some of the more important ones. Most settings have meaningful default values. If, for example, we do not specify the number of replicas, then Docker defaults it to `1`. The name and image of a service are of course mandatory. Note that the name of the service must be unique in the swarm.

To create the preceding service, we use the `docker stack deploy` command. Assuming that the file in which the preceding content is stored is called `stack.yaml`, we have:

```
$ docker stack deploy -c stack.yaml sample-stack
```

Here, we have created a stack called `sample-stack` that consists of one service, `whoami`. We can list all stacks on our swarm, whereupon we should get this:

```
$ docker stack ls
NAME              SERVICES
sample-stack      1
```

If we list the services defined in our swarm, we get the following output:

List of all services running in the swarm

In the output, we can see that currently we have only one service running, which was to be expected. The service has an ID. The format of the ID, contrary, what you have used so far for containers, networks, or volumes, is alphanumeric. We can also see that the name of the service is a combination of the service name we defined in the stack file and the name of the stack, which is used as a prefix. This makes sense, since we want to be able to deploy multiple stacks (with different names) using the same stack file into our swarm. To make sure that service names are unique, Docker decided to combine service name and stack name.

In the third column we see the mode, which is `replicated`. The number of replicas is shown as `6/6`. This tells us that six out of the six requested replicas are running. This corresponds to the desired state. In the output we also see the image that the service uses and the port mappings of the service.

Inspecting the service and its tasks

In the preceding output, we cannot see the details of the `6` replicas that have been created. To get some deeper insight into that, we can use the `docker service ps` command. If we execute this command for our service, we will get the following output:

Details of the whoami service

In the preceding output, we can see the list of six tasks that correspond to the requested six replicas of our `whoami` service. In the `NODE` column, we can also see the node to which each task has been deployed. The name of each task is a combination of the service name plus an increasing index. Also note that, similar to the service itself, each task gets an alphanumeric ID assigned.

In my case, apparently task 2, with the name `sample-stack_whoami.2`, has been deployed to `node-1`, which is the leader of our swarm. Thus, I should find a container running on this node. Let's see what we get if we list all containers running on `node-1`:

List of containers on node-1

As expected, we find a container running from the `training/whoami:latest` image with a name that is a combination of its parent task name and ID. We can try to visualize the whole hierarchy of objects that we generated when deploying our sample stack:

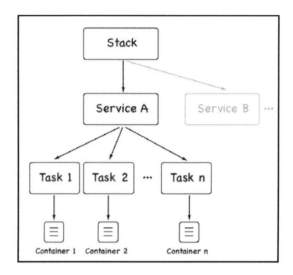

Object hierarchy of a Docker Swarm stack

A stack can consist of one to many services. Each service has a collection of tasks. Each task has a one-to-one association with a container. Stacks and services are created and stored on the Swarm manager nodes. Tasks are then scheduled to swarm worker nodes, where the worker node creates the corresponding container. We can also get some more information about our service by inspecting it. Execute the following command:

```
$ docker service inspect sample-stack_whoami
```

This provides a wealth of information about all the relevant settings of the service. This includes those we have explicitly defined in our `stack.yaml` file, but also those which we didn't specify and which therefore got their default values assigned. We're not going to list the whole output here, as it is too long, but I encourage the reader to inspect it on their own machine. We will discuss part of the information in more detail in the *The Swarm Routing Mesh* section.

Logs of a service

In an earlier chapter we worked with the logs produced by a container. Here we're concentrating on a service. Remember that, ultimately, a service with many replicas has many containers running. Thus, we would expect that, if we ask the service for its logs, that Docker returns an aggregate of all logs of those containers belonging to the service. And indeed, that's what we get if we use the `docker service logs` command:

```
docker@node-1:~$ docker service logs sample-stack_whoami
sample-stack_whoami.2.n21e7ktyvo4b@node-1    | Listening on :8000
sample-stack_whoami.1.mtvvunqieacg@node-5    | Listening on :8000
sample-stack_whoami.6.3hvu4qul0dzs@node-4    | Listening on :8000
sample-stack_whoami.4.xymlohw68639@node-2    | Listening on :8000
sample-stack_whoami.3.lozzitfydlad@node-2    | Listening on :8000
sample-stack_whoami.5.yn84l8fc83el@node-3    | Listening on :8000
docker@node-1:~$
```

Logs of the whoami service

There is not much information in the logs at this point, but it is enough to discuss what we get. The first part of each line in the log always contains the name of the container combined with the node name from which the log entry originates. Then, separated by the vertical bar (|), we get the actual log entry. So if we would, say, ask for the logs of the first container in the list directly, we would only get a single entry, and the value we would see in this case would be `Listening on :8000`.

The aggregated logs that we get with the `docker service logs` command are not sorted in any particular way. So, if correlation of events is happening in different containers you should add information to your log output that makes this correlation possible. Typically, this is a timestamp for each log entry. But this has to be done at the source; for example, the application that produces a log entry needs to also make sure a timestamp is added.

We can also query the logs of an individual task of the service by providing the task ID instead of the service ID or name. So, querying the logs from task 2 gives us the following screenshot:

```
docker@node-1:~$ docker service logs n21e7ktyvo4b
sample-stack_whoami.2.n21e7ktyvo4b@node-1     | Listening on :8000
docker@node-1:~$
```

Logs of an individual task of the whoami service

Reconciling the desired state

We have learned that a swarm service is a description or manifest of the desired state that we want an application or application service to run in. Now, let's see how Docker Swarm reconciles this desired state if we do something that causes the actual state of the service to be different from the desired state. The easiest way to do this is to forcibly kill one of the tasks or containers of the service.

Let's do this with the container that has been scheduled on `node-1`:

```
$ docker container rm -f sample-stack_whoami.2.n21e7ktyvo4b2sufalk0aibzy
```

If we do that and then do a `docker service ps` right thereafter, we will see the following output:

Docker Swarm reconciling the desired state after one task failed

We see that task 2 failed with exit code `137` and that the swarm immediately reconciled the desired state by rescheduling the failed task on a node with free resources. In this case, the scheduler selected the same node as the failed tasks, but this is not always the case. So, without us intervening, the swarm completely fixed the problem, and since the service is running in multiple replicas, at no time was the service down.

Let's try another failure scenario. This time we're going to shut down an entire node and are going to see how the swarm reacts. Let's take `node-2` for this, as it has two tasks (tasks 3 and 4) running on it. For this we need to open a new terminal window and use Docker machine to stop `node-2`:

```
$ docker-machine stop node-2
```

Back on `node-1`, we can now again run `docker service ps` to see what happened:

Swarm reschedules all tasks of a failed node

In the preceding screenshot, we can see that immediately task 3 was rescheduled on `node-1` whilst task 4 was rescheduled on `node-3`. Even this more radical failure is handled gracefully by Docker Swarm.

It is important to note though that if `node-2` ever comes back online in the swarm, the tasks that had previously been running on it will not automatically be transferred back to it. But the node is now ready for a new workload.

Deleting a service or a stack

If we want to remove a particular service from the swarm, we can use the `docker service rm` command. If on the other hand we want to remove a stack from the swarm, we analogously use the `docker stack rm` command. This command removes all services that are part of the stack definition. In the case of the `whoami` service, it was created by using a stack file and thus we're going to use the latter command:

```
docker@node-1:~$ docker stack rm sample-stack
Removing service sample-stack_whoami
Removing network sample-stack_test-net
docker@node-1:~$
```

Removing a stack

The preceding command will make sure that all tasks of each service of the stack are terminated, and the corresponding containers are stopped by first sending a `SIGTERM`, and then, if not successful, a `SIGKILL` after 10 seconds of timeout.

It is important to note that the stopped containers are not removed from the Docker host. Thus, it is advised to purge containers from time to time on worker nodes to reclaim unused resources. Use `docker container purge -f` for this purpose.

Deploying a multi-service stack

In Chapter 8, *Docker Compose*, we used an application consisting of two services that were declaratively described in a Docker compose file. We can use this compose file as a template to create a stack file that allows us to deploy the same application into a swarm. The content of our stack file called `pet-stack.yaml` looks like this:

```
version: "3.5"
services:
  web:
    image: fundamentalsofdocker/ch08-web:1.0
    networks:
      - pets-net
    ports:
      - 3000:3000
    deploy:
      replicas: 3
  db:
    image: fundamentalsofdocker/ch08-db:1.0
    networks:
      - pets-net
    volumes:
      - pets-data:/var/lib/postgresql/data

volumes:
  pets-data:

networks:
  pets-net:
    driver: overlay
```

We request that the service `web` has three replicas, and both services are attached to the overlay network `pets-net`. We can deploy this application using the `docker stack deploy` command:

```
docker@node-1:~$ docker stack deploy -c pet-stack.yaml pets
Creating network pets_pets-net
Creating service pets_db
Creating service pets_web
docker@node-1:~$ 4
```

Deploy the pets stack

Docker creates the `pets_pets-net` overlay network and then the two services `pets_web` and `pets_db`. We can then list all the tasks in the `pets` stack:

```
docker@node-1:~$ docker stack ps pets
ID            NAME         IMAGE                               NODE    DESIRED STATE  CURRENT STATE         ERROR
08f14cawm4if  pets_db.1    fundamentalsofdocker/ch08-db:1.0    node-2  Running        Running 2 seconds ago
qbbefgj97ijp  pets_web.1   fundamentalsofdocker/ch08-web:1.0   node-4  Running        Running 8 seconds ago
o5fblzf86588  pets_web.2   fundamentalsofdocker/ch08-web:1.0   node-3  Running        Running 8 seconds ago
nfrez66ssvix  pets_web.3   fundamentalsofdocker/ch08-web:1.0   node-5  Running        Running 8 seconds ago
docker@node-1:~$
```

List of all the tasks in the pets stack

Finally, let's test the application using `curl`. And, indeed, the application works as expected:

```
docker@node-1:~$ curl localhost:3000/pet
<html>
<head>
    <link rel="stylesheet" href="main.css">
</head>
<body>
    <div class="container">
        <h4>Cat Gif of the day</h4>
        <img src="http:&#x2F;&#x2F;ak-hdl.buzzfed.com&#x2F;static&#x2F;2013-10&#x2F;enhanced&#;
        <p><small>Courtesy: <a href="http://www.buzzfeed.com/copyranter/the-best-cat-gif-post-'
        <p>Delivered to you by container c9aa9dacd9b2<p>
    </div>
</body>
</html>docker@node-1:~$
```

Testing the pets application using curl

The container ID is in the output, where it says `Delivered to you by container c9aa9dacd9b2`. If you run the `curl` command multiple times, the ID should cycle between three different values. These are the ID's of the three containers (or replicas) that we have requested for the service `web`.

Once we're done, we can remove the stack with `docker stack rm pets`.

The swarm routing mesh

If you have been paying attention, then you might have noticed something interesting in the last section. We had the pets application deployed and it resulted in the fact that an instance of the service **web** was installed on the three nodes `node-3`, `node-4`, and `node-5`. Yet, we were able to access the **web** service on `node-1` with `localhost` and we reached each container from there. *How is that possible?* Well, this is due to the so-called swarm routing mesh. The routing mesh makes sure that when we publish a port of a service, that port is then published on all nodes of the swarm. Thus, network traffic that hits any node of the swarm and requests to use the specific port, will be forwarded to one of the service containers by routing the mesh. Let's look at the following figure to see how that works:

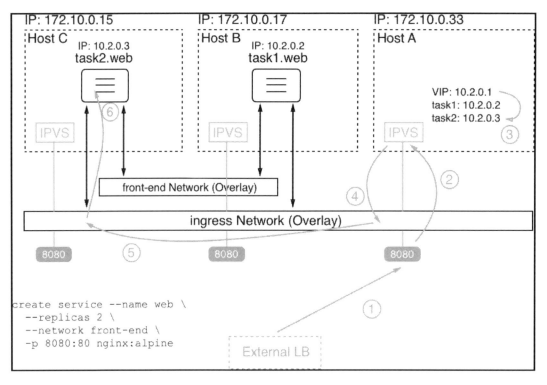

Docker Swarm routing mesh

In this situation we have three nodes, called **Host A** to **Host C**, with the IP addresses 172.10.0.15, 172.10.0.17, and 172.10.0.33. In the lower left-corner of the figure, we see the command that created a service **web** with two replicas. The corresponding tasks have been scheduled on **Host B** and **Host C**. Task 1 landed on host B while task 2 landed on host C.

When a service is created on Docker Swarm it automatically gets a **virtual IP (VIP)** address assigned. This IP address is stable and reserved during the whole life cycle of the service. Let's assume that in our case the VIP is 10.2.0.1.

If now a request for port 8080 coming from an external **load balancer (LB)** is targeted at one of the nodes of our swarm, then this request is handled by the Linux **IP Virtual Server (IPVS)** service on that node. This service makes a lookup with the given port 8080 in the IP table and will find that this corresponds to the VIP of service **web**. Now, since the VIP is not a real target, the IPVS service will load balance the IP addresses of the tasks that are associated with this service. In our case it picked task 2, with the IP address 10.2.0.3. Finally, the **ingress** overlay network is used to forward the request to the target container on host C.

It is important to note that it doesn't matter which swarm node the external request is forwarded to by the external LB. The routing mesh will always handle the request correctly and forward it to one of the tasks of the targeted service.

Summary

In this chapter, we have introduced Docker Swarm, which, next to Kubernetes, is the second most popular orchestrator for containers. We have looked into the architecture of a swarm, discussed all the types of resources running in a swarm, such as services, tasks, and more, and we have created services in the swarm and deployed an application that consists of multiple related services.

In the next chapter, we are going to explore how to deploy services or applications onto a Docker Swarm with zero downtime and automatic rollback capabilities. We are also going to introduce secrets as a means to protect sensitive information.

Questions

To assess your learning progress please answer the following questions:

1. How do you initialize a new Docker Swarm?
   1. docker init swarm
   2. docker swarm init --advertise-addr <IP address>
   3. docker swarm join --token <join token>
2. You want to remove a worker node from a Docker Swarm. What steps are necessary?
3. How do you create an overlay network called front-tier? Make the network attachable.
4. How will you create a service called web from the nginx:alpine image with five replicas, which exposes port 3000 on the ingress network and is attached to the front-tier network?
5. How will you scale the web service down to three instances?

Further reading

Please consult the following link for more in-depth information about selected topics:

- *Amazon AWS EC2 example* at http://dockr.ly/2FFelyT

11

Zero Downtime Deployments and Secrets

In the last chapter, we explored Docker Swarm and its resources in detail. We learned how to build a highly available swarm locally, and in the cloud. Then, we discussed swarm services and stacks in depth. Finally, we created services and stacks in the swarm.

In this chapter, we will show you how we can update services and stacks running in Docker Swarm without interrupting their availability. This is called **zero downtime deployment**. We are also going to introduce swarm secrets as a means to securely provide sensitive information to containers of a service using those secrets.

The topics of this chapter are:

- Zero downtime deployment
- Secrets

After finishing this chapter, you will be able to:

- List two to three different deployment strategies commonly used to update a service without downtime
- Update a service in batches without causing a service interruption
- Define a rollback strategy for a service that is used if an update fails
- Use a secret with a service
- Update the value of a secret without causing downtime

Technical requirements

The code files for this chapter can be found at the link `https://github.com/` `fundamentalsofdocker/labs/tree/master/ch11`.

Zero downtime deployment

One of the most important aspects of a mission-critical application that needs frequent updates is the ability to do updates in a fashion that requires no outage at all. We call this a zero downtime deployment. At all times, the application which is updated is fully operational.

Popular deployment strategies

There are various ways how this can be achieved. Some of them are as follows:

- Rolling updates
- Blue-green deployments
- Canary releases

Docker Swarm supports rolling updates out of the box. The other two types of deployments can be achieved with some extra effort from our side.

Rolling updates

In a mission-critical application, each application service has to run in multiple replicas. Depending on the load, that can be as few as two to three instances and as many as dozens, hundreds, or thousands of instances. At any given time, we want to have a clear majority of all service instances running. So, if we have three replicas, we want to have at least two of them up and running all the time. If we have 100 replicas, we can content ourselves with a minimum of, say 90 replicas, that need to be available. We can then define a batch size of replicas that we may take down to upgrade. In the first case, the batch size would be 1 and in the second case, it would be 10.

When we take replicas down, Docker Swarm will automatically take those instances out of the load balancing pool and all traffic will be load balanced across the remaining active instances. Those remaining instances will thus experience a slight increase in traffic. In the following diagram, prior to the start of the rolling update, if **Task A3** wanted to access **Service B,** it could have been load balanced to any of the three tasks of service B by SwarmKit. Once the rolling update had started, SwarmKit took down **Task B1** for updates. Automatically, this task is then taken out of the pool of targets. So, if **Task A3** now requests to connect to **Service B**, the load balancing will only select from the remaining tasks B2 and B3. Thus, those two tasks might experience a higher load temporarily:

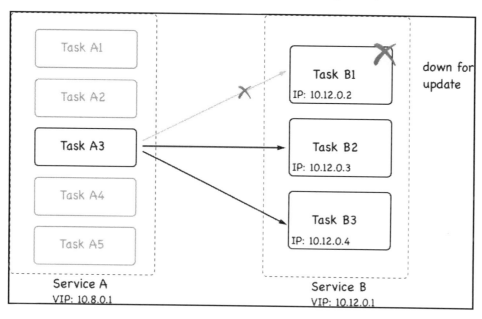

Task B1 is taken down for update

The stopped instances are then replaced by an equivalent number of new instances of the new version of the application service. Once the new instances are up and running, we can have the swarm observe them for a given period of time and make sure they're healthy. If all is good, then we can continue by taking down the next batch of instances and replacing them with instances of the new version. This process is repeated until all instances of the application service are replaced.

In the the following diagram, we see that **Task B1** of **Service B** has been updated to version 2. The container of **Task B1** got a new IP address assigned, and it got deployed to another worker node with free resources:

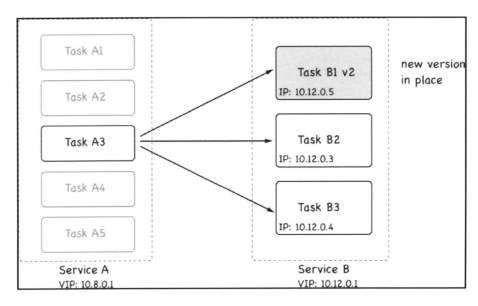

First batch updated in a rolling update

It is important to understand that when a task of a service is updated, it, in most cases, gets deployed to a different worker node than the one it used to live on. But that should be fine as long as the corresponding service is stateless. If we have a stateful service that is location or node aware and we'd like to update it, then we have to adjust our approach, but this is outside of the scope of this book.

Now, let's look into how we can actually instruct the swarm to perform a rolling update of an application service. When we declare a service in a stack file, we can define multiple options that are relevant in this context. Let's look at a snippet of a typical stack file:

```
version: "3.5"
services:
  web:
    image: nginx:alpine
    deploy:
      replicas: 10
      update_config:
        parallelism: 2
        delay: 10s
...
```

In this snippet, we see a section, `update_config`, with the properties `parallelism` and `delay`. Parallelism defines the batch size of how many replicas are going to be updated at a time during a rolling update. Delay defines how long Docker Swarm is going to wait between the update of individual batches. In the preceding case, we have `10` replicas that are updated in two instances at a time and, between each successful update, Docker Swarm waits for `10` seconds.

Let's test such a rolling update. We navigate to subfolder `ch11` of our `labs` folder and use the file `stack.yaml` to create a web service configured for a rolling update. The service uses the Alpine-based Nginx image with version `1.12-alpine`. We will then later update the service to a newer version `1.13-alpine`.

We will deploy this service to our swarm that we created locally in VirtualBox. First, we make sure we have our Terminal window configured to access one of the master nodes of our cluster. We can take the leader `node-1`:

```
$ eval $(docker-machine env node-1)
```

Now, we can deploy the service using the stack file:

```
$ docker stack deploy -c stack.yaml web
```

The output of the preceding command looks like this:

```
$ docker stack deploy -c stack.yaml web
Creating network web_default
Creating service web_web
$ 
```

Deployment of the stack called web

Once the service is deployed, we can monitor it using the following command:

```
$ watch docker stack ps web
```

And we will see the following output:

```
Every 2.0s: docker stack ps web

ID            NAME         IMAGE              NODE      DESIRED STATE   CURRENT STATE          ERROR        PORTS
ze29yvu4jyyc  web_web.1    nginx:1.12-alpine  node-2    Running         Running 3 minutes ago
i1cy5v4o9ld3  web_web.2    nginx:1.12-alpine  node-2    Running         Running 3 minutes ago
kzqylcub4o49  web_web.3    nginx:1.12-alpine  node-1    Running         Running 3 minutes ago
ynt8n4ke8yld  web_web.4    nginx:1.12-alpine  node-3    Running         Running 3 minutes ago
qai8xv1u9v1d  web_web.5    nginx:1.12-alpine  node-5    Running         Running 3 minutes ago
5inv9mkxlpkv  web_web.6    nginx:1.12-alpine  node-4    Running         Running 3 minutes ago
iyjntpgy6cwe  web_web.7    nginx:1.12-alpine  node-1    Running         Running 3 minutes ago
q230vi6rlwrv  web_web.8    nginx:1.12-alpine  node-5    Running         Running 3 minutes ago
nh6jm2fyzwre  web_web.9    nginx:1.12-alpine  node-3    Running         Running 3 minutes ago
iuuS6iot6dxm  web_web.10   nginx:1.12-alpine  node-4    Running         Running 3 minutes ago
```

Service web of stack web running in swarm with 10 replicas

 If you're working on a Mac, you need to make sure your watch tool is installed. Use this command to do so: `brew install watch`.

The previous command will continuously update the output and provide us with a good overview on what's happening during the rolling update.

Now, we need to open a second Terminal and also configure it for remote access to a manager node of our swarm. Once we have done that, we can execute the `docker` command that will update the image of the `web` service of the stack also called `web`:

```
$ docker service update --image nginx:1.13-alpine web_web
```

The preceding command leads to the following output, indicating the progress of the rolling update:

```
overall progress: 4 out of 10 tasks
1/10: running   [==================================================>]
2/10: running   [==================================================>]
3/10: running   [==================================================>]
4/10: running   [==================================================>]
5/10: preparing [=============================>                       ]
6/10: preparing [=============================>                       ]
7/10:
8/10:
9/10:
10/10:
```

Screen showing progress of rolling update

The output indicates that the first two batches with each two tasks have been successful and that the third batch is preparing.

In the first terminal window, where we're watching the stack, we should now see how Docker Swarm updates the service batch by batch with an interval of 10 seconds. After the first batch, it should look like the following screenshot:

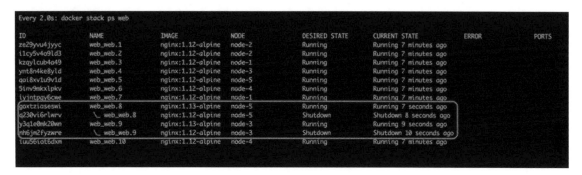

Rolling update of a service in Docker Swarm

In the preceding screenshot, we can see that the first batch of the two tasks, 8 and 9, has been updated. Docker Swarm is waiting for 10 seconds to proceed with the next batch.

It is interesting to note that in this particular case, SwarmKit deploys the new version of the task to the same node as the previous version. This is accidental since we have five nodes and two tasks on each node. SwarmKit always tries to balance the workload evenly across the nodes. So, when SwarmKit takes down a task, then the corresponding node has less workload than all the others and thus gets the new instance scheduled. Normally, you cannot expect to find the new instance of a task on the same node. Just try it out yourself by deleting the stack with `docker stack rm web` and changing the number of replicas to say, seven, and then redeploy and update.

Once all the tasks are updated, the output of our watch `docker stack ps web` command looks similar to the following screenshot:

```
Every 2.0s: docker stack ps web

ID              NAME          IMAGE              NODE      DESIRED STATE    CURRENT STATE               ERROR    PORTS
v99yet3urtyf    web_web.1     nginx:1.13-alpine  node-2    Running          Running 2 minutes ago
ze29yvu4jyyc     \_ web_web.1 nginx:1.12-alpine  node-2    Shutdown         Shutdown 2 minutes ago
s6was0b36hoa    web_web.2     nginx:1.13-alpine  node-2    Running          Running 2 minutes ago
i1cy5v4o9ld3     \_ web_web.2 nginx:1.12-alpine  node-2    Shutdown         Shutdown 2 minutes ago
m2fvxq7yxfqc    web_web.3     nginx:1.13-alpine  node-1    Running          Running 2 minutes ago
kzqylcub4o49     \_ web_web.3 nginx:1.12-alpine  node-1    Shutdown         Shutdown 2 minutes ago
xsjjudndb7jm    web_web.4     nginx:1.13-alpine  node-3    Running          Running 2 minutes ago
ynt8n4ke8yld     \_ web_web.4 nginx:1.12-alpine  node-3    Shutdown         Shutdown 2 minutes ago
fuk4xpb5g5un    web_web.5     nginx:1.13-alpine  node-5    Running          Running about a minute ago
qai8xv1u9v1d     \_ web_web.5 nginx:1.12-alpine  node-5    Shutdown         Shutdown about a minute ago
ipa1sc5hee7d    web_web.6     nginx:1.13-alpine  node-4    Running          Running about a minute ago
5inv9mkxlpkv     \_ web_web.6 nginx:1.12-alpine  node-4    Shutdown         Shutdown about a minute ago
feyu3l2ufjgr    web_web.7     nginx:1.13-alpine  node-1    Running          Running 2 minutes ago
iyjntpgy6cwe     \_ web_web.7 nginx:1.12-alpine  node-1    Shutdown         Shutdown 2 minutes ago
goxtziaseswi    web_web.8     nginx:1.13-alpine  node-5    Running          Running 2 minutes ago
q230vi6rlwrv     \_ web_web.8 nginx:1.12-alpine  node-5    Shutdown         Shutdown 2 minutes ago
y3q1e0mk20wn    web_web.9     nginx:1.13-alpine  node-3    Running          Running 2 minutes ago
nh6jm2fyzwre     \_ web_web.9 nginx:1.12-alpine  node-3    Shutdown         Shutdown 2 minutes ago
7r93m02hhizg    web_web.10    nginx:1.13-alpine  node-4    Running          Running 2 minutes ago
iuu56iot6dxm     \_ web_web.10 nginx:1.12-alpine node-4    Shutdown         Shutdown 2 minutes ago
```

All tasks have been updated successfully

Please note that SwarmKit does not immediately remove the containers of the previous versions of the tasks from the corresponding nodes. This makes sense as we might want to, for example, retrieve the logs from those containers for debugging purposes, or we might want to retrieve their metadata using `docker container inspect`. SwarmKit keeps the four latest terminated task instances around before it purges older ones to not clog the system with unused resources.

Once we're done, we can tear down the stack using the following command:

```
$ docker stack rm web
```

Although using stack files to define and deploy applications is the recommended best practice, we can also define the update behavior in a service `create` statement. If we just want to deploy a single service, this might be the preferred way. Let's look at such a `create` command:

```
$ docker service create --name web \
    --replicas 10 \
    --update-parallelism 2 \
    --update-delay 10s \
    nginx:alpine
```

This command defines the same desired state as the preceding stack file. We want the service to run with 10 replicas and we want a rolling update to happen in batches of 2 tasks at a time, with a 10 second interval between consecutive batches.

Health checks

To make informed decisions, for example, during a rolling update of a swarm service whether or not the just-installed batch of new service instances is running OK or if a rollback is needed, the SwarmKit needs a way to know about the overall health of the system. On its own, SwarmKit (and Docker) can collect quite a bit of information. But there is a limit. Imagine a container containing an application. The container, as seen from outside, can look absolutely healthy and chuckle away just fine. But that doesn't necessarily mean that the application running inside the container is also doing well. The application could, for example, be in an infinite loop or be in a corrupt state, yet still running. But, as long as the application runs, the container runs and from outside, everything looks perfect.

Thus, SwarmKit provides a seam where we can provide it with some help. We, the authors of the application services running inside the containers in the swarm, know best whether or not our service is in a healthy state. SwarmKit gives us the opportunity to define a command that is executed against our application service to test its health. *What exactly this command does is not important to Swarm*, the command just needs to return OK or NOT OK or time out. The latter two situations, namely NOT OK or timeout, will tell SwarmKit that the task it is investigating is potentially unhealthy. Here, I am writing *potentially* on purpose and later, we will see why:

```
FROM alpine:3.6
...
HEALTHCHECK --interval=30s \
    --timeout=10s
    --retries=3
    --start-period=60s
    CMD curl -f http://localhost:3000/health || exit 1
...
```

In the preceding snippet from a Dockerfile, we see the keyword HEALTHCHECK. It has a few options or parameters and an actual command CMD. Let's first discuss the options:

- --interval defines the wait time between health checks. Thus, in our case the orchestrator executes a check every 30 seconds.
- The --timeout parameter defines how long Docker should wait if the health check does not respond until it times out with an error. In our sample, this is 10 seconds. Now, if one health check fails, the SwarmKit retries a couple of times until it gives up and declares the corresponding task as unhealthy and opens the door for Docker to kill this task and replace it by a new instance.

- The number of retries is defined with the parameter `--retries`. In the preceding code, we want to have three retries.
- Next, we have the start period. Some containers need some time to start up (not that this is a recommended pattern, but sometimes it is inevitable). During this start up time, the service instance might not be able to respond to health checks. With the start period, we can define how long the SwarmKit should wait before it executes the very first health check and thus give the application time to initialize. To define the start up time, we use the `--start-period` parameter. In our case, we do the first check after 60 seconds. How long this start period needs to be totally depends on the application and its start up behavior. The recommendation is to start with a relatively low value and if you have a lot of false positives and tasks that are restarted many times, you might want to increase the time interval.
- Finally, we define the actual probing command on the last line with the CMD keyword. In our case, we are defining a request to the `/health` endpoint of `localhost` at port 3000 as a probing command. This call is expected to have three possible outcomes:
  - The command succeeds
  - The command fails
  - The command times out

The latter two are treated the same way by SwarmKit. It is an indication to the orchestrator that the corresponding task might be unhealthy. I did say *might* with intent since SwarmKit does not immediately assume the worst case scenario but assumes that this might just be a temporary fluke of the task and that it will recover from it. This is the reason why we have a `--retries` parameter. There, we can define how many times SwarmKit should retry before it can assume that the task is indeed unhealthy, and consequently kill it and reschedule another instance of this task on another free node to reconcile the desired state of the service.

Why can we use localhost in our probing command? This is a very good question, and the reason is because SwarmKit, when probing a container running in the swarm, executes this `probing` command inside the container (that is, it does something like `docker container exec <containerID> <probing command>`). Thus, the command executes in the same network namespace as the application running inside the container. In the following diagram, we see the life cycle of a service task from its beginning:

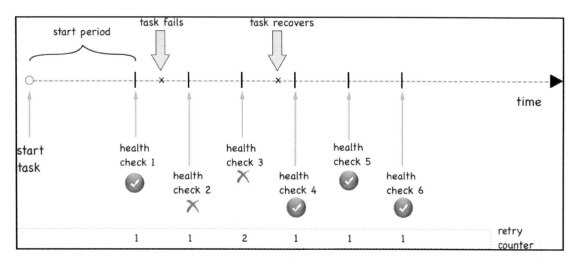

Service task with transient health failure

First, SwarmKit waits with probing until the start period is over. Then, we have a first health check. Shortly thereafter, the task fails when probed. It fails two consecutive times but then it recovers. Thus, health check number 4 is again successful and SwarmKit leaves the task running.

Here, we, see a task that is permanently failing:

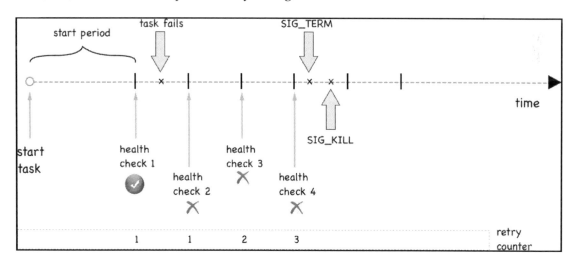

Permanent failure of task

If the task does not recover and after having three retries (or as many as you have defined), then SwarmKit first sends a `SIGTERM` to the container of the task, and if that times out after 10 seconds, it sends a `SIGKILL` signal.

We have just learned how we can define a health check for a service in the Dockerfile of its image. But this is not the only way. We can also define the health check in a stack file that we use to deploy our application into a Docker Swarm. Here is a short snippet of what such a stack file would look like:

```
version: "3.5"
services:
  web:
    image: example/web:1.0
    healthcheck:
      test: ["CMD", "curl", "-f", "http://localhost:3000/health"]
      interval: 30s
      timeout: 10s
      retries: 3
      start_period: 60s
...
```

In this snippet, we see how the health check-related information is defined in the stack file. First and foremost, it is important to realize that we have to define a health check for every service individually. There is no health check on an application or global level.

Similar to what we have defined previously in the Dockerfile, the command that is used to execute the health check by the SwarmKit is `curl -f http://localhost:3000/health`. We also have definitions for `interval`, `timeout`, `retries`, and `start_period`. These latter four key-value pairs have the same meaning as the corresponding parameters we used in the Dockerfile. If there are health check-related settings defined in the image, then the ones defined in the stack file override the ones from the Dockerfile.

Now, let's try to use a service that has a health check defined. In our `lab` folder, we have a file called `stack-health.yaml` with the following content:

```
version: "3.5"
services:
  web:
    image: nginx:alpine
    healthcheck:
      test: ["CMD", "wget", "-qO", "-", "http://localhost"]
      interval: 5s
      timeout: 2s
      retries: 3
      start_period: 15s
```

That we're going to deploy now:

```
$ docker stack deploy -c stack-health.yaml myapp
```

We can find out where the single task got deployed to by using `docker stack ps myapp`. On that particular node, we can list all containers to find the one of our stack. In my example, the task had been deployed to `node-3`:

Displaying the health status of a running task instance

The interesting thing in this screenshot is the `STATUS` column. Docker, or more precisely SwarmKit, has recognized that the service has a health check function defined and is using it to determine the health of each task of the service.

Rollback

Sometimes, things don't go as expected. A last minute fix in an application release inadvertently introduced a new bug, or the new version significantly decreases the throughput of the component, and so on. In such cases, we need to have a plan B which in most cases means the ability to roll back the update to the previous good version.

As with the update, the rollback has to happen in a such a way that it does not cause any outages of the application; it needs to cause zero downtime. In that sense, a rollback can be looked at as a reverse update. We are installing a new version, yet this new version is actually the previous version.

As with the update behavior, we can declare, either in our stack files or in the Docker service `create` command, how the system should behave in case it needs to execute a rollback. Here, we have the stack file that we used before, but this time with some rollback-relevant attributes:

```
version: "3.5"
services:
  web:
    image: nginx:1.12-alpine
    ports:
      - 80:80
    deploy:
      replicas: 10
```

```
        update_config:
          parallelism: 2
          delay: 10s

          failure_action: rollback
          monitor: 10s

    healthcheck:
      test: ["CMD", "wget", "-qO", "-", "http://localhost"]
      interval: 2s
      timeout: 2s
      retries: 3
      start_period: 2s
```

In this stack file, which is available in our lab as `stack-rollback.yaml`, we have defined the details about the rolling update, the health checks, and the behavior during rollback. The health check is defined so that after an initial wait time of 2 seconds, the orchestrator starts to poll the service on `http://localhost` every 2 seconds and it retries 3 times before it considers a task as unhealthy. If we do the math, then it takes at least 8 seconds until a task will be stopped if it is unhealthy due to a bug. So, now under deploy, we have a new entry `monitor`. This entry defines how long newly deployed tasks should be monitored for health as a decision point whether or not to continue with the next batch in the rolling update. Here, in this sample, we have given it 10 seconds. This is slightly more than the 8 seconds we calculated it takes to discover that a defective service has been deployed. So this is good.

We also have a new entry, `failure_action`, which defines what the orchestrator will do if it encounters a failure during the rolling update such as that the service is unhealthy. By default, the action is just to stop the whole update process and leave the system in an intermediate state. The system is not down since it is a rolling update and at least some healthy instances of the service are still operational, but some operations engineer better at taking a look and fixing the problem.

In our case, we have defined the action to be `rollback`. Thus, in case of failure, SwarmKit will automatically revert all tasks that have been updated back to their previous version.

Blue–green deployments

We have discussed in Chapter 6, *Distributed Application Architecture*, what blue–green deployments are, in an abstract way. It turns out that on Docker Swarm we cannot really implement blue–green deployments for arbitrary services. The service discovery and load balancing between two services running in Docker Swarm are part of the swarm routing mesh and cannot be (easily) customized. If **Service A** wants to call **Service B**, then Docker does it all implicitly. Docker, given the name of the target service, will use the Docker DNS service to resolve this name to a **virtual IP (VIP)** address. When the request is then targeted at the VIP, the Linux IPVS service will do another lookup in the Linux kernel IP tables with the VIP and load balances the request to one of the physical IP addresses of the tasks of the service represented by the VIP, as shown in the following figure:

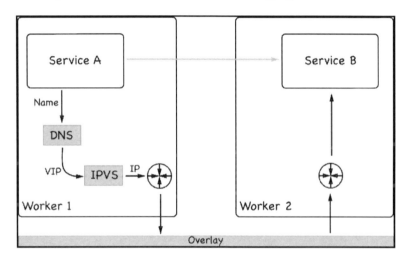

How service discovery and load balancing work in Docker Swarm

Unfortunately, there is no easy way to intercept this mechanism and replace it with a custom behavior. But this would be needed to allow for a true blue–green deployment of **Service B**, which is the target service in our example. As we will see in Chapter 13, *Deploying, Updating, and Securing an Application with Kubernetes*, Kubernetes it is more flexible in this area.

That said, we can always deploy the public-facing services in a blue–green fashion. We can use interlock 2 and its layer 7 routing mechanism to allow for a true blue–green deployment.

Canary releases

Technically, rolling updates are a kind of canary release. But due to their lack of seams, where you could plug customized logic into the system, rolling updates are only a very limited version of canary releases.

True canary releases require us to have more fine-grained control about the update process. Also, true canary releases do not take down the old version of the service until 100% of the traffic has been funneled through the new version. In that regard, they are treated like blue–green deployments.

In a canary release scenario, we want to not just use things such as health checks as deciding factors whether or not to funnel more and more traffic through the new version of the service, but we also want to consider external input in the decision making, such as metrics collected and aggregated by a log aggregator or tracing information. Examples that could be used as decision makers are the conformance to **service level agreements** (SLAs), namely if the new version of the service shows response times that are outside of the tolerance band. This can happen if we add new functionality to an existing service, yet this new functionality degrades the response time.

Secrets

Secrets are used to work with confidential data in a secure way. Swarm secrets are secure at rest and in transit. That is, when a new secret is created on a manager node, and it can only be created on a manager node, its value is encrypted and stored in the raft consensus storage. This is why it is secure at rest. If a service gets a secret assigned to it, then the manager reads the secret from storage, decrypts it, and forwards it to all the containers who are instances of the Swarm service that requests the secret. Since the node-to-node communication in swarm is using mutual **transport layer security** (TLS), the secret value, although decrypted, is still secure in transit. The manager forwards the secret only to the worker nodes on which a service instance is running. Secrets are then mounted as files into the target container. Each secret corresponds to a file. The name of the secret will be the name of the file inside the container, and the value of the secret is the content of the respective file. Secrets are never stored on the filesystem of a worker node but are mounted using `tmpFS` into the container. By default, secrets are mounted into the container at `/run/secrets`, but you can change that to any custom folder.

Creating secrets

First let's see how we can actually create a secret:

```
$ echo "sample secret value" | docker secret create sample-secret -
```

This command creates a secret called `sample-secret` with the value `sample secret value`. Please note the hyphen at the end of the `docker secret create` command. This means that Docker expects the value of the secret from standard input. This is exactly what we're doing by piping the value, `sample secret value` into the `create` command.

Alternatively, we can use a file as the source for the secret value:

```
$ docker secret create other-secret ~/my-secrets/secret-value.txt
```

Here, the value of the secret with the name `other-secret` is read from a file, `~/my-secrets/secret-value.txt`. Once a secret has been created, there is no way to access the value of it. We can, for example, list all our secrets and we will get the following screenshot:

```
$ docker secret ls
ID                          NAME            DRIVER          CREATED           UPDATED
axykb7msipit1g5so63ef02it   other-secret                    28 seconds ago    28 seconds ago
puns1op5wr5hi21st5h3wjd64   sample-secret                   3 minutes ago     3 minutes ago
$
```

List of all secrets

In this list, we only see the ID and name of the secret plus some other metadata, but the actual value of the secret is not visible. We can also use inspect on a secret, for example, to get more information about the `other-secret`:

```
$ docker secret inspect other-secret
[
    {
        "ID": "axykb7msipit1g5so63ef02it",
        "Version": {
            "Index": 135
        },
        "CreatedAt": "2018-03-16T01:29:14.367872931Z",
        "UpdatedAt": "2018-03-16T01:29:14.367872931Z",
        "Spec": {
            "Name": "other-secret",
            "Labels": {}
        }
    }
]
$
```

Inspecting a swarm secret

Even here, we do not get the value of the secret back. This is of course intentional, a secret is a secret and thus needs to remain confidential. We can assign labels to secrets if we want and we can even use a different driver to encrypt and decrypt the secret, if we're not happy with what Docker delivers out of the box.

Using a secret

Secrets are used by services that run in the swarm. Usually, secrets are assigned to a service at creation time. Thus, if we want to run a service called web and assign it a secret, api-secret-key, the syntax would look like the following command:

```
$ docker service create --name web \
    --secret api-secret-key \
    --publish 8000:8000 \
    fundamentalsofdocker/whoami:latest
```

This command creates a service called `web` based on the image `fundamentalsofdocker/whoami:latest`, publishes the container port `8000` to port `8000` on all swarm nodes, and assigns it the secret, `api-secret-key`.

This will only work if the secret called `api-secret-key` is defined in the swarm, otherwise an error will be generated with the text `secret not found: api-secret-key`. Thus, let's create this secret now:

```
$ echo "my secret key" | docker secret create api-secret-key -
```

And now, if we rerun the service `create` command, it will succeed:

```
$ docker service create --name web \
>       --secret api-secret-key \
>       --publish 8000:8000 \
>       fundamentalsofdocker/whoami:latest
dzxxme8kmo0bglr2ufwrhcztm
overall progress: 1 out of 1 tasks
1/1: running   [==============================================>]
verify: Service converged
$
```

Creating a service with a secret

We can now do a `docker service ps web` to find out on which node the sole service instance has been deployed, and then exec into this container. In my case, the instance has been deployed to `node-3`, thus I SSH into that node:

```
$ docker-machine ssh node-3
```

And then I list all my containers on that node to find the one instance belonging to my service and copy its container ID. We can then run the following command to make sure that the secret is indeed available inside the container under the expected filename containing the secret value in clear text:

```
$ docker exec -it <container ID> cat /run/secrets/api-secret-key
```

Once again, in my case, this looks like this:

```
docker@node-1:~$ docker container exec -it d5133b0e3eb3 cat /run/secrets/api-secret-key
my secret key
docker@node-1:~$
```

A secret as a container sees it

If, for some reason, the default location where Docker mounts the secrets inside the container is not acceptable to you, you can define a custom location. In the following command, we mount the secret to `/app/my-secrets`:

```
$ docker service create --name web \
    --name web \
    -p 8000:8000 \
    --secret source=api-secret-key,target=/run/my-secrets/api-secret-key \
    fundamentalsofdocker/whoami:latest
```

In this command, we are using the extended syntax to define a secret which includes the destination folder.

Simulating secrets in a development environment

When working in development, we usually don't have a local swarm on our machine. But secrets only work in a swarm. So, *what can we do*? Well, luckily it is really simple. Due to the fact that secrets are treated as files, we can easily mount a volume that contains the secrets into the container to the expected location, which by default is at `/run/secrets`.

Assume that we have a folder `./dev-secrets` on our local workstation. For each secret, we have a file called the same way as the secret name and with the un-encrypted value of the secret as content of the file. For example, we can simulate a secret called `demo-secret` with a secret value `demo secret value` by executing the following command on our workstation:

```
$ echo "demo secret value" > ./dev-secrets/sample-secret
```

We can then create a container that mounts this folder like this:

```
$ docker container run -d --name whoami \
    -p 8000:8000 \
    -v $(pwd)/dev-secrets:/run/secrets \
    fundamentalsofdocker/whoami:latest
```

And the process running inside the container will not be able to distinguish these mounted files from ones originating from a secret. So, for example, the `demo-secret` is available as file `/run/secrets/demo-secret` inside the container and has the expected value `demo secret value`.

To test this, we can exec a shell inside the preceding container:

```
$ docker container exec -it whoami /bin/bash
```

And then navigate to the folder, `/run/secrets` and display the content of the file `demo-secret`:

```
/# cd /run/secrets
/# cat demo-secret
demo secret value
```

Secrets and legacy applications

Sometimes, we want to containerize a legacy application that we cannot easily, or do not want to, change. This legacy application might expect a secret value to be available as an environment variable. *How are we going to deal with this now?* Docker presents us with the secrets as files but the application is expecting them in the form of environment variables.

In this situation, it is helpful to define a script that runs when the container is started (a so-called entrypoint or start up script). This script will read the secret value from the respective file and define an environment variable with the same name as the file, assigning the new variable the value read from the file. In the case of a secret called `demo-secret` whose value should be available in an environment variable called `DEMO_SECRET`, the necessary code snippet in this start up script could look like this:

```
export DEMO_SECRET=`cat /run/secrets/demo-secret`
```

Similarly, if the legacy application expects the secret values to be present as an entry in say, a YAML configuration file located in the `/app/bin` folder, and called `app.config` whose relevant part looks like this:

```
...
secrets:
  demo-secret: "<<demo-secret-value>>"
  other-secret: "<<other-secret-value>>"
  yet-another-secret: "<<yet-another-secret-value>>"
...
```

Our initialization script now needs to read the secret value from the `secret` file and replace the corresponding placeholder in the config file with the secret value. For the `demo-secret`, this could look like this:

```
file=/app/bin/app.conf
demo_secret=`cat /run/secret/demo-secret`
sed -i "s/<<demo-secret-value>>/$demo_secret/g" "$file"
```

In this snippet, we're using the `sed` tool to replace a placeholder with a value in place. We can use the same technique for the other two secrets in the config file.

We put all the initialization logic into a file called `entrypoint.sh`, make this file executable and, for example, add it to the root of the container's filesystem, and then we define this file as `ENTRYPOINT` in the Dockerfile, or we can override the existing `ENTRYPOINT` of an image in the `docker container run` command.

Let's make a sample. Assume that we have a legacy application running inside a container defined by the image `fundamentalsofdocker/whoami:latest` that expects a secret `db_password` to be defined in a file, `whoami.conf`, in the application folder. We can define a file, `whoami.conf`, on our local machine with this content:

```
database:
  name: demo
  db_password: "<<db_password_value>>"
others:
  val1=123
  val2="hello world"
```

The important part is line 3 of this snippet. It defines where the secret value has to be put by the start up script. Let's add a file called `entrypoint.sh` to the local folder with the following content:

```
file=/app/whoami.conf
db_pwd=`cat /run/secret/db-password`
sed -i "s/<<db_password_value>>/$db_pwd/g" "$file"

/app/http
```

The last line in this script stems from the fact that this is the start command used in the original Dockerfile. Now, change the mode of this file to be executable:

```
$ sudo chmod +x ./entrypoint.sh
```

Now, we define a Dockerfile which inherits from the image `fundamentalsofdocker/whoami:latest`. Add a file called `Dockerfile` to the current folder with the following content:

```
FROM fundamentalsofdocker/whoami:latest
COPY ./whoami.conf /app/
COPY ./entrypoint.sh /
CMD ["/entrypoint.sh"]
```

Let's build the image from this Dockerfile:

```
$ docker image build -t secrets-demo:1.0 .
```

Once the image is built, we can run a service from it. But before we can do that, we need to define the secret in the swarm:

```
$ echo "passw0rD123" | docker secret create demo-secret -
```

And now we can create the service that uses the following secret:

```
$ docker service create --name demo \
    --secret demo-secret \
    secrets-demo:1.0
```

Updating secrets

At times, we need to update a secret in a running service, the reason being that secrets could be leaked out to the public or be stolen by malicious people, such a hackers. In this case, we need to change our confidential data since the moment it has leaked to a non-trusted entity, it has to be considered as insecure.

The updating of secrets, like any other update, has to happen in a way which requires zero downtime. SwarmKit supports us in this regard.

First, we create the new secret in the Swarm. It is recommended to use a versioning strategy when doing so. In our example, we use a version as a postfix of the secret name. We originally started with the secret named db-password and now the new version of this secret is called db-password-v2:

```
$ echo "newPassw0rD" | docker secret create db-password-v2 -
```

Assume that the original service that used the secret had been created like this:

```
$ docker service create --name web \
    --publish 80:80
    --secret db-password
    nginx:alpine
```

The application running inside the container was able to access the secret at /run/secrets/db-password. Now, SwarmKit does not allow us to update an existing secret in a running service, thus we have to first remove the now obsolete version of the secret and then add the new one. Let's start with the removal with the following command:

```
$ docker service update --secret-rm db-password web
```

And then we can add the new secret with the following command:

```
$ docker service update \
    --secret-add source=db-password-v2, target=db-password \
    web
```

Summary

In this chapter, we learned how SwarmKit allows us to update services without requiring downtime. We also discussed the current limits of SwarmKit in regards to zero downtime deployments. In the second part of the chapter, we introduced secrets as a means to provide confidential data to services in a highly secure way.

In the next chapter, we will introduce the currently most popular container orchestrator, Kubernetes. We'll discuss the objects that are used to define and run a distributed, resilient, robust, and highly available application in a Kubernetes cluster. Furthermore, the chapter will familiarize us with MiniKube, a tool used to locally deploy a Kubernetes application, and also demonstrate the integration of Kubernetes with Docker for Mac and Docker for Windows.

Questions

To assess your understanding of the topics discussed in this chapter, please answer the following questions:

1. Explain to an interested layman in a few simple sentences what *zero downtime deployment* means.
2. How does SwarmKit achieve zero downtime deployments?
3. Contrary to traditional (non-containerized) systems, why does a rollback in Docker Swarm *just work*? Explain in a few short sentences.
4. Describe two to three characteristics of a Docker secret.
5. You need to roll out a new version of the `inventory` service. What does your command look like? Here is some more information:
    1. The new image is called `acme/inventory:2.1`.
    2. We want to use a rolling update strategy with a batch size of two tasks.
    3. We want the system to wait for one minute after each batch.

6. You need to update an existing service named `inventory` with a new password that is provided through a Docker secret. The new secret is called `MYSQL_PASSWORD_V2`. The code in the service expects the secret to be called `MYSQL_PASSWORD`. What does the update command look like? (Note: we do not want the code of the service to be changed!)

Further reading

Here are some links to external sources:

- *Apply rolling updates to a service* at https://dockr.ly/2HfGjlD
- *Manage sensitive data with Docker secrets* at https://dockr.ly/2vUNbuH
- *Introducing Docker secrets management* at https://dockr.ly/2k7zwzE
- *From env variables to Docker secrets* at https://bit.ly/2GY3UUB

12
Introduction to Kubernetes

In the previous chapter, we learned how SwarmKit uses rolling updates to achieve zero downtime deployments. We were also introduced to Docker secrets, which are used to share confidential data with an application service running in a Docker Swarm.

In this chapter, we're going to introduce Kubernetes. Kubernetes is currently the clear leader in the container orchestration space. We are starting with a high-level overview of the architecture of a Kubernetes cluster and then we will discuss the main objects used in Kubernetes to define and run containerized applications.

The topics discussed in this chapter are:

- Architecture
- Kubernetes masters
- Cluster nodes
- Introduction to MiniKube
- Kubernetes support in Docker for Mac and Docker for Windows
- Pods
- Kubernetes ReplicaSet
- Kubernetes deployment
- Kubernetes service
- Context-based routing
- Comparing SwarmKit with Kubernetes

After finishing this chapter, you will be able to:

- Draft the high-level architecture of a Kubernetes cluster on a napkin
- Explain three to four main characteristics of a Kubernetes pod
- Describe the role of Kubernetes ReplicaSets in two to three short sentences
- Explain the two to three main responsibilities of a Kubernetes service
- Create a pod in Minikube

- Configure Docker for Mac or Windows to use Kubernetes as orchestrator
- Create a deployment in Docker for Mac or Windows
- Create a Kubernetes service to expose an application service internally (or externally) to the cluster

Technical requirements

The link to the code files can be found here at `https://github.com/ fundamentalsofdocker/labs/tree/master/ch12.`

Architecture

A Kubernetes cluster consists of a set of servers. These servers can be VMs or physical servers. The latter are also called *bare metal*. Each member of the cluster can have one of two roles. It is either a Kubernetes master or a (worker) node. The former is used to manage the cluster while the latter will run application workload. I have put the worker in parentheses since in Kubernetes parlance you only talk about a node when talking about a server that runs application workload. But in Docker parlance and in the Swarm, the equivalent is a *worker node*. I think that the notion of a worker node better describes the role of the server than a simple node.

In a cluster, you have a small and odd number of masters and as many worker nodes as needed. Small clusters might only have a few worker nodes while more realistic clusters might have dozens or even hundreds of worker nodes. Technically, there is no limit on how many worker nodes a cluster can have; in reality, you might experience a significant slowdown in some management operations when dealing with thousands of nodes, though. All members of the cluster need to be connected by a physical network, the so-called **underlay network**.

Kubernetes defines one flat network for the whole cluster. Kubernetes does not provide any networking implementation out of the box, but relies on plugins from third parties. Kubernetes only defines the **Container Network Interface** (CNI) and leaves the implementation to others. The CNI is pretty simple. It basically states that each pod running in the cluster must be able to reach any other pod also running in the cluster without any **Network Address Translation** (NAT) happening in-between. The same must be true between cluster nodes and pods, that is, applications or daemons running directly on a cluster node must be able to reach each pod in the cluster and vice versa.

In the following diagram, I try to illustrate the high-level architecture of a Kubernetes cluster:

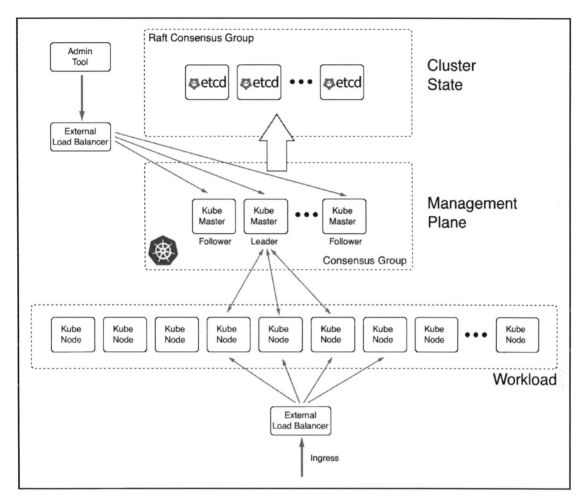

High-level architecture diagram of Kubernetes

The preceding diagram is explained as follows:

- On the top, in the middle we have a cluster of **etcd** nodes. etcd is a distributed key-value store that, in a Kubernetes cluster, is used to store all the state of the cluster. The number of etcd nodes has to be odd as mandated by the Raft consensus protocol which they use to coordinate among themselves. When we talk about the cluster state, we do not include data that is produced or consumed by applications running in the cluster, but rather we're talking about all the information on the topology of the cluster, what services are running, network settings, secrets used, and more. That said, this etcd cluster is really mission critical to the cluster and thus, we should never run only one etcd server in a production environment or any environment that needs to be highly available.
- We then have a cluster of Kubernetes **master** nodes that also form a consensus group among themselves, similar to the etcd nodes. The number of master nodes also has to be an odd number. We can run the cluster with a single master but we should never do that in a production or mission-critical system. There, we always should have at least three master nodes. Since the master nodes are used to manage the whole cluster, we are also talking about the management plane. The master nodes use the etcd cluster as their backing store. It is a good practice to put a **Load Balancer (LB)** in front of the master nodes with a well-known **Fully Qualified Domain Name (FQDN)**, such as `https://admin.example.com`. All tools that are used to manage the Kubernetes cluster should access it through this LB rather than using the public IP address of one of the master nodes. This is shown in the left upper side of the preceding diagram.
- Towards the bottom of the diagram, we have a cluster of worker nodes. The number of nodes can be as low as one and does not have an upper limit. Kubernetes master and worker nodes communicate with each other. It is a bidirectional form of communication which is different to the one we know from Docker Swarm. In Docker Swarm, only the manager nodes communicate with the worker nodes and never the other side around. All ingress traffic accessing the applications running in the cluster should be going through another load balancer. This is the application load balancer or reverse proxy. We never want external traffic to directly access any of the worker nodes.

Now that we have an idea about the high-level architecture of a Kubernetes cluster, let's dive a bit deeper and first look at the Kubernetes master and worker nodes.

Kubernetes master nodes

Kubernetes master nodes are used to manage a Kubernetes cluster. The following is a high-level diagram of such a master:

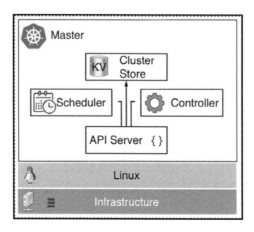

Kubernetes master

At the bottom of the preceding diagram, we have the **Infrastructure**, which can be a VM on-premise or in the cloud or a server (often called bare metal), as well as on-premise or in the cloud. Currently, Kubernetes masters only run on Linux. Most popular Linux distributions such as RHEL, CentOS, and Ubuntu are supported. On this Linux machine, we then have at least the following four Kubernetes services running:

- **API server**: This is the gateway to Kubernetes. All requests to list, create, modify, or delete any resources in the cluster must go through this service. It exposes a REST interface that tools such as `kubectl` use to manage the cluster and applications in the cluster.
- **Controller**: The controller, or more precisely the controller manager, is a control loop that observes the state of the cluster through the API server and makes changes, attempting to move the current or effective state towards the desired state.
- **Scheduler**: The scheduler is a service that tries its best to schedule pods on worker nodes considering various boundary conditions, such as resource requirements, policies, quality of service requirements, and more.
- **Cluster store**: This is an instance of etcd which is used to store all information about the state of the cluster.

To be more precise, etcd, which is used as a cluster store, does not necessarily have to be installed on the same node as the other Kubernetes services. Sometimes, Kubernetes clusters are configured that use standalone clusters of etcd servers, as shown in the architecture diagram in the previous section. But which variant to use is an advanced management decision and is outside of the scope of this book.

We need at least one master, but to achieve high availability, we need three or more master nodes. This is very similar to what we have learned about the manager nodes of a Docker Swarm. In this regard, a Kubernetes master is equivalent to a Swarm manager node.

Kubernetes masters never run application workload. Their sole purpose is to manage the cluster. Kubernetes masters build a Raft consensus group. The Raft protocol is a standard protocol used in situations where a group of members need to make decisions. It is used in many well-known software products such as MongoDB, Docker SwarmKit, and Kubernetes. For a more thorough discussion of the Raft protocol, see the link in the *Further reading* section.

As we have mentioned in the previous section, the state of the Kubernetes cluster is stored in etcd. If the Kubernetes cluster is supposed to be highly available, then etcd must also be configured in HA mode, which normally means that one has at least three etcd instances running on different nodes.

Let's state once again that the whole cluster state is stored in etcd. This includes all the information about all the cluster nodes, all the replica sets, deployments, secrets, network policies, routing information, and so on. It is, therefore, crucial that we have a robust backup strategy in place for this key-value store.

Now, let's look at the nodes that will be running the actual workload of the cluster.

Cluster nodes

Cluster nodes are the nodes onto which Kubernetes schedules application workload. They are the workhorses of the cluster. A Kubernetes cluster can have a few, dozens, hundreds, or even thousands of cluster nodes. Kubernetes has been built from the ground up for high scalability. Don't forget that Kubernetes has been modeled after Google Borg, which has been running tens of thousands of containers for years:

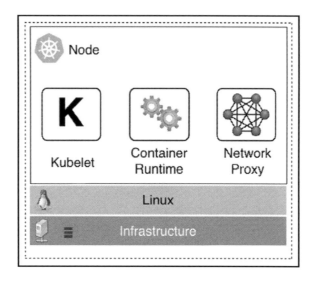

Kubernetes worker node

A worker node can run on a VM or on bare metal, on-premise, or in the cloud. Originally, worker nodes could only be configured on Linux. But since version 1.10 of Kubernetes, worker nodes can also run on Windows Server 2010. It is perfectly fine to have a mixed cluster with Linux and Windows worker nodes.

On each node, we have three services that need to run, which are described as follows:

- **Kubelet**: This is the first and foremost service. Kubelet is what's called the primary node agent. The kubelet service uses pod specifications to make sure all of the containers of the corresponding pods are running and healthy. Pod specifications are files written in YAML or JSON format and they declaratively describe a pod. We will get to know what pods are in the next section. PodSpecs are provided to Kubelet primarily through the API server.
- **Container runtime**: The second service that needs to be present on each worker node is a container runtime. Kubernetes, by default, uses containerd since version 1.9 as its container runtime. Previous to that, it would use the Docker daemon. Other container runtimes such as rkt or CRI-O can be used. The container runtime is responsible for managing and running the individual containers of a pod.

- **kube-proxy**: Finally, there is the kube-proxy. It runs as a daemon and is a simple network proxy and load balancer for all application services running on that particular node.

Now that we have learned about the architecture of Kubernetes and the master and worker nodes, it is time to introduce the tooling that we can use to develop applications targeted at Kubernetes.

Introduction to Minikube

Minikube is a tool that creates a single node Kubernetes cluster in VirtualBox or Hyper-V (other hypervisors are supported) ready to be used during development of a containerized application. We have shown in Chapter 2, *Setting up a Working Environment,* how Minikube and with it the tool `kubectl` can be installed on your Mac or Windows laptop. As stated, Minikube is a single node Kubernetes cluster and thus the node is, at the same time, a Kubernetes master as well as a worker node.

Let's make sure that Minikube is running with the following command:

```
$ minikube start
```

Once Minikube is ready, we can access its single node cluster using `kubectl`. And we should see something similar to the following screenshot:

Listing all nodes in Minikube

As mentioned before, we have a single node cluster with a node called `minikube` . Don't get confused by the value `<none>` in the column `ROLES`; the node plays the role of a worker and a master node at the same time.

Now, let's try to deploy a pod to this cluster. Don't worry about what a pod exactly is at this time; we will dive into all the details about it further along in this chapter. For the moment, just take it as is.

We can use the file `sample-pod.yaml` in the subfolder `ch12` of our `labs` folder to create such a pod. It has the following content:

```
apiVersion: v1
kind: Pod
metadata:
  name: nginx
spec:
  containers:
  - name: nginx
    image: nginx:alpine
    ports:
    - containerPort: 80
    - containerPort: 443
```

Let's use the Kubernetes CLI called `kubectl` to deploy this pod:

```
$ kubectl create -f sample-pod.yaml
pod "nginx" created
```

If we now list all of the pods, we should see this:

```
$ kubectl get pods
NAME    READY   STATUS    RESTARTS   AGE
nginx   1/1     Running   0          51s
```

To be able to access this pod, we need to create a service. Let's use the `sample-service.yaml` file, which has the following content:

```
apiVersion: v1
kind: Service
metadata:
  name: nginx-service
spec:
  type: LoadBalancer
  ports:
  - port: 8080
    targetPort: 80
    protocol: TCP
    name: http
  - port: 443
    protocol: TCP
    name: https
  selector:
    app: nginx
```

Again, don't worry about what exactly a service is at this time. We'll explain it all in detail further down. Let's just create this service:

```
$ kubectl create -f sample-service.yaml
```

Now we can use `curl` to access the service:

```
$ curl -4 http://localhost
```

And we should be receiving the Nginx welcome page as an answer. Before you continue, please remove the two objects you just created:

```
$ kubectl delete po/nginx
$ kubectl delete svc/nginx-service
```

Kubernetes support in Docker for Desktop

Starting from version `18.01-ce`, Docker for Mac and Docker for Windows have started to support Kubernetes out of the box. Developers that want to deploy their containerized applications to Kubernetes can use this orchestrator instead of SwarmKit. Kubernetes support by default is turned off and has to be enabled in the settings. The first time Kubernetes is enabled, Docker for Mac or Windows will need a moment to download all components that are needed to create a single node Kubernetes cluster. Contrary to Minikube, which is also a single node cluster, the version provided by the Docker tools uses containerized versions of all Kubernetes components:

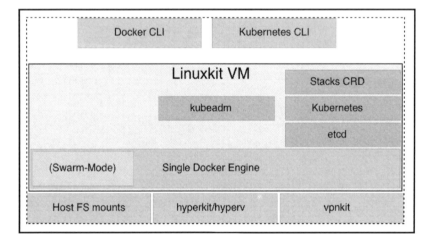

Kubernetes support in Docker for Mac and Windows

The preceding image gives a rough overview on how Kubernetes support has been added to Docker for Mac and Windows. Docker for Mac uses hyperkit to run a LinuxKit-based VM. Docker for Windows uses Hyper-V to achieve the same. Inside the VM, the Docker engine is installed. Part of the engine is SwarmKit, which enables Swarm Mode. Docker for Mac or Windows uses the **kubeadm** tool to set up and configure Kubernetes in that VM. The following three facts are worth mentioning: Kubernetes stores its cluster state in etcd, thus we have etcd running on this VM. Then, we have all the services that make up Kubernetes and finally, some services that support the deployment of Docker stacks from the Docker CLI into Kubernetes. This service is not part of the official Kubernetes distribution, but is Docker specific.

All components of Kubernetes are running in containers in the LinuxKit-based VM. These containers can be hidden through a setting in Docker for Mac or Windows. See further down in the section for a complete list of Kubernetes system containers running on your laptop, if you have Kubernetes support enabled. To avoid repetition, from now on I will only talk about Docker for Desktop instead of Docker for Mac and Docker for Windows. Everything that I will be saying equally applies to both editions.

One big advantage of Docker for Desktop with Kubernetes enabled over Minikube is that the former allows developers to use a single tool to build, test, and run a containerized application targeted at Kubernetes. It is even possible to deploy a multi-service application into Kubernetes using a Docker Compose file.

Now, let's get our hands dirty. First we, have to enable Kubernetes. On the Mac, click on the Docker icon in the menu bar and select **Preferences**. In the dialog box that opens, select **Kubernetes**, as shown in the following screenshot:

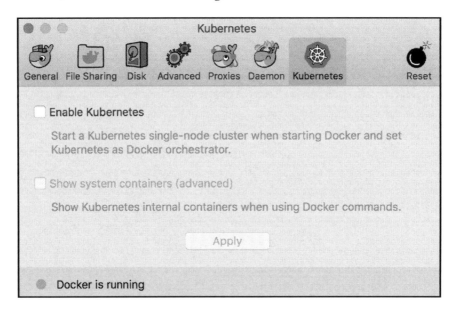

Enabling Kubernetes in Docker for Mac

Then, select the **Enable Kubernetes** checkbox. Also, tick the other checkbox **Show system containers (advanced)**. Then, click the **Apply** button. You will be warned that the installation and configuration of Kubernetes takes a few minutes:

Warning that installation and configuration of Kubernetes takes a while

Click **Install** to start the installation. Now it's time that you take a break and enjoy a nice cup of tea.

Once the installation is finished (which Docker notifies us, by showing a green status icon in the settings dialog), we can test it. Since we now have two Kubernetes clusters running on our laptop, Minikube and Docker for Mac, we need to configure `kubectl` to access the latter one. First, let's list all contexts that we have:

List of contexts for kubectl

Here, we can see that on my laptop, I have the two contexts mentioned before. Currently still, the Minikube context is active, visible by the asterisk in the CURRENT column. We can switch to the `docker-for-desktop` context using the following command:

Changing the context for the Kubernetes CLI

Now, we can use `kubectl` to access the cluster that Docker for Mac just created. We should see this:

```
$ kubectl get nodes
NAME                  STATUS    ROLES    AGE    VERSION
docker-for-desktop    Ready     master   15m    v1.9.2
$
```

The single node Kubernetes cluster created by Docker for Mac

OK, this looks very familiar. It is pretty much the same as what we saw when working with Minikube. The version of Kubernetes that my Docker for Mac is using is 1.9.2. We can also see that the node is a master node.

If we list all containers that are currently running on our Docker for Mac, we get this list (note that I use the `--format` argument to only output the `Container ID` and `Names` of the containers), as shown in the following screenshot:

```
$ docker container ls --format "table {{.ID}}\t{{.Names}}"
CONTAINER ID        NAMES
0cddff5e5a86        k8s_compose_compose-5d4f4d67b6-gbrjh_docker_c3f07e06-2e3b-11e8-860f-025000000001_0
0edd323f6cbb        k8s_compose_compose-api-7bb7b5968f-f98jk_docker_c3e89385-2e3b-11e8-860f-025000000001_0
218514b4fc00        k8s_POD_compose-5d4f4d67b6-gbrjh_docker_c3f07e06-2e3b-11e8-860f-025000000001_0
af8a64fc9f7e        k8s_POD_compose-api-7bb7b5968f-f98jk_docker_c3e89385-2e3b-11e8-860f-025000000001_0
f64fbcd5070c        k8s_sidecar_kube-dns-6f4fd4bdf-9b8kn_kube-system_ab66aab5-2e3b-11e8-860f-025000000001_0
4b6138bd34e7        k8s_dnsmasq_kube-dns-6f4fd4bdf-9b8kn_kube-system_ab66aab5-2e3b-11e8-860f-025000000001_0
bf1394d8e48a        k8s_kubedns_kube-dns-6f4fd4bdf-9b8kn_kube-system_ab66aab5-2e3b-11e8-860f-025000000001_0
a16b63a8f614        k8s_kube-proxy_kube-proxy-p4cf8_kube-system_ab6e9881-2e3b-11e8-860f-025000000001_0
655f8dca4a1c        k8s_POD_kube-proxy-p4cf8_kube-system_ab6e9881-2e3b-11e8-860f-025000000001_0
108b5a2fe05c        k8s_POD_kube-dns-6f4fd4bdf-9b8kn_kube-system_ab66aab5-2e3b-11e8-860f-025000000001_0
23f1808a6f8a        k8s_kube-scheduler_kube-scheduler-docker-for-desktop_kube-system_3a369b3ba7d6d3b6fa014295eab94925_0
89a1032beee7        k8s_kube-controller-manager_kube-controller-manager-docker-for-desktop_kube-system_b098d9f7b8b45512f23bcb04fe3f64f5_0
bb25965301d8        k8s_etcd_etcd-docker-for-desktop_kube-system_7278f85057e8bf5cb81c9f96d3b25320_0
126d0edc29f0        k8s_kube-apiserver_kube-apiserver-docker-for-desktop_kube-system_8d19d05a3d7b137bafa35348cb849dd5_0
d87992c3ea6e        k8s_POD_kube-scheduler-docker-for-desktop_kube-system_3a369b3ba7d6d3b6fa014295eab94925_0
063fdf120ea5        k8s_POD_kube-controller-manager-docker-for-desktop_kube-system_b098d9f7b8b45512f23bcb04fe3f64f5_0
22a1c70f6c4e        k8s_POD_kube-apiserver-docker-for-desktop_kube-system_8d19d05a3d7b137bafa35348cb849dd5_0
91ec502f1467        k8s_POD_etcd-docker-for-desktop_kube-system_7278f85057e8bf5cb81c9f96d3b25320_0
$
```

Kubernetes system containers

In the list, we can identify all the now familiar components that make up Kubernetes such as the:

- API server
- etcd
- Kube proxy
- DNS service
- Kube controller
- Kube scheduler

There are also containers that have the word `compose` in them. These are Docker-specific services and are used to allow us to deploy Docker Compose applications onto Kubernetes. Docker translates the Docker Compose syntax and implicitly creates the necessary Kubernetes objects such as deployments, pods, and services.

Normally, we don't want to clutter our list of containers with these system containers. We can thus uncheck the checkbox **Show system containers** in the settings for Kubernetes.

Now let's try to deploy a Docker Compose application to Kubernetes. Navigate to the subfolder `ch12` of our `labs` folder. We deploy the app as a stack using the `docker-compose.yaml` file:

```
$ docker stack deploy -c docker-compose.yml app
```

This is what we see:

```
$ docker stack deploy -c docker-compose.yml app
Stack app was created
Waiting for the stack to be stable and running...
 - Service db has one container running
 - Service web has one container running
Stack app is stable and running
```

Deploy stack to Kubernetes

We can test the application, for example, using `curl`, and we will see that it is running as expected:

```
$ curl localhost:3000/pet
<html>
<head>
    <link rel="stylesheet" href="main.css">
</head>
<body>
    <div class="container">
        <h4>Cat Gif of the day</h4>
        <img src="http:&#x2F;&#x2F;ak-hdl.buzzfed.com&#x2F;static&#x2F;2013-10&#x2F;en
        <p><small>Courtesy: <a href="http://www.buzzfeed.com/copyranter/the-best-cat-g
        <p>Delivered to you by container web-5c5964c9b8-b5jq9<p>
    </div>
</body>
$
```

Pets application running in Kubernetes on Docker for Mac

Now, you should be curious and wonder what exactly Docker did, when we executed the `docker stack deploy` command. We can use `kubectl` to find out:

```
$ kubectl get all
NAME            DESIRED   CURRENT   UP-TO-DATE   AVAILABLE   AGE
deploy/web      1         1         1            1           9m

NAME              DESIRED   CURRENT   READY   AGE
rs/web-5c5964c9b8 1         1         1       9m

NAME            DESIRED   CURRENT   UP-TO-DATE   AVAILABLE   AGE
deploy/web      1         1         1            1           9m

NAME              DESIRED   CURRENT   READY   AGE
rs/web-5c5964c9b8 1         1         1       9m

NAME              DESIRED   CURRENT   AGE
statefulsets/db   1         1         9m

NAME                      READY   STATUS    RESTARTS   AGE
po/db-0                   1/1     Running   0          9m
po/web-5c5964c9b8-b5jq9   1/1     Running   0          9m

NAME              TYPE           CLUSTER-IP     EXTERNAL-IP   PORT(S)         AGE
svc/db            ClusterIP      None           <none>        55555/TCP       9m
svc/kubernetes    ClusterIP      10.96.0.1      <none>        443/TCP         45m
svc/web           ClusterIP      None           <none>        55555/TCP       9m
svc/web-published LoadBalancer   10.111.43.147  localhost     3000:32590/TCP  9m
$
```

Listing all Kubernetes objects created by docker stack deploy

Docker created a deployment for the `web` service and a stateful set for the `db` service. It also automatically created Kubernetes services for `web` and `db` so that they can be accessed inside the cluster. It also created the Kubernetes service `svc/web-published` which is used for external access.

This is pretty cool to say the least and tremendously decreases friction in the development process for teams targeting Kubernetes as the orchestrator.

Before you continue, please remove the stack from the cluster:

```
$ docker stack rm app
```

And also make sure you reset the context for `kubectl` back to Minikube, as we will be using Minikube for all our samples in this chapter:

```
$ kubectl config use-context minikube
```

Now that we have had an introduction to the tools we can use to develop applications that will eventually run in a Kubernetes cluster, it is time to learn about all the important Kubernetes objects that are used to define and manage such an application. We are starting with the pod.

Pods

Contrary to what is possible in a Docker Swarm, you cannot run containers directly in a Kubernetes cluster. In a Kubernetes cluster, you can only run pods. Pods are the atomic unit of deployment in Kubernetes. A pod is an abstraction of one or many co-located containers that share the same Kernel namespaces, such as the network namespace. No equivalent exists in the Docker SwarmKit. The fact that more than one container can be co-located and sharing the same network namespace is a very powerful concept. The following diagram illustrates two pods:

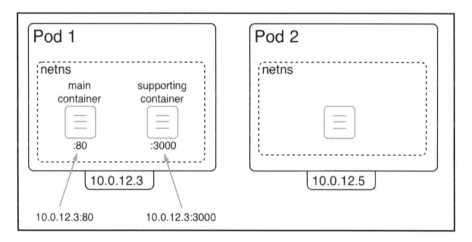

Kubernetes pods

In the preceding diagram, we have two pods, **Pod 1** and **Pod 2**. The first pod contains two containers, while the second one only contains a single container. Each pod gets an IP address assigned by Kubernetes that is unique in the whole Kubernetes cluster. In our case, these are the IP addresses 10.0.12.3 and 10.0.12.5. Both are part of a private subnet managed by the Kubernetes network driver.

A pod can contain one to many containers. All those containers share the same kernel namespaces, and in particular they share the network namespace. This is marked by the dashed rectangle surrounding the containers. Since all containers running in the same pod share the network namespace, each container needs to make sure to use their own port since duplicate ports are not allowed in a single network namespace. In this case, in **Pod 1**, the main container is using port 80 while the supporting container is using port 3000.

Requests from other pods or nodes can use the pod's IP address combined with the corresponding port number to access the individual containers. For example, you could access the application running in the main container of **Pod 1** through 10.0.12.3:80.

Comparing Docker container and Kubernetes pod networking

Now, let's compare Docker's container networking and the networking of a Kubernetes pod. In the diagram here, we have the former on the left hand and the latter on the right hand side:

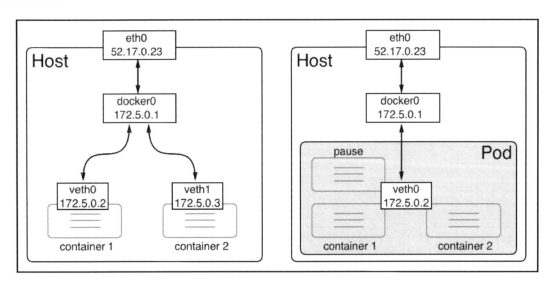

Containers in Pod sharing network namespace

When a Docker container is created and no specific network is specified, then the Docker engine creates a **virtual ethernet** (**veth**) endpoint. The first container gets **veth0** and the next one **veth1**, and so on. These virtual ethernet endpoints are connected to the Linux bridge **docker0** that Docker automatically creates upon installation. Traffic is routed from the bridge **docker0** to every connected veth endpoint. Every container has its own network namespace. No two containers use the same namespace. This is on purpose, to isolate applications running inside the containers from each other.

For a Kubernetes pod, the situation is different. When creating a new pod, Kubernetes first creates a so-called pause container whose only purpose is to create and manage the namespaces that the pod will share with all containers. Other than that, it does nothing useful, but is just sleeping. The **pause** container is connected to the bridge **docker0** through **veth0**. Any subsequent container that will be part of the pod is using a special feature of the Docker engine that allows it to reuse an existing network namespace. The syntax to do so looks like this:

```
$ docker container create --net container:pause ...
```

The important part is the `--net` argument, which uses as a value `container:<container name>`. If we create a new container this way, then Docker does not create a new veth endpoint, but the container uses the same one as the `pause` container.

Another important consequence of multiple containers sharing the same network namespace is the way they communicate with each other. Let's consider the following situation of a pod containing two containers, one listening at port `80` and the other at port `3000`:

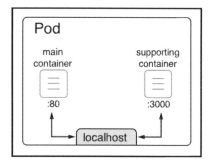

Containers in pods communicate via localhost

When two containers use the same Linux kernel network namespace, they can communicate with each other through localhost, similar to when two processes are running on the same host they can communicate with each other through localhost too. This is illustrated in the preceding diagram. From the main container, the containerized application inside it can reach out to the service running inside the supporting container through `http://localhost:3000`.

Sharing the network namespace

After all this theory, you might be wondering how a pod is actually created by Kubernetes. Kubernetes is only using what Docker provides. So, *how does this network namespace share work?* First, Kubernetes creates the so-called `pause` container as mentioned previously. This container has no other function than to reserve the kernel namespaces for that pod and keep them alive, even if no other container inside the pod is running. Let's simulate the creation of a pod, then. We start by creating the `pause` container and take Nginx for this purpose:

```
$ docker container run -d --name pause nginx:alpine
```

And now we add a second container called `main`, attaching it to the same network namespace as the `pause` container:

```
$ docker container run --name main -dit \
    --net container:pause \
    alpine:latest /bin/sh
```

Since the `pause` and the sample container are both part of the same network namespace, they can reach each other through `localhost`. To show this, we first have to `exec` into the main container:

```
$ docker exec -it main /bin/sh
```

Now, we can test the connection to Nginx running in the `pause` container and listening on port `80`. Here is what we get if we use the `wget` utility to do so:

```
/ # wget -qO - localhost
<!DOCTYPE html>
<html>
<head>
<title>Welcome to nginx!</title>
<style>
    body {
        width: 35em;
        margin: 0 auto;
        font-family: Tahoma, Verdana, Arial, sans-serif;
    }
</style>
</head>
<body>
<h1>Welcome to nginx!</h1>
<p>If you see this page, the nginx web server is successfully installed and
working. Further configuration is required.</p>

<p>For online documentation and support please refer to
<a href="http://nginx.org/">nginx.org</a>.<br/>
Commercial support is available at
<a href="http://nginx.com/">nginx.com</a>.</p>

<p><em>Thank you for using nginx.</em></p>
</body>
</html>
/ #
```

Two containers sharing the same network namespace

The output shows that we can indeed access Nginx on `localhost`. This is proof that the two containers share the same namespace. If that is not enough, we can use the `ip` tool to show `eth0` inside both containers and we will get the exact same result, specifically, the same IP address which is one of the characteristics of a pod, where all its containers share the same IP address:

```
/ # ip a show eth0
11: eth0@if12: <BROADCAST,MULTICAST,UP,LOWER_UP,M-DOWN> mtu 1500 qdisc noqueue state UP
    link/ether 02:42:ac:11:00:02 brd ff:ff:ff:ff:ff:ff
    inet 172.17.0.2/16 brd 172.17.255.255 scope global eth0
       valid_lft forever preferred_lft forever
/ #
```

Displaying the properties of eth0 with the ip tool

If we inspect the `bridge` network, we can only see that the `pause` container is listed. The other container didn't get an entry in the `Containers` list since it is reusing the `pause` container's endpoint:

```
$ docker network inspect bridge
[
    {
        "Name": "bridge",
        "Id": "41909c08794041cabc3a9d2e034426f2344f5310bd1cbfcbae65c5f25a05f541",
        "Created": "2018-03-26T22:16:44.790966007Z",
        "Scope": "local",
        "Driver": "bridge",
        "EnableIPv6": false,
        "IPAM": {
            "Driver": "default",
            "Options": null,
            "Config": [
                {
                    "Subnet": "172.17.0.0/16",
                    "Gateway": "172.17.0.1"
                }
            ]
        },
        "Internal": false,
        "Attachable": false,
        "Ingress": false,
        "ConfigFrom": {
            "Network": ""
        },
        "ConfigOnly": false,
        "Containers": {
            "8965ec65ca4a1de1f1d9c987b68e888c1115cf64f44ba3842953d29a2b9a0ea8": {
                "Name": "pause",
                "EndpointID": "890fc0527f7cb6484d24b7886772db23bb5a0502fe34269fc306277ea7a6f95e",
                "MacAddress": "02:42:ac:11:00:02",
                "IPv4Address": "172.17.0.2/16",
                "IPv6Address": ""
            }
        },
        "Options": {
            "com.docker.network.bridge.default_bridge": "true",
            "com.docker.network.bridge.enable_icc": "true",
            "com.docker.network.bridge.enable_ip_masquerade": "true",
            "com.docker.network.bridge.host_binding_ipv4": "0.0.0.0",
            "com.docker.network.bridge.name": "docker0",
            "com.docker.network.driver.mtu": "1500"
        },
        "Labels": {}
    }
]
$
```

Inspecting the Docker default bridge network

Pod life cycle

We have learned earlier in this book that containers have a life cycle. A container is initialized, run, and ultimately exited. When a container exits, it can do this gracefully with an exit code zero or it can terminate with an error, which is equivalent to a nonzero exit code.

Similarly, a pod has a life cycle. Due to the fact that a pod can contain more than one container, this life cycle is slightly more complicated than the one of a single container. The life cycle of a pod is sketched in the following diagram:

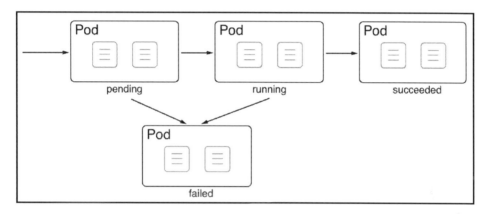

Life cycle of Kubernetes pods

When a pod is created on a cluster node, it first enters into **pending** status. Once all containers of the pod are up and running, the pod enters into **running** status. The pod only enters into this state if all its containers run successfully. If the pod is asked to terminate, it will request all its containers to terminate. If all containers terminate with exit code zero, then the pod enters into **succeeded** status. This is the happy path.

Now, let's look at some scenarios that lead to the pod being in **failed** state. There are three possible scenarios:

- If, during the startup of the pod, at least one container is not able to run and fails (that is it exits with a nonzero exit code), the pod enters from the **pending** state into the **failed** state

- If the pod is in running status and one of the containers suddenly crashes or exits with a nonzero exit code then the pod transitions from the **running** state into the **failed** state
- If the pod is asked to terminate and during the shutdown at least one of the containers exits with a nonzero exit code, then the pod also enters into the **failed** state

Pod specification

When creating a pod in a Kubernetes cluster, we can use either an imperative or a declarative approach. We have discussed the difference of the two approaches earlier in this book, but to rephrase the important aspect, using a declarative approach signifies that we write a manifest which describes the end state we want to achieve. We leave the details of the *how* to the orchestrator. The end state that we want to achieve is also called the **desired state**. In general, the declarative approach is strongly preferred in all of the established orchestrators, and Kubernetes is no exception.

Thus, in this chapter, we will exclusively concentrate on the declarative approach. Manifests or specifications for a pod can be written using either YAML or JSON format. In this chapter, we will concentrate on YAML since it is easier to read for us humans. Let's look at a sample specification. Here is the content of the pod.yaml file that can be found in the ch12 subfolder of our labs folder:

```
apiVersion: v1
kind: Pod
metadata:
  name: web-pod
spec:
  containers:
  - name: web
    image: nginx:alpine
    ports:
    - containerPort: 80
```

Each specification in Kubernetes starts with the version information. Pods have been around for quite some time and thus the API version is v1. The second line specifies the type of Kubernetes object or resource we want to define. Obviously, in this case, we want to specify a pod. Next follows a block with metadata. At a bare minimum, we need to give the pod a name. Here, we call it web-pod. The next block that follows is the spec block, which contains the specification of the pod. The most important part (and the only one in this simple sample) is the list of all containers that are part of this pod. We only have one container here, but multiple containers are possible. The name we choose for our container is web and the container image is nginx:alpine. Finally, we define the list of ports the container is exposing.

Once we have authored such a specification, we can apply it to the cluster using the Kubernetes CLI kubectl. In a Terminal, navigate to the ch12 subfolder and execute the following command:

```
$ kubectl create -f pod.yaml
```

Which will respond with pod "web-pod" created. We can then list all pods in the cluster with kubectl get pods:

```
$ kubectl get pods
NAME        READY    STATUS     RESTARTS    AGE
web-pod     1/1      Running    0           2m
```

As expected, we have one of one pods in running status. The pod is called `web-pod`, as defined. We can get more detailed information about the running pod by using the `describe` command:

```
$ kubectl describe pod/web-pod
Name:           web-pod
Namespace:      default
Node:           minikube/192.168.99.105
Start Time:     Sun, 25 Mar 2018 22:47:49 -0500
Labels:         <none>
Annotations:    <none>
Status:         Running
IP:             172.17.0.3
Containers:
  web:
    Container ID:   docker://e8784dfc2e3fcf1de4bfb9ab1508176799b6024b96d9447126e1db5dd5e2201f
    Image:          nginx:alpine
    Image ID:       docker-pullable://nginx@sha256:17c4704e19a11cd47545fa3c17e6903fc88672021f7f907f212d6663baf6ab57
    Port:           80/TCP
    State:          Running
      Started:      Sun, 25 Mar 2018 22:47:50 -0500
    Ready:          True
    Restart Count:  0
    Environment:    <none>
    Mounts:
      /var/run/secrets/kubernetes.io/serviceaccount from default-token-fhdsm (ro)
Conditions:
  Type           Status
  Initialized    True
  Ready          True
  PodScheduled   True
Volumes:
  default-token-fhdsm:
    Type:         Secret (a volume populated by a Secret)
    SecretName:   default-token-fhdsm
    Optional:     false
QoS Class:        BestEffort
Node-Selectors:   <none>
Tolerations:      <none>
Events:
  Type     Reason                Age    From                 Message
  ----     ------                ----   ----                 -------
  Normal   Scheduled             5m     default-scheduler    Successfully assigned web-pod to minikube
  Normal   SuccessfulMountVolume 5m     kubelet, minikube    MountVolume.SetUp succeeded for volume "default-token-fhdsm"
  Normal   Pulled                5m     kubelet, minikube    Container image "nginx:alpine" already present on machine
  Normal   Created               5m     kubelet, minikube    Created container
  Normal   Started               5m     kubelet, minikube    Started container
$
```

Describing a pod running in the cluster

Please note the notation `pod/web-pod` in the previous `describe` command. Other variants are possible, for example, `pods/web-pod` or `po/web-pod`. `pod` and `po` are aliases of `pods`. The `kubectl` tool defines many aliases to make our lives a bit easier.

The `describe` command gives us a plethora of valuable information about the pod, not the least of which is the list of events that happened with this pod affected. The list is shown at the end of the output.

The information in the `Containers` section is very similar to what we find in a `docker container inspect` output.

We also see a `Volumes` section with some entry of type `Secret`. We will discuss Kubernetes secrets in the next chapter. Volumes, on the other hand, are discussed next.

Pods and volumes

In the chapter about containers, we have learned about volumes and their purpose to access and store persistent data. As containers can mount volumes, pods can do so as well. In reality, it is really the containers inside the pod that mount the volumes, but that is just a semantic detail. Let's first see how we can define a volume in Kubernetes. Kubernetes supports a plethora of volume types and we're not diving into too much detail about this. Let's just create a local volume implicitly by defining a `PersistentVolumeClaim` called `my-data-claim`:

```
apiVersion: v1
kind: PersistentVolumeClaim
metadata:
  name: my-data-claim
spec:
  accessModes:
    - ReadWriteOnce
  resources:
    requests:
      storage: 2Gi
```

We have defined a claim that requests 2 GB of data. Let's create this claim:

```
$ kubectl create -f volume-claim.yaml
```

We can list the claim using `kubectl` (`pvc` is the shortcut for `PersistentVolumeClaim`):

List of PersistentStorageClaim objects in the cluster

In the output, we can see that the claim has implicitly created a volume called `pvc-<ID>`. We are now ready to use the volume created by the claim in a pod. Let's use a modified version of the pod specification that we used previously. We can find this updated specification in the `pod-with-vol.yaml` file in the `ch12` folder. Let's look at this specification in detail:

```
apiVersion: v1
kind: Pod
metadata:
  name: web-pod
spec:
  containers:
  - name: web
    image: nginx:alpine
    ports:
    - containerPort: 80
    volumeMounts:
    - name: my-data
      mountPath: /data
  volumes:
  - name: my-data
    persistentVolumeClaim:
      claimName: my-data-claim
```

In the last four lines, in the block `volumes`, we define the list of volumes we want to use for this pod. The volumes that we list here can be used by any of the containers of the pod. In our particular case, we only have one volume. We define that we have a volume `my-data` that is a persistent volume claim whose claim name is the one we just created before. Then in the container specification, we have the `volumeMounts` block where we define the volume we want to use and the (absolute) path inside the container where the volume will be mounted. In our case, we mount the volume to the `/data` folder of the container filesystem. Let's create this pod:

```
$ kubectl create -f pod-with-vol.yaml
```

Then, we can `exec` into the container to double-check that the volume has mounted by navigating to the `/data` folder, create a file there, and exit the container:

```
$ kubectl exec -it web-pod -- /bin/sh
/ # cd /data
/data # echo "Hello world!" > sample.txt
/data # exit
```

If we are right, then the data in this container must persist beyond the life cycle of the pod. Thus, let's delete the pod and then recreate it and exec into it to make sure the data is still there. This is the result:

```
$ kubectl delete po/web-pod
pod "web-pod" deleted
$ kubectl create -f pod-with-vol.yaml
pod "web-pod" created
$ kubectl exec -it web-pod -- /bin/sh
/ # cat /data/sample.txt
Hello world!
/ #
```

Data stored in volume survives pod recreation

Kubernetes ReplicaSet

A single pod in an environment with high availability requirements is insufficient. *What if the pod crashes? What if we need to update the application running inside the pod but cannot afford any service interruption?* These questions and more can only indicate that pods alone are not enough and we need a higher-level concept that can manage multiple instances of the same pod. In Kubernetes, the **ReplicaSet** is used to define and manage such a collection of identical pods that are running on different cluster nodes. Among other things, a ReplicaSet defines which container images are used by the containers running inside a pod and how many instances of the pod will run in the cluster. These properties and the many others are called the desired state.

The ReplicaSet is responsible for reconciling the desired state at all times, if the actual state ever deviates from it. Here is a Kubernetes ReplicaSet:

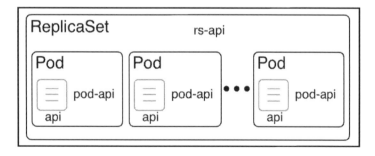

Kubernetes ReplicaSet

In the preceding diagram, we see such a ReplicaSet called **rs-api,** which governs a number of pods. The pods are called **pod-api**. The ReplicaSet is responsible for making sure that at any given time there are always the desired number of pods running. If one of the pods crashes for whatever reason, the ReplicaSet schedules a new pod on a node with free resources instead. If there are more pods than the desired number, then the ReplicaSet kills the superfluous pods. We can thus say that the ReplicaSet guarantees a self-healing and scalable set of pods. There is no limit on how many pods a ReplicaSet can be comprised of.

ReplicaSet specification

Similar to what we have learned about pods, Kubernetes also allows us to either imperatively or declaratively define and create a `ReplicaSet`. Since the declarative approach is by far the recommended one in most cases, we're going to concentrate on this approach. Here is a sample specification for a Kubernetes `ReplicaSet`:

```
apiVersion: apps/v1
kind: ReplicaSet
metadata:
  name: rs-web
spec:
  selector:
    matchLabels:
      app: web
  replicas: 3
  template:
    metadata:
      labels:
        app: web
    spec:
      containers:
      - name: nginx
        image: nginx:alpine
        ports:
        - containerPort: 80
```

This looks an awful lot like the pod specification we introduced earlier. Let's concentrate on the differences, then. First, on line 2, we have the kind which was `Pod` and is now `ReplicaSet`. Then, on lines 6–8, we have a selector which determines the pods that will be part of the `ReplicaSet`. In this case, it is all pods that have a label `app` with the value `web`. Then, on line 9, we define how many replicas of the pod we want to run; three, in this case. Finally, we have the `template` section which first defines the `metadata` and then the `spec` which defines the containers that run inside the pod. In our case, we have a single container using the `nginx:alpine` image and exporting port `80`.

The really important elements are the number of replicas and the selector which specifies the set of pods governed by the ReplicaSet.

In our ch12 folder, we have a file called replicaset.yaml that contains the preceding specification exactly. Let's use this file to create the ReplicaSet:

```
$ kubectl create -f replicaset.yaml
replicaset "rs-web" created
```

If we list all the ReplicaSets in the cluster, we get this (rs is a shortcut for replicaset):

```
$ kubectl get rs
NAME        DESIRED    CURRENT    READY    AGE
rs-web      3          3          3        51s
```

In the preceding output, we can see that we have a single ReplicaSet called rs-web whose desired state is three (pods). The current state also shows three pods and all three pods are ready. We can also list all pods in the system and we get this:

```
$ kubectl get pods
NAME             READY    STATUS     RESTARTS    AGE
rs-web-6qzld     1/1      Running    0           4m
rs-web-frj2m     1/1      Running    0           4m
rs-web-zd2kt     1/1      Running    0           4m
```

Here, we see our three expected pods. The names of the pods are using the name of the ReplicaSet with a unique ID appended for each pod. In the READY column, we see how many containers are defined in the pod and how many of them are ready. In our case, we have only a single container per pod and in each case, it is ready. Thus, the overall status of the pod is Running. We also see how many times each pod had to be restarted. In our case, we did not have any restarts yet.

Self-healing

Now let's test the magic powers of the self-healing of the ReplicaSet by randomly killing one of its pods and observing what's going to happen. Let's delete the first pod from the previous list:

```
$ kubectl delete po/rs-web-6qzld
pod "rs-web-6qzld" deleted
```

And then, let's list all pods again. We expect to see only two pods, *right*? Wrong:

```
$ kubectl get pods
NAME            READY    STATUS      RESTARTS    AGE
rs-web-frj2m    1/1      Running     0           22h
rs-web-q6cr7    1/1      Running     0           41s
rs-web-zd2kt    1/1      Running     0           22h
$
```

List of pods after having killed a pod of the ReplicaSet

OK, evidently the second pod in the list has been recreated as we can see from the AGE column. This is auto-healing in action. Let's see what we discover if we describe the ReplicaSet:

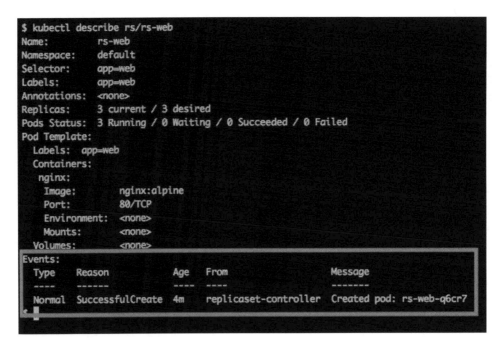

```
$ kubectl describe rs/rs-web
Name:          rs-web
Namespace:     default
Selector:      app=web
Labels:        app=web
Annotations:   <none>
Replicas:      3 current / 3 desired
Pods Status:   3 Running / 0 Waiting / 0 Succeeded / 0 Failed
Pod Template:
  Labels:  app=web
  Containers:
   nginx:
    Image:         nginx:alpine
    Port:          80/TCP
    Environment:   <none>
    Mounts:        <none>
  Volumes:         <none>
Events:
  Type     Reason            Age    From                    Message
  ----     ------            ---    ----                    -------
  Normal   SuccessfulCreate  4m     replicaset-controller   Created pod: rs-web-q6cr7
```

Describe the ReplicaSet

And indeed, we find an entry under Events that tells us that the ReplicaSet created the new pod rs-web-q6cr7.

Kubernetes deployment

Kubernetes takes the single responsibility principle very seriously. All Kubernetes objects are designed to do one thing and one thing only. And they are designed to do this one thing very well. In this regard, we have to understand Kubernetes **ReplicaSets** and **Deployments**. The ReplicaSet, as we have learned, is responsible for achieving and reconciling the desired state of an application service. This means that the ReplicaSet manages a set of pods.

The **Deployment** augments a ReplicaSet by providing rolling update and rollback functionality on top of it. In Docker Swarm, the swarm service would incorporate the functionality of both the ReplicaSet and the Deployment. In this regard, SwarmKit is much more monolithic than Kubernetes. The following diagram shows the relationship of a Deployment to a ReplicaSet:

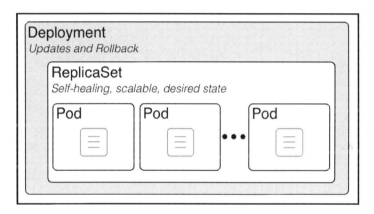

Kubernetes deployment

In the preceding diagram, the **ReplicaSet** is defining and governing a set of identical pods. The main characteristics of the ReplicaSet are that it is self-healing, scalable, and always does its best to reconcile the desired state. The Kubernetes deployment in turn adds rolling update and rollback functionality to the plate. In this regard, a deployment is really a wrapper object to a ReplicaSet.

We will learn more about rolling updates and rollbacks in the next chapter of this book.

Kubernetes service

The moment we start to work with applications consisting of more than one application service, we have a need for service discovery. In the following diagram, we illustrate this problem:

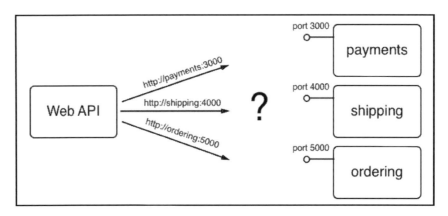

Service discovery

In this diagram, we have a **Web API** service that needs access to three other services—**payments**, **shipping**, and **ordering**. The Web API should at no time have to care how and where to find those three services. In the API code, we just want to use the name of the service we want to reach and its port number. A sample would be the URL `http://payments:3000` that is used to access an instance of the payments service.

In Kubernetes, the payments application service is represented by a ReplicaSet of pods. Due to the nature of highly distributed systems, we cannot assume that pods have stable endpoints. A pod can come and go in a wimp. But that's a problem if we need to access the corresponding application service from an internal or external client. If we cannot rely on pod endpoints being stable, *what else can we do?*

This is where Kubernetes services come into play. They are meant to provide stable endpoints to ReplicaSets or Deployments, as shown here:

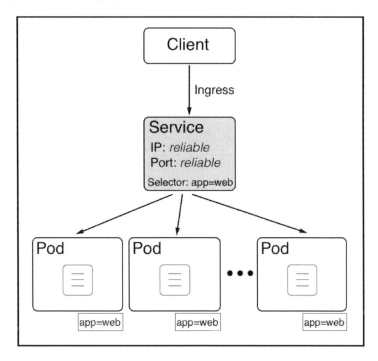

Kubernetes service providing stable endpoints to clients

In the preceding diagram, in the center, we see such a Kubernetes service. It provides a reliable cluster-wide IP address also called a **virtual IP (VIP)**, as well as a reliable port that's unique in the whole cluster. The pods that the Kubernetes service is proxying are determined by the selector defined in the service specification. Selectors are always based on labels. Every Kubernetes object can have zero to many labels assigned. In our case, the selector is **app=web**, that is, all pods that have a label called app with a value of web are proxied.

Context-based routing

Often, we want to configure context-based routing for our Kubernetes cluster. Kubernetes offers us various ways to do so. The preferred and most scalable way at this time is to use an **IngressController** for this job. The following diagram tries to illustrate how this ingress controller works:

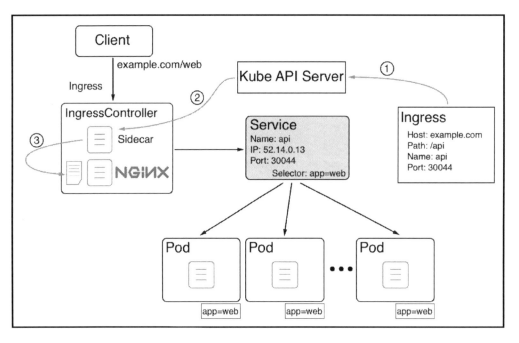

Context-based routing using a Kubernetes ingress controller

In this diagram, we can see how context-based (or layer 7) routing works when using an ingress controller, such as Nginx. Here, we have a deployment of an application service called **web**. All the pods of this application service have a label **app=web**. We then have a Kubernetes service called web that provides a stable endpoint to those pods. The service has a (virtual) IP of 52.14.0.13 and exposes port 30044. That is, if a request comes to any node of the Kubernetes cluster for the name **web** and port 30044, then it is forwarded to this service. The service then load balances the request to one of the pods.

So far so good, *but how is an ingress request from a client to the URL* `http[s]://example.com/web` *routed to our web service?* First, we have to define the routing from a context-based request to a corresponding `<service name>/<port>` request. This is done through an **Ingress** object:

1. In the Ingress object, we define the host and path as the source and the (service) name, and the port as the target. When this Ingress object is created by the Kubernetes API server, then a process that runs as sidecar in the IngressController picks this change up
2. Modifies the configuration file of the Nginx reverse proxy
3. By adding the new route, Nginx is then asked to reload its configuration and thus will be able to correctly route any incoming requests to `http[s]://example.com/web`.

Comparing SwarmKit with Kubernetes

Now that we have learned a lot of details about the most important resources in Kubernetes, it is helpful to compare the two orchestrators, SwarmKit and Kubernetes, by matching the important resources. Here is the table:

SwarmKit	Kubernetes	Description
Swarm	Cluster	Set of servers/nodes managed by the respective orchestrator.
Node	Cluster member	Single host (physical or virtual) which is a member of the swarm/cluster.
Manager node	Master	Node managing the swarm/cluster. This is the control plane.
Worker node	Node	Member of the swarm/cluster running application workload.
Container	Container**	Instance of a container image running on a node. In a Kubernetes cluster, we cannot run a container.
Task	Pod	Instance of a service (swarm) or ReplicaSet (Kubernetes) running on a node. A task manages a single container while a Pod contains one to many containers that are all sharing the same network namespace.

Service	ReplicaSet	Defines and reconciles the desired state of an application service consisting of multiple instances.
Service	Deployment	A deployment is a ReplicaSet augmented with rolling update and rollback capabilities.
Routing Mesh	Service	The Swarm Routing Mesh provides L4 routing and load balancing using IPVS. A Kubernetes service is an abstraction which defines a logical set of pods and a policy by which to access them. It is a stable endpoint for a set of pods.
Stack	Stack **	Definition of an application consisting of multiple (Swarm) services. While stacks are not native to Kubernetes, Docker's tool Docker for Mac or Windows, will translate them for deployment onto a Kubernetes cluster.
Network	Network policy	Swarm **software-defined networks** (**SDNs**) are used to firewall containers. Kubernetes only defines a single flat network. Every pod can reach every other pod and or node, unless network policies are explicitly defined to constrain inter-pod communication.

Summary

In this chapter, we have learned the basics of Kubernetes. We had an overview of its architecture and an introduction into the main resources used to define and run applications in a Kubernetes cluster. We also introduced Minikube and Kubernetes support in Docker for Mac and Windows.

In the next chapter, we're going to deploy an application into a Kubernetes cluster. Then, we're going to be updating one of the services of this application using a zero downtime strategy. Finally, we're going to instrument application services running in Kubernetes with sensitive data using secrets. Stay tuned.

Questions

Please answer the following questions to assess your learning progress:

1. Explain in a few short sentences what the role of a Kubernetes master is.
2. List the elements that need to be present on each Kubernetes (worker) node.
3. Yes or No: We cannot run individual containers in a Kubernetes cluster.
4. Explain the reason why containers of a pod can use `localhost` to communicate with each other.
5. What is the purpose of the so-called pause container in a pod?
6. Bob tells you: *Our application consists of three Docker images:* `web`, `inventory`, *and* `db`. *Since we can run multiple containers in a Kubernetes pod, we are going to deploy all the services of our application in a single pod.* List three to four reasons why this is a bad idea.
7. Explain in your own words why we need Kubernetes ReplicaSets.
8. Under which circumstances do we need Kubernetes deployments?
9. List at least three types of Kubernetes services and explain their purposes and their differences.

Further reading

Here is a list of articles with more detailed information on various topics discussed in this chapter:

- *The Raft Consensus Algorithm* at `https://raft.github.io/`
- *Docker Compose and Kubernetes with Docker for Desktop* at `https://dockr.ly/2G8Iqb9`

13

Deploying, Updating, and Securing an Application with Kubernetes

In the last chapter, we learned about the basics of the container orchestrator, Kubernetes. We got a high-level overview of the architecture of Kubernetes and learned much about the important objects used by Kubernetes to define and manage a containerized application.

In this chapter, we will learn how to deploy, update, and scale applications into a Kubernetes cluster. We will also explain how zero downtime deployments are achieved to enable disruption-free updates and rollbacks of mission critical applications. Finally, in this chapter, we are introducing Kubernetes secrets as a means to configure services with and protect sensitive data.

The chapter covers the following topics:

- Deploying a first application
- Zero-downtime deployments
- Kubernetes secrets

After working through this chapter, you will be able to:

- Deploy a multi-service application into a Kubernetes cluster
- Update an application service running in Kubernetes without causing downtime
- Define secrets in a Kubernetes cluster
- Configure an application service to use Kubernetes secrets

Technical requirements

In this chapter, we're going to use Minikube on our local computer. Please refer to `Chapter 2`, *Setting up a Working Environment,* for more information on how to install and use Minikube.

The code for this chapter can be found in the `ch13` subfolder of the `labs` folder. Please make sure you have cloned the GitHub repository at `https://github.com/fundamentalsofdocker/labs`, as described in `Chapter 2`, *Setting up a Working Environment.*

In your Terminal, navigate to the folder `labs/ch13`.

Deploying a first application

We will take our pets application, which we first introduced in `Chapter 8`, *Docker Compose,* and deploy it into a Kubernetes cluster. Our cluster will be Minikube, which, as you know, is a single-node cluster. But, from the perspective of a deployment, it doesn't really matter how big the cluster is and where the cluster is located—in the cloud, in your company's data center, or on your personal workstation.

Deploying the web component

Just as a reminder, our application consists of two application services, the Node.js-based web component and the backing PostgreSQL database. In the previous chapter, we learned that we need to define a Kubernetes `Deployment` object for each application service we want to deploy. Let's do this first for the web component. As always in this book, we will choose the declarative way of defining our objects. Here is the YAML defining a `Deployment` object for the web component:

```
! web-deployment.yaml  ✕                                    ⌕
 1    apiVersion: extensions/v1beta1
 2    kind: Deployment
 3    metadata:
 4      name: web
 5    spec:
 6      replicas: 1
 7      selector:
 8        matchLabels:
 9          app: pets
10          service: web
11      template:
12        metadata:
13          labels:
14            app: pets
15            service: web
16        spec:
17          containers:
18            - image: fundamentalsofdocker/ch08-web:1.0
19              name: web
20              ports:
21                - containerPort: 3000
22                  protocol: TCP
23
```

Kubernetes deployment definition for the web component

The preceding deployment definition can be found in the `web-deployment.yaml` file in the `labs` folder `ch13`. The lines of code are as follows:

- **On line 4**: We define the `name` for our `Deployment` object as `web`
- **On line 6**: We declare that we want to have one instance of the `web` component running
- **From line 8 to 10**: We define which pods will be part of our deployment, namely those which have the labels `app` and `service` with values, `pets` and `web` respectively
- **On line 11**: In the template for the pods starting at line 11, we define that each pod will have the two labels `app` and `service` applied

- **From line 17**: We define the single container that will be running in the pod. The image for the container is our well-known `fundamentalsofdocker/ch08-web:1.0` image and the name of the container will be `web`

- **Ports**: Finally, we declare that the container exposes port 3000 for TCP-type traffic

 Please make sure that you have set the context of `kubectl` to `Minikube`. See `Chapter 2`, *Setting up a Working Environment*, for details on how to do that.

We can deploy this `Deployment` object using `kubectl`:

```
$ kubectl create -f web-deployment.yaml
```

We can double-check that the deployment has been created again using our Kubernetes CLI, and we should see the following output:

```
$ kubectl get all
NAME           DESIRED   CURRENT   UP-TO-DATE   AVAILABLE   AGE
deploy/web     1         1         1            1           5m

NAME                DESIRED   CURRENT   READY   AGE
rs/web-769b88f67    1         1         1       5m

NAME           DESIRED   CURRENT   UP-TO-DATE   AVAILABLE   AGE
deploy/web     1         1         1            1           5m

NAME                DESIRED   CURRENT   READY   AGE
rs/web-769b88f67    1         1         1       5m

NAME                     READY   STATUS    RESTARTS   AGE
po/web-769b88f67-4fccx   1/1     Running   0          5m

NAME             TYPE        CLUSTER-IP   EXTERNAL-IP   PORT(S)   AGE
svc/kubernetes   ClusterIP   10.96.0.1    <none>        443/TCP   8d
$
```

Listing all resources running in Minikube

 At the time of writing, there seems to be a bug in Minikube or `kubectl` that displays certain resources twice when using the command `kubectl get all`. You can just ignore the duplicate output.

In the preceding output, we see that Kubernetes created three objects—the deployment, a pertaining `ReplicaSet`, and a single pod (remember we specified that we want one replica only). The current state corresponds to the desired state for all three objects, thus we are fine so far.

Now, the web service needs to be exposed to the public. For this, we need to define a Kubernetes `Service` object of type `NodePort`. Here is the definition, which can be found in the `web-service.yaml` file in the `labs` folder `ch13`:

```
web-service.yaml  ×
1    apiVersion: v1
2    kind: Service
3    metadata:
4      name: web
5    spec:
6      type: NodePort
7      ports:
8      - port: 3000
9        protocol: TCP
10     selector:
11       app: pets
12       service: web
```

Definition of the Service object for our web component

The preceding lines of codes are as follows:

- **On line 4**: We set the name of this `Service` object to `web`.
- **On line 6**: We define the type of `Service` object we're using. Since the `web` component has to be accessible from outside of the cluster, this cannot be a `Service` object of type `ClusterIP` but must be either of type `NodePort` or `LoadBalancer`. We have discussed the various types of Kubernetes services in the previous chapter and so will not go into further detail about this. In our sample, we're using a `NodePort` type of service.

- **On lines 8 and 9**: We specify that we want to expose port `3000` for access through the TCP protocol. Kubernetes will map container port `3000` automatically to a free host port in the range of 30,000 to 32,768. Which port Kubernetes effectively chooses can be determined using the `kubectl get service` or `kubectl describe` command for the service after it has been created.
- **From line 10 to 12**: We define the filter criteria for the pods for which this service will be a stable endpoint. In this case, it is all pods that have the labels `app` and `service` with values `pets` and `web` respectively.

Having this specification for a `Service` object, we can create it using `kubectl`:

```
$ kubectl create -f web-service.yaml
```

We can list all services to see the result of the preceding command:

```
$ kubectl get services
NAME          TYPE        CLUSTER-IP      EXTERNAL-IP   PORT(S)           AGE
kubernetes    ClusterIP   10.96.0.1       <none>        443/TCP           9d
web           NodePort    10.103.113.40   <none>        3000:30125/TCP    3m
$
```

The Service object created for the web component

In the output, we see that a service called `web` has been created. A unique `clusterIP` `10.103.113.40` has been assigned to this service, and the container port `3000` has been published on port `30125` on all cluster nodes.

If we want to test this deployment, we need to first find out what IP address Minikube has, and then use this IP address to access our `web` service. The following is the command that we can use to do this:

```
$ IP=$(minikube ip)
$ curl -4 $IP:30125/
Pets Demo Application
```

OK, the response is `Pets Demo Application`, which is what we expected. The web service is up and running in the Kubernetes cluster. Next, we want to deploy the database.

Deploying the database

A database is a stateful component and has to be treated differently to stateless components, such as our web component. We have discussed the difference between stateful and stateless components in a distributed application architecture in detail in `Chapter 6`, *Distributed Application Architecture,* and `Chapter 9`, *Orchestrators.*

Kubernetes has defined a special type of `ReplicaSet` object for stateful components. The object is called a `StatefulSet`. Let's use this kind of object to deploy our database. The definition can be found in the `labs/ch13/db-stateful-set.yaml` file. The details are as follows:

```yaml
db-stateful-set.yaml ×
1   apiVersion: apps/v1
2   kind: StatefulSet
3   metadata:
4     name: db
5   spec:
6     selector:
7       matchLabels:
8         app: pets
9         service: db
10    serviceName: db
11    template:
12      metadata:
13        labels:
14          app: pets
15          service: db
16      spec:
17        containers:
18        - image: fundamentalsofdocker/ch08-db:1.0
19          name: db
20          ports:
21          - containerPort: 5432
22          volumeMounts:
23          - mountPath: /var/lib/postgresql/data
24            name: pets-data
25    volumeClaimTemplates:
26    - metadata:
27        name: pets-data
28      spec:
29        accessModes:
30        - ReadWriteOnce
31        resources:
32          requests:
33            storage: 100Mi
34
```

A StatefulSet for the DB component

OK, this looks a bit scary, but it is not. It is a bit longer than the definition of the deployment for the web component due to the fact that we also need to define a volume where the PostgreSQL database can store the data. The volume claim definition is on lines 25 to 33. We want to create a volume with the name `pets-data` and of a maximum size equal to 100 MB. On lines 22 to 24, we use this volume and mount it into the container at `/var/lib/postgresql/data` where PostgreSQL expects it. On line 21, we also declare that PostgreSQL is listening at port `5432`.

As always, we use `kubectl` to deploy the `StatefulSet`:

```
$ kubectl create -f db-stateful-set.yaml
```

If we now list all resources in the cluster we can see the additional objects created:

```
$ kubectl get all
NAME          DESIRED   CURRENT   UP-TO-DATE   AVAILABLE   AGE
deploy/web    1         1         1            1           27m

NAME              DESIRED   CURRENT   READY   AGE
rs/web-769b88f67  1         1         1       27m

NAME          DESIRED   CURRENT   UP-TO-DATE   AVAILABLE   AGE
deploy/web    1         1         1            1           27m

NAME              DESIRED   CURRENT   READY   AGE
rs/web-769b88f67  1         1         1       27m

NAME               DESIRED   CURRENT   AGE
statefulsets/db    1         1         49s

NAME                    READY   STATUS    RESTARTS   AGE
po/db-0                 1/1     Running   0          49s
po/web-769b88f67-qd2xf  1/1     Running   0          27m

NAME             TYPE        CLUSTER-IP     EXTERNAL-IP   PORT(S)          AGE
svc/kubernetes   ClusterIP   10.96.0.1      <none>        443/TCP          10d
svc/web          NodePort    10.103.113.40  <none>        3000:30125/TCP   27m
$ 
```

The StatefulSet and its pod

We see that a `StatefulSet` and a pod have been created. For both, the current state corresponds to the desired state and thus the system is healthy. But that doesn't mean that the web component can access the database at this time. Service discovery would not work so far. Remember that the web component wants to access the db service under the name db.

To make service discovery work inside the cluster, we have to define a Kubernetes `Service` object for the database component too. Since the database should only ever be accessible from within the cluster, the type of `Service` object we need is `ClusterIP`. Here is the specification, which can be found in the `labs/ch13/db-service.yaml` file:

```
! db-service.yaml  ✕

         Gabriel Schenker, 2 days ago | 1
    1    apiVersion: v1
    2    kind: Service
    3    metadata:
    4      name: db
    5    spec:
    6      type: ClusterIP
    7      ports:
    8      - port: 5432
    9        protocol: TCP
   10      selector:
   11        app: pets
   12        service: db          Gab
```

Definition of the Kubernetes Service object for the database

The database component will be represented by this `Service` object and it will be reachable by the name `db`, which is the name of the service, as defined on line 4. The database component does not have to be publicly accessible, so we decided to use a `Service` object of type `ClusterIP`. The selector on lines 10 to 12 defines that this service represents a stable endpoint for all pods that have the according labels defined, that is, `app: pets` and `service: db`.

Let's deploy this service with the following command:

```
$ kubectl create -f db-service.yaml
```

And we should now be ready to test the application. We can use the browser this time to enjoy the funny cat images:

Testing the pets application running in Kubernetes

 192.168.99.100 is the IP address of my Minikube. Verify your address using the command `minikube ip`. The port number `30125` is the number that Kubernetes automatically selected for my web `Service` object. Replace this number with the port that Kubernetes assigned to your service. Get the number by using the command `kubectl get services`.

Now we have successfully deployed the pets application to Minikube, which is a single-node Kubernetes cluster. We had to define four artifacts to do so, which are as follows:

- A `Deployment` and a `Service` object for the web component
- A `StatefulSet` and a `Service` object for the database component

To remove the application from the cluster, we can use the following small script:

```
kubectl delete svc/web
kubectl delete deploy/web
kubectl delete svc/db
kubectl delete statefulset/db
```

Streamlining the deployment

So far, we have created four artifacts that needed to be deployed to the cluster. And this is only a very simple application, consisting of two components. Imagine having a much more complex application. It would quickly become a maintenance nightmare. Luckily, we have several options as to how we can simplify the deployment. The method that we are going to discuss here is the possibility of defining all the components that make up an application in Kubernetes in a single file.

Other solutions that lie outside of the scope of this book would include the use of a package manager, such as **Helm**.

If we have an application consisting of many Kubernetes objects such as `Deployment` and `Service` objects, then we can keep them all in one single file and separate the individual object definitions by three dashes. For example, if we wanted to have the deployment and the service definition for the web component in a single file, this would look as follows:

```
apiVersion: extensions/v1beta1
kind: Deployment
metadata:
  name: web
spec:
  replicas: 1
  selector:
    matchLabels:
      app: pets
      service: web
  template:
    metadata:
      labels:
        app: pets
        service: web
    spec:
      containers:
      - image: fundamentalsofdocker/ch08-web:1.0
        name: web
        ports:
        - containerPort: 3000
          protocol: TCP
---
apiVersion: v1
kind: Service
metadata:
  name: web
spec:
  type: NodePort
```

```
ports:
- port: 3000
  protocol: TCP
selector:
  app: pets
  service: web
```

We have collected all the four object definitions for the pets application in the `labs/ch13/pets.yaml` file, and we can deploy the application in one go:

```
$ kubectl create -f pets.yaml
deployment "web" created
service "web" created
statefulset "db" created
service "db" created
$
```

Using a single script to deploy the pets application

Similarly, we have created a script, `labs/ch13/remove-pets.sh`, to remove all artifacts of the pets application from the Kubernetes cluster:

```
$ ./remove-pets.sh
deployment "web" deleted
service "web" deleted
statefulset "db" deleted
service "db" deleted
$
```

Removing pets from the Kubernetes cluster

We have taken our pets application we introduced in `Chapter 8`, *Docker Compose*, and defined all the Kubernetes objects that are necessary to deploy this application into a Kubernetes cluster. In each step, we have made sure that we got the expected result, and once all artifacts existed in the cluster, we have shown the running application.

Zero downtime deployments

In a mission-critical environment, it is important that the application is always up and running. These days we cannot afford any downtime anymore. Kubernetes gives us various means of achieving this. An update of an application in the cluster that causes no downtime is called a **zero downtime deployment**. In this chapter, we will present two ways of achieving this. These are as follows:

- Rolling updates
- Blue-green deployments

Let's start by discussing rolling updates.

Rolling updates

In the previous chapter, we learned that the Kubernetes `Deployment` object distinguishes itself from the `ReplicaSet` object in that it adds rolling updates and rollbacks on top of the latter's functionality. Let's use our `web` component to demonstrate this. Evidently, we will have to modify the manifest or description of the deployment for the `web` component.

We will use the same deployment definition as in the previous section, with one important difference—we will have five replicas of the web component running. The following definition can also be found in the `labs/ch13/web-deploy-rolling-v1.yaml` file:

```
apiVersion: extensions/v1beta1
kind: Deployment
metadata:
  name: web
spec:
  replicas: 5
  selector:
    matchLabels:
      app: pets
      service: web
  template:
    metadata:
      labels:
        app: pets
        service: web
    spec:
      containers:
      - image: fundamentalsofdocker/ch08-web:1.0
        name: web
```

```
ports:
- containerPort: 3000
  protocol: TCP
```

We can now create this deployment as usual and also, at the same time, the service that makes our component accessible:

```
$ kubectl create -f web-deploy-rolling-v1.yaml
$ kubectl create -f web-service.yaml
```

Once we have deployed the pods and the service, we can test our web component with the following command:

```
$ PORT=$(kubectl get svc/web -o yaml | grep nodePort | cut -d' ' -f5)
$ IP=$(minikube ip)
$ curl -4 ${IP}:${PORT}/
Pets Demo Application
```

As we can see, the application is up and running and returns us the expected message, `Pets Demo Application`.

Now our developers have created a new version, `2.0`, of the `web` component. The code of the new version of the `web` component can be found in the `labs/ch13/web` folder, and the only change is located on line 12 of the file `server.js`:

```
 9     app.set('views', __dirname);
10
11     app.get('/',function(req,res){
12         res.status(200).send('Pets Demo Application v2\n');
13     });
14
```

Code change for version 2.0 of the web component

The developers have built the new image as follows:

```
$ docker image build -t fundamentalsofdocker/ch13-web:2.0 web
```

And, subsequently, they pushed the image to Docker Hub:

```
$ docker image push fundamentalsofdocker/ch13-web:2.0
```

We now want to update the image used by our pods that are part of the web Deployment object. We can do this by using the set image command of kubectl:

```
$ kubectl set image deployment/web \
    web=fundamentalsofdocker/ch13-web:2.0
```

If we then test the application again, we get the confirmation that the update has indeed happened:

```
curl -4 ${IP}:${PORT}/
Pets Demo Application v2
```

Now, *how do we know that there hasn't been any downtime during this update? Did the update really happen in a rolling fashion? What does rolling update mean at all?* Let's investigate. First, we can get a confirmation from Kubernetes that the deployment has indeed happened and was successful by using the rollout status command:

```
$ kubectl rollout status deploy/web
deployment "web" successfully rolled out
```

If we describe the deployment web with kubectl describe deploy/web, we get the following list of events at the end of the output:

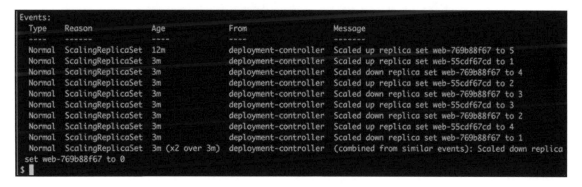

List of events found in the output of the deployment description of the web component

The first event tells us that when we created the deployment, a `ReplicaSet` `web-769b88f67` with five replicas was created. Then we executed the `update` command and the second event in the list tells us that this meant creating a new `ReplicaSet` called `web-55cdf67cd` with, initially, one replica only. Thus, at that particular moment there existed six pods on the system, the five initial pods, and one pod with the new version. But since the desired state of the `Deployment` object states that we want five replicas only, Kubernetes now scales down the old `ReplicaSet` to four instances, which we see in the third event. Then, again, the new `ReplicaSet` is scaled up to two instances and, subsequently, the old `ReplicaSet` scaled down to three instances, and so on, until we have five new instances and all the old instances have been decommissioned. Although, we cannot see any precise time (other than three minutes) when that happened, the order of the events tells us that the whole update happened in a rolling fashion.

During a short time period, some of the calls to the web service would have had an answer from the old version of the component and some calls would have received an answer from the new version of the component. But at no time would the service have been down.

We can also list the `Recordset` objects in the cluster and will get the confirmation of what I said in the preceding section:

```
$ kubectl get rs
NAME             DESIRED    CURRENT    READY    AGE
web-55cdf67cd    5          5          5        27m
web-769b88f67    0          0          0        36m
$
```

List all Recordset objects in the cluster

We see that the new recordset has five instances running and the old one has been scaled down to zero instances. The reason why the old `Recordset` object is still lingering around is that Kubernetes provides us with the possibility of rolling back the update and, in that case, will reuse the `Recordset`.

To roll back the update of the image in case some undetected bug sneaked in to the new code, we can use the `rollout undo` command:

```
$ kubectl rollout undo deploy/web
deployment "web"
$ curl -4 ${IP}:${PORT}/
Pets Demo Application
```

I have also listed the test command using `curl` in the preceding snippet to verify that the rollback indeed happened. If we list the recordsets, we see the following output:

```
$ kubectl get rs
NAME            DESIRED   CURRENT   READY   AGE
web-55cdf67cd   0         0         0       36m
web-769b88f67   5         5         5       45m
$
```

Listing RecordSet objects after rollback

This confirms that the old `RecordSet` (`web-769b88f67`) object has been reused and the new one has been scaled down to zero instances.

Sometimes though we cannot, or do not want to, tolerate the mixed state of an old version coexisting with new version. We want an all-or-nothing strategy. This is where blue–green deployments come into play, which we will discuss next.

Blue–green deployment

If we want to do a blue–green style deployment for our component web of the pets application, then we can do so by using labels creatively. Let's first remind ourselves how blue–green deployments work. Here is a rough step-by-step instruction:

1. Deploy a first version of the component `web` as `blue`. We will label the pods with a label `color: blue` to do so.
2. Deploy the Kubernetes service for these pods with the label, `color: blue` in the `selector` section.
3. Now we can deploy version 2 of the `web` component, but this time the pods have a label, `color: green`.
4. We can test the green version of the service that it works as expected.
5. Now we flip traffic from `blue` to `green` by updating the Kubernetes service for the `web` component. We modify the selector to use the label `color: green`.

Let's define a `Deployment` object for version 1, blue:

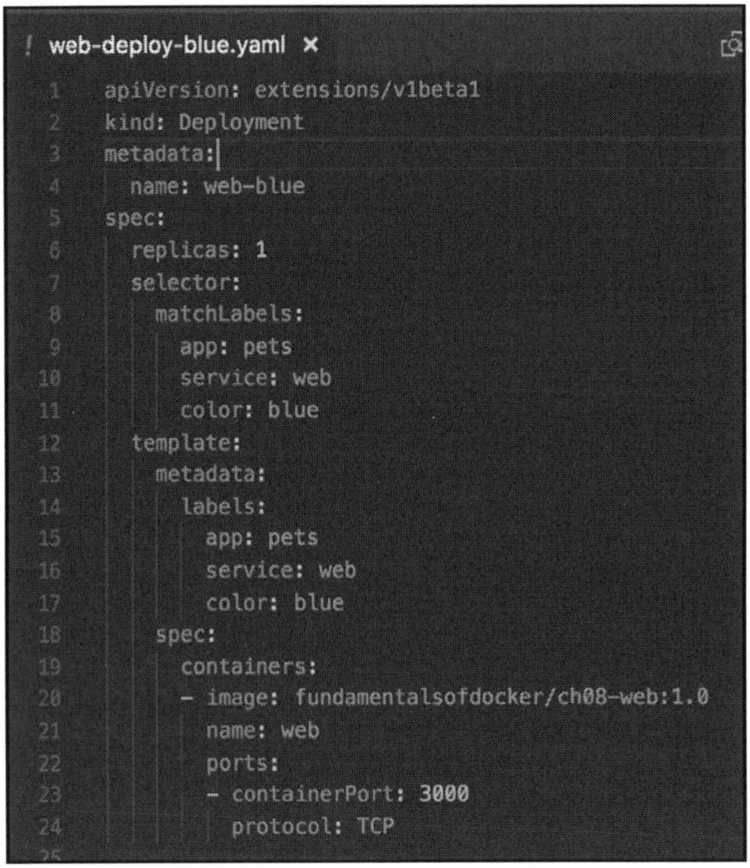

```
web-deploy-blue.yaml ✕
1    apiVersion: extensions/v1beta1
2    kind: Deployment
3    metadata:
4      name: web-blue
5    spec:
6      replicas: 1
7      selector:
8        matchLabels:
9          app: pets
10         service: web
11         color: blue
12     template:
13       metadata:
14         labels:
15           app: pets
16           service: web
17           color: blue
18       spec:
19         containers:
20         - image: fundamentalsofdocker/ch08-web:1.0
21           name: web
22           ports:
23           - containerPort: 3000
24             protocol: TCP
25
```

Specification of the deployment blue for the web component

The preceding definition can be found in the `labs/ch13/web-deploy-blue.yaml` file. Please note line 4 where we define the name of the deployment as `web-blue` to distinguish it from the upcoming deployment `web-green`. Also note that we have added the label `color: blue` on lines 11 and 17. Everything else remains the same as before.

Now we define the `Service` object for the `web` component. It will be the same as we used before with a minor change, as you will see in the following screenshot:

```
! web-svc-blue-green.yaml ✕
   1      apiVersion: v1
   2      kind: Service
   3      metadata:
   4        name: web
   5      spec:
   6        type: NodePort
   7        ports:
   8        - port: 3000
   9          protocol: TCP
  10        selector:
  11          app: pets
  12          service: web
  13          color: blue
  14          |
```

Kubernetes service for the web component supporting blue–green deployments

The only difference to the definition of the service we used earlier in this chapter is line 13, which adds the label `color: blue` to the `selector`. We can find the preceding definition in the `labs/ch13/web-svc-blue-green.yaml` file.

We can then deploy the `blue` version of the web component with the following command:

```
$ kubectl create -f web-deploy-blue.yaml
$ kubectl create -f web-svc-blue-green.yaml
```

Once the service is up and running, we can determine its IP address and port number and test it:

```
$ PORT=$(kubectl get svc/web -o yaml | grep nodePort | cut -d' ' -f5)
$ IP=$(minikube ip)
$ curl -4 ${IP}:${PORT}/
Pets Demo Application
```

As expected, we get the response `Pets Demo Application`.

Now we can deploy the green version of the web component. The definition of its Deployment object can be found in the labs/ch13/web-deploy-green.yaml file and looks as follows:

```yaml
web-deploy-green.yaml
1   apiVersion: extensions/v1beta1
2   kind: Deployment
3   metadata:
4     name: web-green
5   spec:
6     replicas: 1
7     selector:
8       matchLabels:
9         app: pets
10        service: web
11        color: green
12    template:
13      metadata:
14        labels:
15          app: pets
16          service: web
17          color: green
18      spec:
19        containers:
20        - image: fundamentalsofdocker/ch13-web:2.0
21          name: web
22          ports:
23          - containerPort: 3000
24            protocol: TCP
25
```

Specification of the deployment green for the web component

The interesting lines are as follows:

- **Line 4**: With the name web-green to distinguish from web-blue and allow for parallel install
- **Lines 11 and 17**: Having the color green
- **Line 20**: Now using version 2.0 of the image

Now we're ready to deploy this green version of the service, and it should run separate from the blue service:

```
$ kubectl create -f web-deploy-green.yaml
```

We can make sure that both deployments coexist:

```
$ kubectl get deploy
NAME          DESIRED   CURRENT   UP-TO-DATE   AVAILABLE   AGE
web-blue      1         1         1            1           23h
web-green     1         1         1            1           3s
$
```

Displaying the list of Deployment objects running in the cluster

As expected, we have both `blue` and `green` running. We can verify that `blue` is still the active service:

```
$ curl -4 ${IP}:${PORT}/
Pets Demo Application
```

Now comes the interesting part. We can flip traffic from `blue` to `green` by editing the existing service for the web component. So, execute the following command:

```
$ kubectl edit svc/web
```

Change the value of the label `color` from `blue` to `green`. Then save and quit the editor. The Kubernetes CLI will automatically update the service. When we now query the web service again, we get this:

```
$ curl -4 ${IP}:${PORT}/
Pets Demo Application v2
```

This confirms that the traffic has indeed switched to the `green` version of the web component (note the `v2` at the end of the response to the `curl` command).

If we realize that something went wrong with our green deployment and the new version has a defect, we can easily switch back to the `blue` version by editing the service web again and replacing the value of the label color from `green` back to `blue`. This rollback is instantaneous and should always work. We can then remove the buggy green deployment and fix the component. When we have corrected the problem, we can deploy the `green` version once again.

Once the `green` version of the component is running as expected and performing well, we can decommission the `blue` version:

```
$ kubectl delete deploy/web-blue
```

When we're ready to deploy a new version, 3.0, this one becomes the blue version. We update the `labs/ch13/web-deploy-blue.yaml` file accordingly and deploy it. Then we flip the service web from `green` to `blue`, and so on.

We have successfully demonstrated, with our component `web` of the pets application, how blue–green deployment can be achieved in a Kubernetes cluster.

Kubernetes secrets

Sometimes, services that we want to run in the Kubernetes cluster have to use confidential data such as passwords, secret API keys or certificates, to name just a few. We want to make sure that this sensitive information can only ever be seen by the authorized or dedicated service. All other services running in the cluster should not have any access to this data.

For this reason, Kubernetes secrets have been introduced. A secret is a key-value pair where the key is the unique name of the secret and the value is the actual sensitive data. Secrets are stored in etcd. Kubernetes can be configured such that secrets are encrypted at rest, that is, in etcd, and in transit, that is, when the secrets are going over the wire from a master node to the worker nodes on which the pods of the service using this secret are running.

Manually defining secrets

We can create a secret declaratively the same way we created any other object in Kubernetes. Here is the YAML for such a secret:

```
apiVersion: v1
kind: Secret
metadata:
  name: pets-secret
type: Opaque
data:
  username: am9obi5kb2UK
  password: cOVjcmVOLXBhc1N3MHJECg==
```

The preceding definition can be found in the `labs/ch13/pets-secret.yaml` file. Now you might wonder what the values are. *Are these the real (unencrypted) values?* No, they are not. And they are also not really encrypted values but just `base64` encoded values. Thus they are not really secure, since base64-encoded values can be easily reverted to clear text values. *How did I get these values?* That's easy:

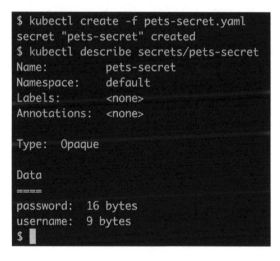

```
$ echo "john.doe" | base64
am9obi5kb2UK
$ echo "sEcret-pasSw0rD" | base64
c0VjcmV0LXBhc1N3MHJECg==
$
```

Creating base64-encoded values for the secret

We can then create the secret and describe it:

```
$ kubectl create -f pets-secret.yaml
secret "pets-secret" created
$ kubectl describe secrets/pets-secret
Name:         pets-secret
Namespace:    default
Labels:       <none>
Annotations:  <none>

Type:  Opaque

Data
====
password:  16 bytes
username:  9 bytes
$
```

Creating and describing the Kubernetes secret

In the description of the secret, the values are hidden and only their length is given. *So maybe the secrets are safe now?* No, not really. We can easily decode this secret using the `kubectl get` command:

```
$ kubectl get secrets/pets-secret -o yaml
apiVersion: v1
data:
  password: cOVjcmV0LXBhc1N3MHJECg==
  username: am9obi5kb2UK
kind: Secret
metadata:
  creationTimestamp: 2018-03-31T20:36:05Z
  name: pets-secret
  namespace: default
  resourceVersion: "154786"
  selfLink: /api/v1/namespaces/default/secrets/pets-secret
  uid: 22d818bd-3523-11e8-a3cb-080027c10823
type: Opaque
$
```

Kubernetes secret decoded

As we can see in the preceding screenshot, we have our original secret values back. And we can decode them:

```
$ echo "cOVjcmV0LXBhc1N3MHJECg==" | base64 --decode
sEcret-pasSw0rD
```

Thus, the consequences are that this method of creating a Kubernetes is not to be used in any other environment than development, where we deal with non-sensitive data. In all other environments, we need a better way to deal with secrets.

Creating secrets with kubectl

A much safer way to define secrets is to use `kubectl`. First, we create files containing the base64-encoded secret values similar to what we did in the preceding section, but this time we store the values in temporary files:

```
$ echo "sue-hunter" | base64 > username.txt
$ echo "123abc456def" | base64 > password.txt
```

Now we can use `kubectl` to create a secret from those files as follows:

```
$ kubectl create secret generic pets-secret-prod \
    --from-file=./username.txt \
    --from-file=./password.txt
secret "pets-secret-prod" created
```

The secret can then be used the same way as the manually-created secret.

Why is this method more secure than the other one you might ask? Well, first of all, there is no YAML that defines a secret and is stored in some source code version control system, such as GitHub, which many people have access to and so can see and decode the secrets. Only the admin person that is authorized to know the secrets ever sees their values and uses them to directly create the secrets in the (production) cluster. The cluster itself is protected by role-based access control so that no unauthorized people have access to it nor can they possibly decode the secrets defined in the cluster.

But now, let's see how we can actually use the secrets that we have defined.

Using secrets in a pod

Let's say we want to create a `Deployment` object where the `web` component uses our secret called `pets-secret` that we introduced in the preceding section. We use the following command to create the secret in the cluster:

```
$ kubectl create -f pets-secret.yaml
```

In the `labs/ch13/web-deploy-secret.yaml` file, we can find the definition of the
`Deployment` object. We had to add the part starting from line 23 to the original definition of
the `Deployment` object:

```yaml
! web-deploy-secret.yaml  ✕
1    apiVersion: extensions/v1beta1
2    kind: Deployment
3    metadata:
4      name: web
5    spec:
6      replicas: 1
7      selector:
8        matchLabels:
9          app: pets
10         service: web
11     template:
12       metadata:
13         labels:
14           app: pets
15           service: web
16       spec:
17         containers:
18         - image: fundamentalsofdocker/ch08-web:1.0
19           name: web
20           ports:
21           - containerPort: 3000
22             protocol: TCP
23           volumeMounts:
24           - name: secrets
25             mountPath: "/etc/secrets"
26             readOnly: true
27         volumes:
28         - name: secrets
29           secret:
30             secretName: pets-secret
31
```

Deployment object for web component with a secret

On lines 27 through 30 we define a volume called `secrets` from our secret `pets-secret`. We then use this volume in the container, as described on lines 23 through 26. We mount the secrets in the container filesystem at `/etc/secrets` and we mount the volume in read-only mode. Thus, the secret values will be available to the container as files in said folder. The names of the files will correspond to the key names, and the content of the files will be the values of the corresponding keys. The values will be provided in unencrypted form to the application running inside the container.

In our case, having the keys' username and password in the secret, we will find two files, named `username` and `password`, in the `/etc/secrets` folder in the container filesystem. The file `username` should contain the value `john.doe`, and the file `password` the value `sEcret-pasSw0rD`. Here is the confirmation:

```
$ kubectl exec -it web-597b7f7749-87mq5 -- /bin/sh
/app # cd /etc/secrets/
/etc/secrets # ls -l
total 0
lrwxrwxrwx    1 root     root            15 Apr  2 01:26 password -> ..data/password
lrwxrwxrwx    1 root     root            15 Apr  2 01:26 username -> ..data/username
/etc/secrets # cat username && cat password
john.doe
sEcret-pasSw0rD
/etc/secrets #
```

Confirming that secrets are available inside the container

On line 1 of the preceding output, we exec into the container where the web component runs. Then, on lines 2 to 5, we list the files in the `/etc/secrets` folder, and finally, on lines 6 to 8, we show the content of the two files which, unsurprisingly, show the secret values in clear text.

Since any application written in any language can read simple files, this mechanism of using secrets is very backwards compatible. Even an old Cobol application can read clear text files from the filesystem.

Sometimes, though, applications expect secrets to be available in environment variables. Let's look at what Kubernetes offers us in this case.

Secret values in environment variables

Let's say our web component expects the username in the environment variable, PETS_USERNAME and the password in PETS_PASSWORD, then we can modify our deployment YAML to look as follows:

```
! web-deploy-secret-env.yaml ✕
 1    apiVersion: extensions/v1beta1
 2    kind: Deployment
 3    metadata:
 4      name: web
 5    spec:
 6      replicas: 1
 7      selector:
 8        matchLabels:
 9          app: pets
10          service: web
11      template:
12        metadata:
13          labels:
14            app: pets
15            service: web
16        spec:
17          containers:
18          - image: fundamentalsofdocker/ch08-web:1.0
19            name: web
20            ports:
21            - containerPort: 3000
22              protocol: TCP
23            env:
24            - name: PETS_USERNAME
25              valueFrom:
26                secretKeyRef:
27                  name: pets-secret
28                  key: username
29            - name: PETS_PASSWORD
30              valueFrom:
31                secretKeyRef:
32                  name: pets-secret
33                  key: password
34
```

Deployment mapping secret values to environment variables

On lines 23 through 33, we define the two environment variables, PETS_USERNAME and PETS_PASSWORD, and map the corresponding key-value pair of the pets-secret to them.

Note, we don't need a volume anymore but we directly map the individual keys of our pets-secret into corresponding environment variables valid inside the container. The following sequence of commands shows that the secret values are indeed available inside the container in the respective environment variables:

```
$ kubectl exec -it web-694f958cd4-6zq89 -- /bin/sh
/app # echo $PETS_USERNAME && echo $PETS_PASSWORD
john.doe
sEcret-pasSw0rD
/app #
```

Secret values are mapped to environment variables

In this section, we have shown how to define secrets in a Kubernetes cluster and how to use those secrets in containers running as part of the pods of a deployment. We have shown two variants on how secrets can be mapped inside a container, the first one using files and the second approach using environment variables.

Summary

In this chapter, we have learned how to deploy an application into a Kubernetes cluster and how to set up application-level routing for this application. Furthermore, we have learned ways to update application services running in a Kubernetes cluster without causing any downtime. Finally, we have used secrets to provide sensitive information to application services running in the cluster.

In the next and final chapter, we are going to learn how to run a containerized sample application in the cloud using different offerings provided by cloud vendors, such as Microsoft Azure, Amazon AWS, and Google Cloud. Stay tuned.

Questions

To assess your learning progress, please answer the following questions:

1. You have an application consisting of two services, the first one being a web API and the second one a DB, such as Mongo. You want to deploy this application into a Kubernetes cluster. In a few short sentences, explain how you proceed.
2. Describe in your own words in a few sentences the components you need to establish layer 7 (or application level) routing for your application.
3. List the main steps needed to implement blue–green deployment for a simple application service. Avoid going into too much detail.
4. Name three or four types of information that you would provide to an application service through Kubernetes secrets.
5. Name the sources that Kubernetes accepts when creating a secret.

Further reading

Here are a few links that provide additional information on the topics discussed in this chapter:

- Performing a rolling update at `https://bit.ly/2o2okEQ`
- Blue–green deployment at `https://bit.ly/2r2IxNJ`
- Secrets in Kubernetes at `https://bit.ly/2C6hMZF`

Running a Containerized App in the Cloud

14

In the previous chapter, we learned how to deploy a multi-service application into a Kubernetes cluster. We configured application-level routing for this application and updated its services using a zero-downtime strategy. Finally, we provided confidential data to the running services by using Kubernetes secrets.

In this chapter, we will give an overview of some of the most popular ways of running containerized applications in the cloud. We will have a closer look at what the most popular cloud vendor, AWS, offers in this regard. We will include self-hosting and hosted solutions and discuss their pros and cons. Offerings of other vendors, such as Microsoft Azure and **Google Cloud Engine (GCE)**, will also be briefly discussed.

Here are the topics we will be discussing in this chapter:

- Deploying our application into AWS ECS
- Deploying and using Docker EE on AWS
- A short peek into Azure's container offerings
- A short peek into Google's container offerings

After reading this chapter, you will be able to:

- Deploy a simple application into AWS ECS
- Create a Kubernetes cluster in AWS using Docker Enterprise Edition
- Deploy a simple application into a Docker Enterprise Edition cluster in AWS
- Name hosted container offerings of Microsoft Azure and Google Cloud
- List two or three pros and cons for each of the cloud-based managed offerings of Amazon, Microsoft, and Google

Technical requirements

We are going to use Amazon AWS, Microsoft Azure, and Google Cloud in this chapter. Thus it is necessary to have an account on each platform. If you do not have an existing account, you can ask for a trial account for all of those cloud providers. We also use the files in folder `ch14` of our labs repository from GitHub at `https://github.com/fundamentalsofdocker/labs/tree/master/ch14`.

Deploying our application into AWS ECS

In this section, we are going to learn how to deploy our pets application to AWS **Elastic Container Service (ECS)**. Next to Kubernetes and Docker Swarm, ECS is one of the most popular container platforms.

 We are assuming that you are somewhat familiar with AWS and its core concepts, such as **security group (SG)**, **virtual private cloud (VPC)**, and **elastic compute cloud (EC2)**.

As a prerequisite, we need an account on AWS. If you do not yet have such an account then please create a free trial account here at `https://aws.amazon.com/free`. Log in to your account using the link at `https://console.aws.amazon.com`. Navigate to the ECS home page at `https://console.aws.amazon.com/ecs/home`.

Introduction to ECS

AWS ECS has a somewhat unique way of defining resources. From a high-level perspective, the resource types AWS use resemble a bit of a mixture of Docker Swarm and Kubernetes resources. At the center to everything is the ECS cluster. There are multiple ways of creating such a cluster. The two main ones are as follows:

- **Fargate**: This is new and at the time of writing only available in the US East region. Infrastructure such as EC2 instances are automatically provisioned and managed by ECS.
- **Manual**: We provision and manage our own infrastructure, such as EC2 instances.

Once we have provisioned a cluster, we're ready to author task definitions. A task definition can be compared to a Kubernetes pod. It is an abstraction of one to many containers that are co-located and run in the same network namespace. Thus, if I have two containers, web and db, where web needs to access the container DB on port 3456, it can do so through a localhost, that is http://127.0.0.1:3456.

A task is an instance of a task definition. When creating a task, we're actually running containers in the cluster based on the settings in the task definition. We can create multiple tasks from one and the same task definition.

In AWS ECS, there is also the concept of a service. A service is very similar to a Docker Swarm service as it makes sure that the life cycle of a set of tasks is orchestrated. Crashed tasks are rescheduled and more.

 As always on AWS, we need to have an SG and a VPC with subnets defined ahead. Unfortunately, if you're not familiar with how to do this then we have to refer you to the online documentation of AWS since this topic lies outside the scope of this book.

Creating a Fargate ECS cluster of AWS

Perform the following steps once you have created a security group and a VPC with at least one subnet:

1. Navigate to https://console.aws.amazon.com/ecs and click on **Create Cluster** button.
2. Choose the **Networking Only (Powered by AWS Fargate)** template and then click **Next Step**.
3. Enter the name of the cluster, for example, pets-cluster, and leave the **Create VPC** checkbox unchecked.
4. Click **Create**. The cluster will be created for you.

This might take a moment or so. Once done, you can click **View Cluster** button.

Authoring a task definition

We're starting with a simple task definition, which we then test and evolve until we have our pets application up and running. Proceed with the following steps:

1. In the navigation pane, choose **Task Definitions**.

2. Then click the **Create new Task Definition** button.
3. Select **FARGATE** as the launch type compatibility and then click **Next Step**.
4. Name the task definition `pets-task-def`.
5. Under the **Task Size** section, select 1 GB for task memory and 0.5 for task CPU.
6. Next, click the **Add container** button. In the dialog box, enter `web` as the name and `nginx:alpine` as the image. Under the **Port mappings** section, add port 80:

Adding a container to the ECS task definition

7. Then click the **Add**. button. Now we're ready to actually run a task from this task description in our pets cluster.

Running a task in ECS

Select the `pets-task-def` task definition and under **Actions,** select **Run Task.** In the window, perform the following steps:

1. Select **FARGATE** as the launch type.
2. Under the **Cluster VPC** dropdown, select the VPC that you have prepared beforehand.
3. Under the **Subnets** dropdown, select one of the subnets of your VPC.
4. Click the **Edit** button under the **Security groups** option and select your security group that you have prepared.
5. Leave all the other fields with their default values:

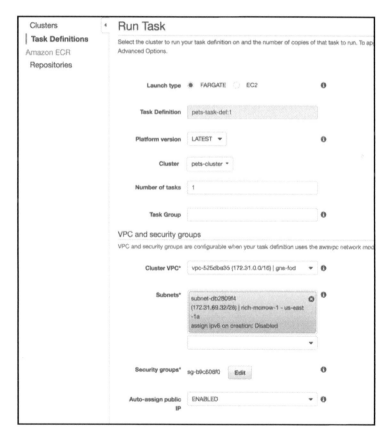

Running a task in our ECS cluster

6. Once done, click the **Run Task** button. It may take a minute or so to provision and run this task. You can see the task in the cluster overview on the **Tasks** tab:

Our first task is running in the pets cluster

7. Click on the task (in the **Tasks** column) to navigate to the task details page. There you will find the public IP address for this task. Copy the IP address and paste it into a new browser tab and hit *Enter*. The welcome page of Nginx should be displayed as follows:

Testing the first task running in our ECS pets cluster

Modifying the task definition

Now that we have successfully run a first task in our ECS cluster, it is time to modify the task definition to use our images of the pets application instead of the Nginx image. We will be using the image `fundamentalsofdocker/ch14-web:1.0` in this task definition ,the source code of which can be found in our code repository in folder `labs/ch14/ecs/web`.

The steps to change the task definition are as follows:

1. Select the `pets-task-def` task definition and then select revision 1.
2. The **Create new revision** button will be enabled. Click it and in the appearing page scroll down to the **Container Definitions** section. There you should see our web container. Click it and modify the image and instead of `nginx:alpine` add the value `fundamentalsofdocker/ch14-web:1.0`.
3. Click **Update** and then click **Create**. This will create a new revision 2 of our task definition called `pets-task-def:2`.
4. Go back to the cluster and stop the current task. Then click **Run new Task**.
5. In the dialog, fill in the same information that you did when running the first task but make sure that under **Task Definition** you select revision 2, namely `pets-task-def:2`.
6. Click **Run Task** and wait until the task is provisioned and running. This may take a while since ECS needs to download the image from Docker Hub. Once the task is ready, navigate to its details and locate the public IP address assigned to it.

Use the browser to verify you can reach our `web` component. If all went well, we should see the following screenshot:

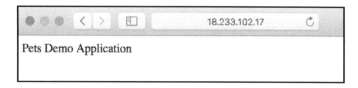

The pets web component is running in our ECS pets cluster

Now our `web` component is running but we also need the database from which it retrieves the nice cat images. So we need to create yet another revision of the task definition, which will include our `db` component.

Adding the database component to the application

Let's modify the task definition and add a volume and the database container that will use that container:

1. Select the `pets-task-def` task definition again and then select revision 2.
2. Click the **Create new revision** button. First we want to add a volume definition. This volume will be used by the `db` container.
3. Scroll down to the **Volumes** section and click the **Add volume** link. Name the volume `pets-data` and click **Add**.
4. In the **Container Definitions** section, click the **Add container** button. Define the name of the container to be `db` and the image to be `fundamentalsofdocker/ch08-db:1.0`.
5. Scroll down to the **STORAGE AND LOGGING** section and under **Mount points,** select `pets-data` as **Source volume** and `/var/lib/postgresql/data` as **Container path**:

Mounting the volume pets-data to the db container

6. Click **Add** to complete this dialog and then click **Create** to create revision 3 of the task definition. This revision 3 contains the full definition of our pets application. Let's find out whether it works, shall we?

7. Navigate to the cluster details and make sure to stop the previous task.
8. Then click **Run Task** and enter the same values as before with the exception of the task definition.
9. There, be sure to select `pets-task-def:3`.

Once the task is provisioned and running, we can locate its public IP address and then in a browser navigate to `http://<IP address>/pet`, where `<IP address>` is the public IP of the task:

52.91.14.57/pet

Cat Gif of the day

Courtesy: Buzzfeed

Delivered to you by container f0dd8a1c4495

The pets application running in AWS ECS

In conclusion, we have created a cluster in AWS and deployed our pets application to it by defining an ECS task definition first and then running a task from this task definition. Since we are using the Fargate version of ECS, we did not have to worry about our own infrastructure, such as EC2 instances.

ECS makes it relatively easy to deploy and run a containerized application in the cloud. When using the Fargate template, we don't even have to provision and manage the infrastructure, as AWS will do that for us. Although this might be appealing for many, it is also one of the biggest drawbacks of this offering. AWS, out of understandable commercial interest, does everything to lock us into their ecosystem. Once we have bought into ECS, it is highly unlikely that we will ever be able to change the cloud provider or even just use a different orchestration engine, such as Kubernetes.

Deploying and using Docker EE on AWS

In this section, we're going to install Docker **Universal Control Plane (UCP)** version 3.0. UCP is part of Docker's enterprise offering and supports the two orchestration engines, Docker Swarm and Kubernetes. UCP can be installed in the cloud or on-premise. Even hybrid clouds are possible with UCP.

To try this, you need a valid license for Docker EE or you can claim a free test license on Docker Store.

Provisioning the infrastructure

Create an **auto scaling group (ASG)** in AWS using the Ubuntu 16.04 server AMI. Configure the ASG to contain three instances of size **t2.xlarge**. Here is the result of this:

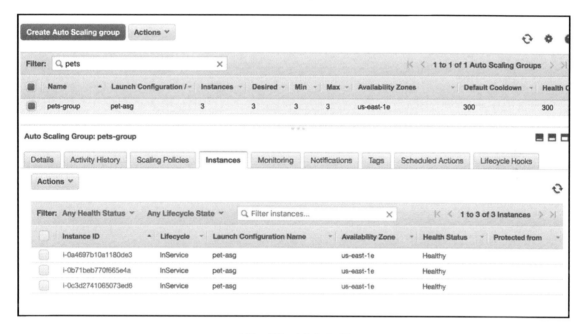

ASG on AWS ready for Docker EE

Once the ASG has been created, and before we continue, we need to open the SG a bit (of which our ASG is part of) so that we can access it through SSH from our laptop and also so that the VMs can communicate with each other. Navigate to your SG and add two new inbound rules, shown here:

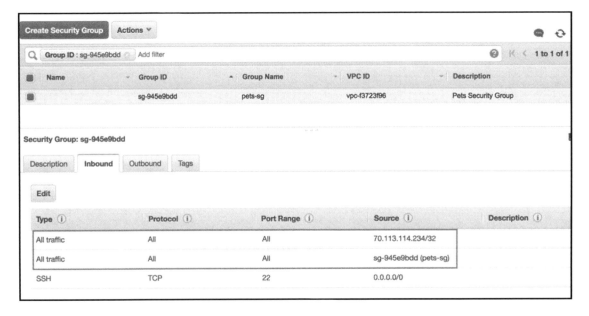

AWS Security Group settings

In the preceding screenshot:

- The first rule allows any traffic from my personal laptop (with IP address 70.113.114.234) to access any resource in the SG.
- The second rule allows any traffic inside the SG itself. These settings are not meant to be used in a production-like environment as they are way too permissive. But for this demo environment, they work well.

Installing Docker

SSH into all three instances and install Docker. Using the downloaded key, SSH into the first machine:

```
$ ssh -i pets.pem ubuntu@<IP address>
```

Here `<IP address>` is the public IP address of the VM we want to SSH into.

Now we can install Docker. For a detailed instruction, refer to `https://dockr.ly/2HiWfBc`. We have a script in the `labs/ch14/aws` folder called `install-docker.sh` that we can use. First we need to clone the `labs` GitHub repository to the VM:

```
$ git clone https://github.com/fundamentalsofdocker/labs.git
$ cd labs/ch14/aws
```

Then run the script to install Docker:

```
$ ./install-docker.sh
```

Once the script is finished, we can verify that Docker is indeed installed using `sudo docker version`. Repeat the preceding code for the two other VMs.

 The `sudo` is only necessary until the next SSH session is opened to this VM since we have added the user `ubuntu` to the group `docker`. Thus exist the current SSH session and connect again. This time `sudo` should not be needed in conjunction with `docker`.

Installing Docker UCP

We need to set a few environment variables, as follows:

```
$ export UCP_IP=<IP address>
$ export UCP_FQDN=<FQDN>
$ export UCP_VERSION=3.0.0-beta2
```

Here `<IP address>` and `<FQDN>` are the public IP address and the public DNS name of the AWS EC2 instance we're installing in UCP.

After that, we can use the following command to download all the images that UCP needs:

```
$ docker run --rm docker/ucp:${UCP_VERSION} images --list \
    | xargs -L 1 docker pull
```

Finally, we can install UCP:

```
ubuntu@ip-172-31-8-100:~$ docker container run --rm -it --name ucp \
>       -v /var/run/docker.sock:/var/run/docker.sock \
>       docker/ucp:${UCP_VERSION} install \
>       --admin-username admin \
>       --admin-password adminadmin \
>       --san ${UCP_IP} \
>       --san ${UCP_FQDN}
INFO[0000] Verifying your system is compatible with UCP 3.0.0-beta2 (4f665c3)
INFO[0000] Your engine version 18.03.0-ce, build 0520e24 (4.4.0-1052-aws) is compatible
INFO[0000] All required images are present
INFO[0000] Initializing a new swarm at 172.31.8.100
INFO[0005] Establishing mutual Cluster Root CA with Swarm
INFO[0008] Installing UCP with host address 172.31.8.100 - If this is incorrect, please sp
INFO[0008] Generating UCP Client Root CA
INFO[0008] Deploying UCP Service
INFO[0049] Installation completed on ip-172-31-8-100 (node jatip5ocsvhighii1o55ho41v)
INFO[0049] UCP Instance ID: 803f54eedvsdlc2wvfju0iv47
INFO[0049] UCP Server SSL: SHA-256 Fingerprint=51:E8:13:FF:5F:2C:89:CC:E8:53:46:5C:D9:2F:3
INFO[0049] Login to UCP at https://172.31.8.100:443
INFO[0049] Username: admin
INFO[0049] Password: (your admin password)
ubuntu@ip-172-31-8-100:~$
```

Installing UCP 3.0.0-beta2 on a VM in AWS

Now we can open a browser window and navigate to `https://<IP address>`. Log in with your username, `admin`, and password, `adminadmin`. When asked for the license, upload your license key or follow the link to procure a trial license.

Once logged in, on the left-hand side under the **Shared Resources** section, select **Nodes** and then click on the **Add Node** button:

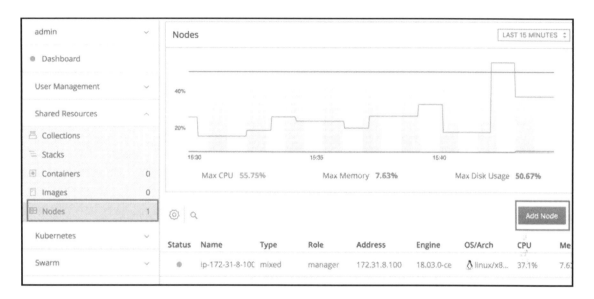

Adding a new node to UCP

In the subsequent **Add Node** dialog box, make sure that the node type is **Linux** and the node role, **Worker** is selected. Then copy the `docker swarm join` command at the bottom of the dialog box. SSH into the other two VMs you created and run this command to have the respective node join the Docker Swarm as a worker node:

```
$ ssh -i pets.pem ubuntu@54.208.149.247
Welcome to Ubuntu 16.04.4 LTS (GNU/Linux 4.4.0-1052-aws x86_64)

 * Documentation:  https://help.ubuntu.com
 * Management:     https://landscape.canonical.com
 * Support:        https://ubuntu.com/advantage

  Get cloud support with Ubuntu Advantage Cloud Guest:
    http://www.ubuntu.com/business/services/cloud

30 packages can be updated.
0 updates are security updates.


*** System restart required ***
Last login: Sun Apr  8 20:58:32 2018 from 70.113.114.234
ubuntu@ip-172-31-6-57:~$ docker swarm join --token SWMTKN-1-4w858a6f37b8v4ozyxn0bxacjoxtcogizu04dmosga
c3j5ocna-983bleo9oaygu03wmyz1ekptb 172.31.8.100:2377
This node joined a swarm as a worker.
ubuntu@ip-172-31-6-57:~$
```

Joining a node as a worker to the UCP cluster

Back in the web UI of UCP, you should see that we now have three nodes ready, as shown here:

Status	Name	Type	Role	Address	Engine	OS/Arch	CPU	Memory	Disk	Details
●	ip-172-31-8-10C	mixed	manager	172.31.8.100	18.03.0-ce	⏷ linux/x8...	31.95%	7.71%	50.73%	Healthy UCP ...
●	ip-172-31-15-11	swarm	worker	172.31.15.110	18.03.0-ce	⏷ linux/x8...	3.5%	1.05%	31.36%	Healthy UCP ...
●	ip-172-31-6-57	swarm	worker	172.31.6.57	18.03.0-ce	⏷ linux/x8...	3.27%	1.07%	31.36%	Healthy UCP ...

List of nodes in the UCP cluster

By default, worker nodes are configured so that they can only run the Docker Swarm work load. This can be changed in the node details though. In this, three settings are possible—Swarm only, Kubernetes only, or mixed workload. Let's start with Docker Swarm as the orchestration engine and deploy our pets application.

Remote admin the UCP cluster

To be able to manage our UCP cluster remotely from our laptop, we need to create and download a so called **client bundle** from UCP. Proceed with the following steps:

1. In the UCP web UI, on the left-hand side under **admin,** select the **My Profile** option
2. In the subsequent dialog, select the **New Client Bundle** option and then **Generate Client Bundle:**

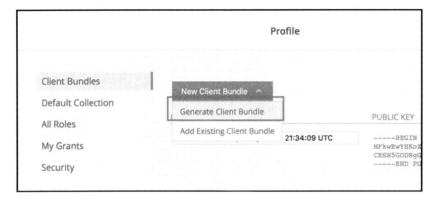

Generating and downloading a UCP client bundle

3. Locate the downloaded bundle on your disk and unzip it

4. In a new terminal window, navigate to that folder and source the env.sh file:

```
$ source env.sh
```

You should get an output similar to this:

```
Cluster "ucp_34.232.53.86:6443_admin" set.
User "ucp_34.232.53.86:6443_admin" set.
Context "ucp_34.232.53.86:6443_admin" created.
```

Now we can verify that we can indeed remote access the UCP cluster by, for example, listing all the nodes of the cluster:

```
$ docker node ls
ID                          HOSTNAME          STATUS    AVAILABILITY    MANAGER STATUS    ENGINE VERSION
wougljiphzk4vmmbm1tlqi2kg   ip-172-31-6-57    Ready     Active                            18.03.0-ce
jatip5ocsvhighii1o55ho41v * ip-172-31-8-100   Ready     Active          Leader            18.03.0-ce
tlkaeww3idlte90ko5zr8xkeu   ip-172-31-15-110  Ready     Active                            18.03.0-ce
$
```

Listing all the nodes of our remote UCP cluster

Let's try to deploy the pets application as a stack using Docker Swarm as the orchestration engine.

Deploying to Docker Swarm

In the Terminal, navigate to the labs/ch14/ucp folder and create the pets stack using the file stack.yml:

```
$ docker stack deploy -c stack.yml pets
Creating network pets_pets-net
Creating service pets_db
Creating service pets_web
$
```

Deploying the pets stack into the UCP cluster

In the UCP web UI, we can verify that the stack has been created:

The pets stack listing in the UCP web UI

To test the application, we can navigate to **Services** under the main menu, **Swarm**. The list of services running in the cluster will be displayed as follows:

Details of the service web of the pets stack

In the preceding screenshot, we see our two services, web and db, of the pets stack. If we click on the web service, its details get displayed on the right-hand side. There we find an entry, **Published Endpoints**. Click on the link and our pets application should be displayed in the browser.

When done, remove the stack from the console with:

```
$ docker stack rm pets
```

Or alternatively, you can try to remove that stack from within the UCP web UI.

Deploying to Kubernetes

From the same Terminal that you used to remote access the UCP cluster to deploy the pets application as a stack using Docker Swarm as the orchestration engine, we can now try to deploy the pets application to the UCP cluster using Kubernetes as the orchestration engine.

Make sure you're still in the `labs/ch14/ucp` folder. Use `kubectl` to deploy the pets application. First test that we can get all the nodes of the cluster with the Kubernetes CLI:

```
$ kubectl get nodes
NAME              STATUS   ROLES     AGE   VERSION
ip-172-31-15-110  Ready    <none>    1h    v1.8.2-docker.128+56ab40b2f3e9b9
ip-172-31-6-57    Ready    <none>    1h    v1.8.2-docker.128+56ab40b2f3e9b9
ip-172-31-8-100   Ready    master    22h   v1.8.2-docker.128+56ab40b2f3e9b9
$
```

Getting all the nodes of the UCP cluster using the Kubernetes CLI

Apparently, my environment is configured correctly and `kubectl` can indeed list all the nodes in the UCP cluster. That means I can now deploy the pets application using the definitions in file `pets.yaml`:

```
$ kubectl create -f pets.yaml
deployment "web" created
service "web" created
deployment "db" created
service "db" created
$
```

Creating the pets application in the UCP cluster using the Kubernetes CLI

We can list the objects created by using `kubectl get all`. In a browser, we can then navigate to `http://<IP address>:<port>` to access the pets application, where `<IP address>` is the public IP address of one of the UCP cluster nodes and `<port>` is the port published by the Kubernetes service `web`.

We have created a cluster of three VMs in an AWS ASG and have installed Docker and UCP 3.0 on them. We then deployed our famous pets application into the UCP cluster, once using Docker Swarm as the orchestration engine and once Kubernetes.

Docker UCP is a platform agnostic container platform that offers a secure enterprise grade software supply chain on any cloud and on-premise, on bare metal, or on virtualized environments. It even offers the freedom of choice when it comes to orchestration engines. The user can choose between Docker Swarm and Kubernetes. It is even possible to run applications in both orchestrators in the same cluster.

A short peek into Azure's container offerings

To play with Microsoft's container-related offerings in Azure, we need an account on Azure. You can create a trial account or use an existing account. Get your trial account here at `https://azure.microsoft.com/en-us/free/`.

Microsoft offers different container-related services on Azure. Probably the easiest one to use is the **Azure Container Instances**, which promises *the fastest and simplest way to run a container in Azure, without having to provision any virtual machines and without having to adopt a higher-level service.* This service is only really useful if you want to run a single container in a hosted environment. The set up is quite easy. In the Azure portal (`portal.azure.com`), first create a new resource group and then create an Azure container instance. You only need to fill out a short form with properties such as the name of the container, the image to use, and the port to open. The container can be made available on a public or private IP address and will be automatically restarted if it crashes. There is a decent management console available, for example, to monitor resource consumption such as CPU and memory.

The second choice is **Azure Container Service (ACS)**, which *provides a way to simplify the creation, configuration, and management of a cluster of virtual machines that are preconfigured to run containerized applications.* ACS uses Docker images and provides a choice between the three orchestrators: Kubernetes, Docker Swarm, or DC/OS (powered by Apache Mesos). Microsoft claims that their service can be scaled to tens of thousands of containers. ACS is free and one is only charged for the computing resources.

Let's try to create a hosted Docker Swarm with one manager and one worker node, to which we will then deploy our pets demo application. First we need to install the Azure CLI 2.0. We can use a Docker image for this:

```
$ docker container run -it microsoft/azure-cli:latest
```

Once the container is running, we need to log in to our account:

```
bash-4.3# az login
```

You will be presented with the following message:

```
To sign in, use a web browser to open the page
https://microsoft.com/devicelogin and enter the code <code> to
authenticate.
```

Follow the instructions and log in through the browser. Once you have successfully authenticated to your Azure account, you can go back to your Terminal and you should be logged in.

First, we create a new resource group named pets-rg:

 Select the location that is closest to you. In my case, it is US East.

```
bash-4.3# az group create --name pets-rg --location eastus
{
  "id": "/subscriptions/186760ad-9152-4499-b317-c9bff441fb9d/resourceGroups/pets-rg",
  "location": "eastus",
  "managedBy": null,
  "name": "pets-rg",
  "properties": {
    "provisioningState": "Succeeded"
  },
  "tags": null
}
bash-4.3#
```

Creating a resource group in Azure

Then we create a new **Azure Container Service,** using Docker Swarm as the orchestration engine. This may take a few minutes. Here is the result:

```
bash-4.3# az acs create -g pets-rg -n pets-cluster --orchestrator-type swarm --generate-ssh-keys
{
  "id": "/subscriptions/186760ad-9152-4499-b317-c9bff441fb9d/resourceGroups/pets-rg/providers/Microso
li1523325303.63794370404",
  "name": "azurecli1523325303.63794370404",
  "properties": {
    "additionalProperties": {
      "duration": "PT10M22.7071402S",
      "outputResources": [
        {
          "id": "/subscriptions/186760ad-9152-4499-b317-c9bff441fb9d/resourceGroups/pets-rg/providers
tainerServices/pets-cluster",
          "resourceGroup": "pets-rg"
        }
      ],
      "templateHash": "14213326594306665848"
    },
    "correlationId": "94aebdbd-b8d0-40fc-b492-e285e1a364bb",
    "debugSetting": null,
    "dependencies": [],
    "mode": "Incremental",
    "outputs": {
      "agentFQDN": {
        "type": "String",
        "value": "pets-clust-pets-rg-186760agent.eastus.cloudapp.azure.com"
      },
      "masterFQDN": {
        "type": "String",
        "value": "pets-clust-pets-rg-186760mgmt.eastus.cloudapp.azure.com"
      },
      "sshMaster0": {
```

Creating an Azure Container Service using Docker Swarm (shortened)

Once our Docker Swarm has been created in Azure, we can issue the following command to retrieve the list of public IPs that we need to connect to the Swarm:

```
bash-4.3# az network public-ip list --resource-group pets-rg \
>       --query "[*].{Name:name,IPAddress:ipAddress}" \
>       -o table
Name                                                          IPAddress
------------------------------------------------------------  -------------
swarm-agent-ip-pets-clust-pets-rg-186760agent-CE7D8170        13.92.172.89
swarm-master-ip-pets-clust-pets-rg-186760mgmt-CE7D8170        13.90.151.207
bash-4.3#
```

The first entry is the IP address of the Docker agent pool and the second one is from the Docker Swarm master. With this information, we can create an SSH tunnel into the master using its IP address. We need to do that directly from our laptop and not within the Azure CLI container since the latter doesn't have the Docker CLI installed. To be able to do so, we also need to copy the private key from the certificate from within the Azure CLI container to our host. Open a new Terminal window and list all the running containers to find the <container ID> of the Azure CLI container and then run the following command to copy the key:

```
$ docker cp <container ID>:/root/.ssh/id_rsa ~/.ssh/fob
```

And now in the same Terminal as the previous command, create the tunnel with this command:

```
$ ssh -i ~/.ssh/fob -p 2200 -fNL 2375:localhost:2375 \
    azureuser@<IPAddress>
```

Replace <IPAddress> with the IP address of your Swarm master.

We will use this tunnel to manage Docker Swarm on Azure remotely. But to do this, we need to also define the DOCKER_HOST environment variable:

```
$ export DOCKER_HOST=:2375
```

Yes, this is not an error. We define just the port and no hostname (due to the SSH tunnel). Once we have done all that, we're ready to remotely manage our Docker Swarm. Let's first run the `docker info` command:

```
$ docker info
Containers: 1
 Running: 1
 Paused: 0
 Stopped: 0
Images: 1
Role: primary
Strategy: spread
Filters: health, port, dependency, affinity, constraint
Nodes: 3
 swarm-agent-CE7D8170000000: 10.0.0.4:2375
  └ Status: Healthy
  └ Containers: 0
  └ Reserved CPUs: 0 / 2
  └ Reserved Memory: 0 B / 7.137 GiB
  └ Labels: executiondriver=<not supported>, kernelversion=3.19.0-65-generic, operatingsystem=Ubuntu 14.04.4 LTS, storagedriver=overlay
  └ Error: (none)
  └ UpdatedAt: 2018-04-07T20:25:56Z
 swarm-agent-CE7D8170000001: 10.0.0.5:2375
  └ Status: Healthy
  └ Containers: 0
  └ Reserved CPUs: 0 / 2
  └ Reserved Memory: 0 B / 7.137 GiB
  └ Labels: executiondriver=<not supported>, kernelversion=3.19.0-65-generic, operatingsystem=Ubuntu 14.04.4 LTS, storagedriver=overlay
  └ Error: (none)
  └ UpdatedAt: 2018-04-07T20:26:22Z
 swarm-agent-CE7D8170000002: 10.0.0.6:2375
  └ Status: Healthy
  └ Containers: 1
  └ Reserved CPUs: 0 / 2
  └ Reserved Memory: 0 B / 7.137 GiB
  └ Labels: executiondriver=<not supported>, kernelversion=3.19.0-65-generic, operatingsystem=Ubuntu 14.04.4 LTS, storagedriver=overlay
  └ Error: (none)
  └ UpdatedAt: 2018-04-07T20:25:59Z
Plugins:
 Volume:
 Network:
 Log:
Swarm:
```

Docker info executed remotely on Docker Swarm in Azure (shortened)

We see that we have a swarm with three worker nodes ready to accept workload. The output also tells us that Azure is using the legacy Docker Swarm instead of SwarmKit.

Let's try to deploy our pets application on this swarm. In your Terminal, navigate to the `labs/ch14/azure` folder and deploy the app as described in the file `docker-compose.yml`:

```
$ docker-compose up
Creating network "azure_default" with the default driver
Creating volume "azure_pets-data" with default driver
Pulling web (fundamentalsofdocker/ch08-web:1.0)...
swarm-agent-CE7D8170000001: Pulling fundamentalsofdocker/ch08-web:1.0... : downloaded
swarm-agent-CE7D8170000002: Pulling fundamentalsofdocker/ch08-web:1.0... : downloaded
swarm-agent-CE7D8170000000: Pulling fundamentalsofdocker/ch08-web:1.0... : downloaded
Pulling db (fundamentalsofdocker/ch08-db:1.0)...
swarm-agent-CE7D8170000000: Pulling fundamentalsofdocker/ch08-db:1.0... : downloaded
swarm-agent-CE7D8170000001: Pulling fundamentalsofdocker/ch08-db:1.0... : downloaded
swarm-agent-CE7D8170000002: Pulling fundamentalsofdocker/ch08-db:1.0... : downloaded
Creating azure_db_1   ... done
Creating azure_web_1 ... done
Attaching to azure_web_1, azure_db_1
web_1  | Listening at 0.0.0.0:3000
db_1   | The files belonging to this database system will be owned by user "postgres".
db_1   | This user must also own the server process.
db_1   |
db_1   | The database cluster will be initialized with locale "en_US.utf8".
db_1   | The default database encoding has accordingly been set to "UTF8".
db_1   | The default text search configuration will be set to "english".
db_1   |
db_1   | Data page checksums are disabled.
db_1   |
db_1   | fixing permissions on existing directory /var/lib/postgresql/data ... ok
db_1   | creating subdirectories ... ok
db_1   | selecting default max_connections ... 100
db_1   | selecting default shared_buffers ... 128MB
db_1   | selecting dynamic shared memory implementation ... posix
db_1   | creating configuration files ... ok
db_1   | running bootstrap script ... ok
db_1   | performing post-bootstrap initialization ... sh: locale: not found
db_1   | 2018-04-07 20:34:10.714 UTC [27] WARNING:  no usable system locales were found
db_1   | ok
db_1   | syncing data to disk ...
db_1   | WARNING: enabling "trust" authentication for local connections
db_1   | You can change this by editing pg_hba.conf or using the option -A, or
```

Running the pets application on Docker Swarm on Azure (shortened)

OK, now let's test the application. For that we need the public IP of the swarm agent pool that we were retrieving earlier in this section. Open your browser at `<IP address>/pet` and you should see the pets application:

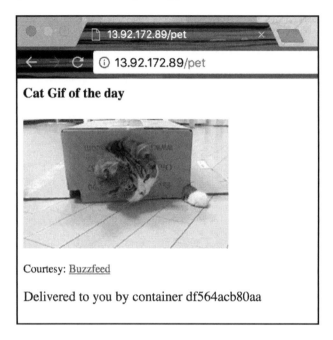

Pets application running on Docker Swarm in Azure

Once we're done playing with Docker Swarm on Azure, we should delete it so as not to incur any unnecessary cost:

```
$ az group delete --name pets-rg --yes --no-wait
```

We have shown in this section how to provision Docker Swarm in Azure using the Azure CLI. We then have successfully deployed our pets application into that swarm.

Azure has a few compelling offerings regarding the container workload and the lock-in is not that evident as it is on AWS due to the fact that Azure does mainly offer open source orchestration engines, such as Kubernetes, Docker Swarm, DC/OS, or Rancher. Technically, we remain mobile if we initially run our containerized applications in Azure and later decide to move to another cloud provider. The cost should be limited.

A short peek into Google's container offerings

Google is the inventor of Kubernetes and, to this date, the driving force behind it. One would thus expect that Google has a compelling offering around hosted Kubernetes. Let's have a peek into it. To continue, you need to either have an existing account with Google Cloud or you can create a test account here at `https://console.cloud.google.com/freetrial`. Proceed with the following steps:

1. In the main menu, select **Kubernetes Engine**. The first time you do that, it will take a few moments until the Kubernetes engine is initialized.
2. Once this is ready, we can create a cluster by clicking on **CREATE CLUSTER**.
3. Name the cluster as `pets-cluster` and leave all other settings in the **Create a Kubernetes Cluster** form with their default values and click on **Create**.

It will again take a few moments to provision the cluster for us. Once the cluster has been created, we can open the **Cloud Shell**. This should look similar to the following screenshot:

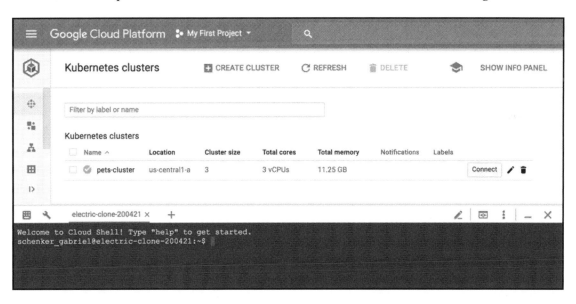

First Kubernetes cluster ready and Cloud Shell open in GCE

We can now clone our `labs` GitHub repository to this environment with the following command:

```
$ git clone https://github.com/fundamentalsofdocker/labs
$ cd labs/ch14/gce
```

We should now find a `pets.yaml` file in the current folder, which we can use to deploy the pets application into our Kubernetes cluster. Have a look at the file:

```
$ less pets.yaml
```

It has pretty much the same content as the same file we used in the previous chapter. The two differences are:

- We use a service of type `LoadBalancer` (instead of `NodePort`) to publicly expose the component `web`.
- We do not use volumes for the PostgreSQL database since configuring StatefulSet correctly on GCE is a bit more involved than in Minikube. The consequence of this is that our pets application will not persist the state if the `db` pod crashes. How to use persistent volumes on GCE lies outside the scope of this book.

Before we can continue, we need to first set up `gcloud` and `kubectl` credentials:

```
$ gcloud container clusters get-credentials pets-cluster \
    --zone us-central1-a
```

Having done that, it's time to deploy the application:

```
$ kubectl create -f pets.yaml
```

Once the objects have been created, we can observe the `LoadBalancer` service `web` until it is assigned a public IP address:

```
$ kubectl get svc/web --watch
```

This should look similar to the following screenshot:

```
schenker_gabriel@electric-clone-200421:~/labs/ch14/gce$ kubectl get svc/web --watch
NAME       TYPE           CLUSTER-IP      EXTERNAL-IP      PORT(S)         AGE
web        LoadBalancer   10.43.244.195   35.184.142.67    3000:32086/TCP  25m
```

Retrieving the public IP address of the service web

We can then use this IP address and navigate to `http://<IP address>:3000/pet` and we should be greeted by the familiar cat image.

To clean up and delete all resources, run this script:

```
kubectl delete deploy/web
kubectl delete deploy/db
kubectl delete svc/web
kubectl delete svc/db
```

We have created a hosted Kubernetes cluster in GCE. We have then used the Cloud Shell provided through the GCE portal to first clone our `labs` GitHub repository and then the `kubectl` tool to deploy the pets application into the Kubernetes cluster.

When looking into a hosted Kubernetes solution, GCE is a compelling solution. It makes it very easy to start and since Google is the main driving force behind Kubernetes, we can rest assured that we will always be able to leverage the full uncrippled functionality of Kubernetes.

Summary

In this final chapter of the book, you learned how to deploy a containerized application into AWS ECS and got a quick introduction on how to install and use Docker's UCP, which is part of the enterprise offering on AWS. Then you were given a glimpse of what the current container-related cloud offerings of Microsoft Azure and Google Cloud Engine are. On each one, we successfully installed our pets application.

Questions

To assess your knowledge, please answer the following questions:

1. Give a high-level description of the tasks needed to provision and run Docker UPC on AWS.
2. Name a handful of reasons when to use a hosted solution such as Azure ACS or AWS ECS and when to use a (hosted) Docker Swarm or Kubernetes-based offering.

Further reading

The following articles give you some more information related to the topics we discussed in this chapter:

- *Deploy Docker Enterprise Edition on Linux servers* at `https://dockr.ly/2vH5dpN`
- Getting Started with Amazon ECS using Fargate at `https://amzn.to/2Hh7pcM`
- Azure Container Service (AKS) at `https://bit.ly/2JglX9d`
- Google Kubernetes Engine at `https://bit.ly/2I8MjJx`

Assessment

Chapter 1

1. Correct answers are: 4, 5.
2. A Docker container is, to IT, what a shipping container is to the transportation industry. It defines a standard on how to package goods. In this case, goods are the application(s) developers write. The suppliers (in this case, the developers) are responsible for packaging the goods into the container and making sure everything fits as expected. Once the goods are packaged into a container, it can be shipped. Since it is a standard container, the shippers can standardize their means of transportation such as lorries, trains, or ships. The shipper doesn't really care what's in a container. Also, the loading and unloading process from one transportation means to another (for example, train to ship) can be highly standardized. This massively increases the efficiency of transportation. Analogous to this is an operations engineer in IT who can take a software container built by a developer and ship it to a production system and run it there in a highly standardized way, without worrying about what's in the container. It will just work.
3. Some of the reasons why containers are game changers are:
   - Containers are self-contained and thus if they run on one system, they run anywhere where a container can run.
   - Containers run on-premise and in the cloud, as well as in hybrid environments. This is important for today's typical enterprises since it allows a mostly smooth transition from on-premise to cloud.
   - Container images are built or packaged by the people who know best – the developers.
   - Container images are immutable which is important for a good release management.
   - Containers are enablers of a secure software supply chain-based on encapsulation (using Linux namespaces and cgroups), secrets, content trust, and image vulnerability scanning.

4. A container runs anywhere where a container can run because:
    - Containers are self-contained black boxes. They encapsulate not only an application but all its dependencies, such as libraries and frameworks, configuration data, certificates, and so on.
    - Containers are based on widely accepted standards such as OCI.
    - TODO: add more reasons.

5. False! Containers are useful for modern applications as well as to containerize traditional applications. The benefit for an enterprise when doing the latter is huge. Cost savings in the maintenance of legacy apps of 50% or more have been reported. The time between new releases of such legacy applications could be reduced by up to 90%. These numbers have been publicly reported by real enterprise customers.

6. 50% or more.

7. Containers are based on Linux namespaces (network, process, user, and so on) and cgroups (control groups).

Chapter 2

1. `docker-machine` can be used to do the following:
    - Create a VM configured as Docker host in different environments, such as VirtualBox
    - SSH into a Docker host
    - Configure the local Docker CLI for access of a remote Docker host
    - List all hosts in a given environment
    - Remove or destroy existing hosts

2. True. Docker for Windows creates a Linux VM in Hyper-V, on which it then runs Linux containers.

3. Container are optimally used in CI/CD, which is all about automation. Each step, from building a container image, shipping the image, and finally running containers from this image, is ideally scripted for maximum productivity. With it, one achieves a repeatable and auditable process.

4. Ubuntu 17.4 or later, CentOS 7.x, Alpine 3.x, Debian, Suse Linux, RedHat Linux, and so on.

5. Windows 10 Professional or Enterprise Edition, Windows Server 2016.

Chapter 3

1. The states of a container are as follows

   - Created
   - Running
   - Exited

2. The following command helps us to find out what is currently running on our host:

   ```
   $ docker container ls
   ```

3. The following command is used to list down the IDs of all containers:

   ```
   $ docker container ls -q
   ```

Chapter 4

Here are possible answers to the questions:

1. Dockerfile:

   ```
   FROM ubuntu:17.04
   RUN apt-get update
   RUN apt-get install -y ping
   ENTRYPOINT ping
   CMD 127.0.0.1
   ```

2. To achieve the result you can execute the following steps:

   ```
   $ docker container run -it --name sample \
       alpine:latest /bin/sh
   / # apk update && \
       apk add -y curl && \
       rm -rf /var/cache/apk/*
   / # exit
   $ docker container commit sample my-alpine:1.0
   $ docker container rm sample
   ```

3. As a sample here is the `Hello World` in C:

    1. Create a file `hello.c` with this content:

```
#include <stdio.h>
int main()
{
    printf("Hello, World!");
    return 0;
}
```

    2. Create a Dockerfile with this content:

```
FROM alpine:3.5 AS build
RUN apk update && \
    apk add --update alpine-sdk
RUN mkdir /app
WORKDIR /app
COPY hello.c /app
RUN mkdir bin
RUN gcc -Wall hello.c -o bin/hello

FROM alpine:3.5
COPY --from=build /app/bin/hello /app/hello
CMD /app/hello
```

4. Some characteristics of a Docker image are:
   - It is immutable
   - It is composed of immutable layers
   - Each layer contains only what has changed (the delta) in regard to the lower lying layers
   - An image is a (big) tarball of files and folders
   - an image is a template for containers

5. Option 3 is correct. First we need to make sure we're logged in and then we tag the image and finally push it. Since it is an image we're using `docker image` . . . and not `docker container` . . . (as in number 4).

Chapter 5

The easiest way to play with volumes is to use the Docker Toolbox as when directly using Docker for Mac or Docker for Windows, then the volumes are stored inside a (somewhat hidden) Linux VM that Docker for Mac/Win uses transparently.

Thus, we suggest the following:

```
$ docker-machine create --driver virtualbox volume-test
$ docker-machine ssh volume-test
```

And now that you're inside a Linux VM called `volume-test`, you can execute the following exercises:

1. To create a named `volume` run the following command:

   ```
   $ docker volume create my-products
   ```

2. Execute the following command:

   ```
   $ docker container run -it --rm \
       -v my-products:/data:ro \
       alpine /bin/sh
   ```

3. To get the path on the host for the volume use, for example, this command:

   ```
   $ docker volume inspect my-products | grep Mountpoint
   ```

   Which (if using docker-machine and VirtualBox) should result in:

   ```
   "Mountpoint": "/mnt/sda1/var/lib/docker/volumes/my-products/_data"
   ```

   Now execute the following command:

   ```
   $ sudo su
   $ cd /mnt/sda1/var/lib/docker/volumes/my-products/_data
   $ echo "Hello world" > sample.txt
   $ exit
   ```

4. Execute the following command:

   ```
   $ docker run -it --rm -v my-products:/data:ro alpine /bin/sh
   # / cd /data
   # / cat sample.txt
   ```

In another terminal execute:

```
$ docker run -it --rm -v my-products:/app-data alpine /bin/sh
# / cd /app-data
# / echo "Hello other container" > hello.txt
# / exit
```

5. Execute a command such as this:

```
$ docker container run -it --rm \
    -v $HOME/my-project:/app/data \
    alpine /bin/sh
```

6. Exit both containers and then back on the host, execute this command:

```
$ docker volume prune
```

7. Run the following command:

```
$ docker system info | grep Version
```

Which should output something similar to this:

```
Server Version: 17.09.1-ce
Kernel Version: 4.4.104-boot2docker
```

If you have been using `docker-machine` to create and use a Linux VM in VirtualBox, don't forget to clean up after you're done:

```
$ docker-machine rm volume-test
```

Chapter 6

1. In a system consisting of many parts, failure of at least one part is only a matter of time. To avoid any downtime if such a situation occurs, one runs multiple instances of each component. If one of the instances fails, there are still others to serve the requests.

2. In a distributed application architecture, we have many moving parts. If Service A needs access to an instance of Service B, then it cannot know where to find such an instance. Instances can be on any random node of the cluster and they can even come and go as the orchestration engine sees fit, so we do not identify the target instance by, say, its IP address and port, but rather by its name and port. A DNS service knows how to resolve a service name into an IP address since it has all the information about all service instances running in the cluster.

3. A circuit breaker is a mechanism that helps to avoid cascading failures in a distributed application triggered by a single failing service. The circuit breaker observes a request from one service to another and measures the latency over time and the number of request failures or timeouts. If a certain target instance causes too many failures, the calls to it are intercepted and an error code is returned to the caller, instantly giving the target time to recover if possible, and the caller, in turn, knows instantly that it either should degrade its own service or try with another instance of the target service.

4. A monolith is an application that consists of one single code base that is highly coupled. If changes to the code are made, no matter how minimal, the whole application has to be compiled, packaged, and redeployed. A monolith is simple to deploy and monitor in production due to the fact that it has very few moving parts. Monoliths are difficult to maintain and extend. A distributed application consists of many loosely coupled services. Each service originates from its own independent source code base. Individual services can and often have independent life cycles. They can be developed and revised independently. Distributed applications are more difficult to manage and monitor.

5. One talks about a blue-green deployment when a currently running version of a service, called blue, is replaced by a new release of the same service, called green. The replacement happens without any downtime since while the blue version is still running, the green version of the service is installed on the system and, once ready, a simple change in the configuration of the router that funnels traffic to the service is needed so that the traffic is now all directed to green instead of blue.

Chapter 7

1. The three core elements are sandbox, endpoint, and network

2. Execute this command:

```
$ docker network create --driver bridge frontend
```

3. Run this command:

```
$ docker container run -d --name n1 \
    --network frontend -p 8080:80 nginx:alpine
$ docker container run -d --name n2 \
    --network frontend -p 8081:80 nginx:alpine
```

Test that both Nginx instances are up and running:

```
$ curl -4 localhost:8080
$ curl -4 localhost:8081
```

You should be seeing the welcome page of Nginx in both cases.

4. To get the IPs of all attached containers, run:

```
$ docker network inspect frontend | grep IPv4Address
```

You should see something similar to the following:

```
"IPv4Address": "172.18.0.2/16",
"IPv4Address": "172.18.0.3/16",
```

To get the subnet used by the network, use the following (for example):

```
$ docker network inspect frontend | grep subnet
```

You should receive something along the lines of the following (obtained from the previous example):

```
"Subnet": "172.18.0.0/16",
```

5. The host network allows us to run a container in the networking namespace of the host.
6. Only use this network for debugging purposes or when building a system-level tool. Never use the host network for an application container running production!
7. The none network is basically saying that the container is not attached to any network. It should be used for containers that do not need to communicate with other containers and do not need to be accessed from outside.
8. The none network could e.g. be used for a batch process running in a container that only needs access to local resources such as files which could be accessed via a host mounted volume.

Chapter 8

1. The following code can be used to run the application in daemon mode.

```
$ docker-compose up -d
```

2. Execute the following command to display the details of the running service.

```
$ docker-compose ps
```

This should result in the following output:

```
Name                        Command                State  Ports
-----------------------------------------------------------------------
mycontent_nginx_1 nginx -g daemon off;  Up    0.0.0.0:3000->80/tcp
```

3. The following command can be used to scale up the web service:

```
$ docker-compose up --scale web=3
```

Chapter 9

Here are the sample answers to the questions of this chapter:

1. Here are some reasons why we need an orchestration engine:
    - Containers are ephemeral and only an automated system (the orchestrator) can handle this efficiently.
    - For high availability reasons, we want to run multiple instances of each container. The number of containers to manage quickly becomes huge.
    - To meet the demand of today's internet, we need to quickly scale up and down.
    - Containers, contrary to VMs, are not treated as pets and fixed or healed when they misbehave, but are treated as cattle. If one misbehaves, we kill it and replace it with a new instance. The orchestrator quickly terminates an unhealthy container and schedules a new instance.

2. Here are some responsibilities of a container orchestration engine:
    - Manages a set of nodes in a cluster
    - Schedules workload to the nodes with sufficient free resources
    - Monitors the health of nodes and workload
    - Reconciles current state with desired state of applications and components
    - Provides service discovery and routing
    - Load balances requests
    - Secures confident data by providing support for secrets

3. Here is an (incomplete) list of orchestrators, sorted by their popularity:
   - Kubernetes by Google, donated to the CNCF
   - SwarmKit by Docker—that is, **Operations Support System (OSS)**
   - AWS ECS by Amazon
   - Azure AKS by Microsoft
   - Mesos by Apache—that is, OSS
   - Cattle by Rancher
   - Nomad by HashiCorp

Chapter 10

1. The correct answer is:

```
$ docker swarm init [--advertise-addr <IP address>]
```

The `--advertise-addr` is optional and only needed if you the host have more than one IP address.

2. On the worker node that you want to remove execute: `$ docker swarm leave`
   On one of the master nodes execute the command `$ docker node rm -f <node ID>`
   where `<node ID>` is the ID of the worker node to remove.

3. The correct answer is:

```
$ docker network create \
    --driver overlay \
    --attachable \
    front-tier
```

4. The correct answer is:

```
$ docker service create --name web \
    --network front-tier \
    --replicas 5 \
    -p 3000:80 \
    nginx:alpine
```

5. The correct answer is:

```
$ docker service update --replicas 3 web
```

Chapter 11

1. Zero downtime means that when updating a service, say from version 1 to version 2, the application to which this service belongs remains up and running all the time. At no time is the application interrupted or not functional.

2. Docker SwarmKit uses rolling updates to achieve zero downtime. Every service runs in multiple instances for high availability. When a rolling update is happening, small batches of the overall set of service instances are replaced by new versions. This happens while the majority of the service instances are up and running to serve incoming requests.

3. Container images are immutable. That is, once created, they can never be changed. When a containerized application or service needs to be updated, a new container image is created. During a rolling update, the old container image is replaced with the new container image. If a rollback is necessary, then the new image is replaced with the old image. This can be looked at as a reverse update. As long as we do not delete the old container image, we can always return to this previous version by reusing it. Since, as we said earlier, images are immutable, we are indeed returning to the previous state.

4. Docker secrets are encrypted at rest; they are stored encrypted in the raft database. Secrets are also encrypted in transit since the node-to-node communication is using mutual TLS.

5. The command would have to look like this:

```
$ docker service update --image acme/inventory:2.1 \
    --update-parallelism 2 \
    --update-delay 60s \
    inventory
```

6. First, we need to remove the old secret:

```
$ docker service update --secret-rm MYSQL_PASSWORD inventory
```

Then we add the new secret and make sure we use the extended format where we can remap the name of the secret, that is, the external and internal name of the secret do not have to match. The latter command could look like this:

```
$ docker service update \
    --secret-add source=MYSQL_PASSWORD_V2,target=MYSQL_PASSWORD \
    inventory
```

Chapter 12

1. The Kubernetes master is responsible for managing the cluster. All requests to create objects, the scheduling of pods, the managing of `ReplicaSets`, and more is happening on the master. The master does not run application workload in a production or production-like cluster.

2. On each worker node, we have the kubelet, the proxy, and a container runtime.

3. The answer is Yes. You cannot run standalone containers on a Kubernetes cluster. Pods are the atomic unit of deployment in such a cluster.

4. All containers running inside a pod share the same Linux kernel network namespace. Thus, all processes running inside those containers can communicate with each other through `localhost` in a similar way that processes or applications directly running on the host can communicate with each other through `localhost`.

5. The `pause` container's sole role is to reserve the namespaces of the pod for the containers that run in the pod.

6. This is a bad idea since all containers of a pod are co-located, which means they run on the same cluster node. But the different component of the application (that is, `web`, `inventory`, and `db`) usually have very different requirements in regards to scalability or resource consumption. The `web` component might need to be scaled up and down depending on the traffic and the `db` component in turn has special requirements on storage that the others don't have. If we do run every component in its own pod, we are much more flexible in this regard.

7. We need a mechanism to run multiple instances of a pod in a cluster and make sure that the actual number of pods running always corresponds to the desired number, even when individual pods crash or disappear due to network partition or cluster node failures. The ReplicaSet is this mechanism that provides scalability and self-healing to any application service.

8. We need deployment objects whenever we want to update an application service in a Kubernetes cluster without causing downtime to the service. Deployment objects add rolling update and rollback capabilities to ReplicaSets.

9. Kubernetes service objects are used to make application services participate in service discovery. They provide a stable endpoint to a set of pods (normally governed by a ReplicaSet or a deployment). Kube services are abstractions which define a logical set of pods and a policy on how to access them. There are four types of Kube services:

   - **ClusterIP**: Exposes the service on an IP address only accessible from inside the cluster; this is a **virtual IP (VIP)**
   - **NodePort**: Publishes a port in the range 30,000–32767 on every cluster node
   - **LoadBalancer**: This type exposes the application service externally using a cloud provider's load balancer such as ELB on AWS
   - **ExternalName**: Used when you need to define a proxy for a cluster external service such as a database

Chapter 13

1. Assuming we have a Docker image in a registry for the two application services, the web API and Mongo DB, we then need to do the following:

   - Define a deployment for Mongo DB using a `StatefulSet`; let's call this deployment `db-deployment`. The `StatefulSet` should have one replica (replicating Mongo DB is a bit more involved and is outside of the scope of this book).
   - Define a Kubernetes service called `db` of type `ClusterIP` for the `db-deployment`.
   - Define a deployment for the web API; let's call it `web-deployment`. Let's scale this service to three instances.
   - Define a Kubernetes service called `api` of type `NodePort` for `web-deployment`.
   - If we use secrets, then define those secrets directly in the cluster using `kubectl`.
   - Deploy the application using `kubectl`.

2. To implement layer 7 routing for an application, we ideally use an `IngressController`. The `IngressController` is a reverse proxy such as Nginx that has a sidecar listening on the Kubernetes Server API for relevant changes and updating the reverse proxy's configuration and restarting it, if such a change has been detected. We then need to define Ingress resources in the cluster which define the routing, for example from a context-based route such as `https://example.com/pets` to `<a service name>/<port>` pair such as `api/32001`. The moment Kubernetes creates or changes this Ingress object, the `IngressController`'s sidecar picks it up and updates the proxy's routing configuration.

3. Assuming this is a **cluster internal** inventory service:
   - When deploying version 1.0 we define a deployment called `inventory-deployment-blue` and label the pods with a label `color: blue`.
   - We deploy the Kubernetes service of type `ClusterIP` called `inventory` for the preceding deployment with the selector containing `color: blue`.
   - When ready to deploy the new version of the payments service, we first define a deployment for version 2.0 of the service and call it `inventory-deployment-green`. We add a label `color: green` to the pods.
   - We can now smoke test the "green" service and when everything is OK, we can update the inventory service such as the selector contains `color: green`.

4. Some type of information that is confidential and thus should be provided to services through Kubernetes secrets include: passwords, certificates, API key IDs, API key secrets or tokens.

5. Sources for secret values can be files or base64 encoded values.

Chapter 14

1. To install UCP in AWS:
    1. Create a VPC with subnets and a security group.
    2. Then provision a cluster of Linux VMs, possibly as part of an auto scaling group. Many Linux distros are supported, such as CentOS, RHEL, Ubuntu, and so on.
    3. Next, install Docker on each VM.
    4. Finally, select one VM on which to install UCP using the docker/ucp image.
    5. Once UCP is installed, join the other VMs to the cluster either as worker nodes or manager nodes.

2. Cloud vendor-specific and proprietary solutions, such as ECS, have the advantages of being tightly and seamlessly integrated with the other services, such as logging, monitoring, or storage, provided by the cloud vendor. Also, often one does not have to provision and manage the infrastructure but this will be automatically done by the provider. On the positive side, it is also noteworthy that to deploy a first containerized application usually happens pretty quickly, meaning that the startup hurdles are pretty low.

    On the other hand, choosing a proprietary service such as ECS locks us into the ecosystem of the respective cloud provider. Also, we have to live with what they give us. In the case of Azure ACS, this meant that when choosing Docker Swarm as the orchestration engine, we were given classic Docker Swarm which is legacy and has long been replaced with SwarmKit by Docker.

    If we chose a hosted or self-managed solution based on the latest versions of Docker Swarm or Kubernetes, we enjoy the latest and greatest features of the respective orchestration engine.

Other Books You May Enjoy

If you enjoyed this book, you may be interested in these other books by Packt:

Docker on Windows

Elton Stoneman

ISBN: 978-1-78528-165-5

- Comprehend key Docker concepts: images, containers, registries, and swarms
- Run Docker on Windows 10, Windows Server 2016, and in the cloud
- Deploy and monitor distributed solutions across multiple Docker containers
- Run containers with high availability and fail-over with Docker Swarm
- Master security in-depth with the Docker platform, making your apps more secure
- Build a Continuous Deployment pipeline by running Jenkins in Docker
- Debug applications running in Docker containers using Visual Studio
- Plan the adoption of Docker in your own organization

Docker for Serverless Applications

Chanwit Kaewkasi

ISBN: 978-1-78883-526-8

- Learn what Serverless and FaaS applications are
- Get acquainted with the architectures of three major serverless systems
- Explore how Docker technologies can help develop Serverless applications
- Create and maintain FaaS infrastructures
- Set up Docker infrastructures to serve as on-premises FaaS infrastructures
- Define functions for Serverless applications with Docker containers

Leave a review - let other readers know what you think

Please share your thoughts on this book with others by leaving a review on the site that you bought it from. If you purchased the book from Amazon, please leave us an honest review on this book's Amazon page. This is vital so that other potential readers can see and use your unbiased opinion to make purchasing decisions, we can understand what our customers think about our products, and our authors can see your feedback on the title that they have worked with Packt to create. It will only take a few minutes of your time, but is valuable to other potential customers, our authors, and Packt. Thank you!

Index

Printed in Great Britain
by Amazon